AF723222

Dreaming the Myth Onwards

Dreaming the Myth Onwards shows how a revised appreciation of myth can enrich our daily lives, our psychological awareness and our human relationships. Lucy Huskinson and her contributors explore the interplay between myth and Jungian thought and practice, demonstrating the philosophical and psychological principles that underlie our experience of psyche and world.

Contributors from multidisciplinary backgrounds throughout the world come together to assess the contemporary relevance of myth, in terms of its utility, its effectual position within Jungian theory and practice, and as a general approach for making sense of life. As well as examining the more conscious facets of myth, this volume discusses the unconscious psychodynamic 'processes of myth', including active imagination, transference and countertransference, to illustrate just how these mythic phenomena give meaning to Jungian theory and therapeutic experience.

This rigorous and scholarly analysis showcases fresh readings of central Jungian concepts, updated in accordance with shifts in the cultural and epistemological concerns of contemporary western consciousness. *Dreaming the Myth Onwards* will be essential reading for practising analysts and academics in the field of the arts and social sciences.

Lucy Huskinson is Lecturer in Philosophy of Religion at Bangor University, Wales, and Visiting Fellow at the Centre for Comparative Literature and Cultural Studies, Monash University, Australia; the Philosophy Program, La Trobe University, Australia; and the Centre for Psychoanalytic Studies, University of Essex, UK. Her first book is *Nietzsche and Jung: The Whole Self in the Union of Opposites* (Routledge, 2004).

'This book will come as a revelation to some readers and as a relief to others. As a most remarkable and astonishing array of perspectives and differing styles of thinking, all offered in the name of C. G. Jung . . . it is about much more than Jungian mythological perspectives. It is also about image, imagination, psychological narrative, and the theory and practice of Jungian analysis . . . a kaleidoscopic richness of Jungiana!'

David L. Miller, PhD, Watson-Ledden Professor, Emeritus, Syracuse University, New York, Core Faculty Member, Retired, Pacifica Graduate Institute, California

'*Dreaming the Myth Onwards* is a timely and thoughtful collection of essays by a distinguished group of Jungian scholars and analysts. The articles stimulate, provoke and challenge us to review our clichés about the relation of myth to modernity – a most useful exercise indeed, and terribly relevant to where we are headed in the twenty-first century.'

Murray Stein, PhD, Training Analyst at the International School for Analytical Psychology in Zurich, and author of *Jung's Map of the Soul*

'While reading *Dreaming the Myth Onwards* with great interest, the following sentence in one of Jung's letters came to mind: "The systematic elaboration of my ideas which were often just thrown out, is a task for those who come after me" [Letter to Jolande Jacobi, 24th September 1948]. To be sure, the contributors to this book take such a task very seriously, but they achieve more than this. Inspired by Jung's ideas, they "dream" and also "think" them onwards, and put forward creative ideas about the interpretation of myth and modernity, together with some new readings of Jung's most original theories.'

Mario Jacoby, PhD, Training Analyst at the International School for Analytical Psychology in Zurich, and author of *Individuation and Narcissism: The Psychology of Self in Jung and Kohut*

Dreaming the Myth Onwards

New directions in Jungian therapy and thought

Edited by
Lucy Huskinson

Routledge
Taylor & Francis Group
LONDON AND NEW YORK

First published 2008
by Routledge
27 Church Road, Hove, East Sussex BN3 2FA

Simultaneously published in the USA and Canada
by Routledge
270 Madison Avenue, New York, NY 10016

Routledge is an imprint of the Taylor & Francis Group an informa business

Copyright © 2008 Selection and editorial matter, Lucy Huskinson; individual chapters, the contributors

Typeset in Times by Garfield Morgan, Swansea, West Glamorgan
Printed and bound in Great Britain by TJ International Ltd, Padstow, Cornwall
Paperback cover design by Lisa Dynan
Paperback cover image © Bettmann/CORBIS

All rights reserved. No part of this book may be reprinted or reproduced or utilised in any form or by any electronic, mechanical, or other means, now known or hereafter invented, including photocopying and recording, or in any information storage or retrieval system, without permission in writing from the publishers.

This publication has been produced with paper manufactured to strict environmental standards and with pulp derived from sustainable forests.

British Library Cataloguing in Publication Data
A catalogue record for this book is available from the British Library

Library of Congress Cataloging in Publication Data
Dreaming the myth onwards : new directions in Jungian therapy and thought / edited by Lucy Huskinson.
p. cm.
Includes bibliographical references and index.
ISBN 978-0-415-43837-7 (hardback) – ISBN 978-0-415-43838-4 (pbk.)
1. Myth–Psychological aspects. 2. Jung, C. G. (Carl Gustav), 1875–1961.
I. Huskinson, Lucy, 1976–
BF175.5.M95D74 2008
150.19'54–dc22

2007026729

ISBN: 978-0-415-43837-7 (hbk)
ISBN: 978-0-415-43838-4 (pbk)

for Ann and the firespitter

Contents

Contributors

Lucy Huskinson is Lecturer in Philosophy of Religion at the University of Wales, Bangor, and Visiting Fellow at the Centre for Comparative Literature and Cultural Studies, Monash University, Australia; the Philosophy Program, La Trobe University, Australia; and the Centre for Psychoanalytic Studies, University of Essex, UK. Her first book is *Nietzsche and Jung: The Whole Self in the Union of Opposites* (Routledge, 2004).

Michael Vannoy Adams (DPhil, LCSW) is a Jungian Psychoanalyst in New York City. He is a Clinical Associate Professor at the New York University Postdoctoral Program in Psychotherapy and Psychoanalysis and a faculty member at the Jungian Psychoanalytic Association. He has published three books: *The Multicultural Imagination: 'Race', Color, and The Unconscious*; *The Mythological Unconscious*; and *The Fantasy Principle: Psychoanalysis of the Imagination*. He has received three Gradiva Awards from the National Association for the Advancement of Psychoanalysis. His website is: http://www.jungnewyork.com

Phil Goss is a Jungian analyst in private practice in the north of England and a Senior Lecturer in Counselling and Psychotherapy at the University of Central Lancashire. His recent publications include a paper 'Discontinuities in the male psyche: waiting, deadness and disembodiment: archetypal and clinical approaches' (*Journal of Analytical Psychology*, 2006) and a chapter for *Education and Imagination* (Routledge, forthcoming).

Frances Gray (PhD) holds a PhD in Philosophy from the Australian National University. She teaches philosophy at the University of New England in Armidale, NSW, Australia. Her research publications include articles on feminism and on philosophy of religion. Her book, *Jung, Irigaray, Individuation* is published by Routledge (2007).

Honor Griffith (PhD) is a Jungian psychotherapist in private practice in British Columbia, Canada. She is author of 'Jung and Postmodernism: Bridging the Self-Other Divide', in *Psychology at the Threshold* (eds.

Dennis Patrick Slattery and Lionel Corbett, 2000), and of various published articles and book reviews.

Birgit Heuer is a Jungian analyst (British Association of Psychotherapists) with a previous training in body-oriented psychotherapy. She practices in West London and at the Hale Clinic. She has 26 years of clinical experience in full-time private practice. She has worked as clinical supervisor at Kingston University Health Centre for a number of years and she has been the theoretical seminar organizer on the BAP training committee. She has written on the body and analysis, on clinical paradigm and on healing and analysis.

Nihan Kaya is a Turkish novelist and author of *Gizli Ozne* (*The Hidden Self*, 2003); *Cati Kati* (*The Attic Storey*, 2004); *Bugu* (*The Mist*, 2006); *Uc Koseli Yazilar: Edebiyat-Psikoloji-Kadin* (*Essays with Three Corners: Literature-Psychology-Femininity*, forthcoming); and *Disparoni* (*Dyspareunia*, forthcoming). She has an MA in Psychoanalytic Studies from the University of Essex, UK.

Shiho Main (PhD) is a visiting fellow at the Centre for Psychoanalytic Studies at the University of Essex, UK, and an associate lecturer with the Open University. Her book, provisionally titled *Childhood Re-Imagined: Images and Narratives of Development in Analytical Psychology*, is forthcoming from Routledge.

Konoyu Nakamura (PhD) graduated from Doshisha University in Kyoto in 1974 and obtained her PhD from Konan University in Kobe in 1997 for her dissertation *Shinkeisei-shokuyoku-hushin-sho no Shinri-rinsho* (*Clinical Psychology for Anorexia Nervosa*). She has been working at many clinical arenas for more than 20 years as a Jungian oriented psychotherapist and she is a Professor at Otemon Gakuin University in Osaka and is involved in clinical work at her practice in Kyoto.

Susan Rowland (PhD) is Reader in English and Jungian Studies, at the University of Greenwich, UK. She was Chair of the International Association For Jungian Studies, 2003–6. Her publications include: *Jung as a Writer* (Routledge, 2005); *Jung: A Feminist Revision* (Polity, 2002); and *C.G. Jung and Literary Theory* (Palgrave, 1999).

Vincenzo Sanguineti is an Associate Professor of Psychiatry at Jefferson Medical College, Philadelphia, USA, and is a therapist in private practice. He is author of numerous psychiatric articles and of two books: *Landscapes in My Mind: The Origins and Structure of the Subjective Experience* (International Press, 1999); and *The Rosetta Stone for the Human Mind: Three Languages to Integrate Neurobiology and Psychology* (Springer, 2007).

Joy Schaverien (PhD) is a professional member of the SAP, with a private practice in the East Midlands. She is also Visiting Professor at the Northern Programme for Art Psychotherapy in Sheffield and a Training Therapist and Supervisor for the British Association of Psychotherapists. She is a member of the editorial board of the *Journal of Analytical Psychology*. Her contributions include: *Desire and the Female Therapist: Engendered Gazes in Psychotherapy and Art Therapy* (1995); *The Revealing Image* (1991); and (edited) *Gender, Countertransference and the Erotic Transference* (2006).

Leon Schlamm (PhD) is Lecturer in Religious Studies at the University of Kent, UK, and director of its MA programme in the study of mysticism and religious experience. He is author of numerous scholarly articles on Jung (particularly in *Harvest*), as well as on Rudolf Otto (*Religious Studies*) and transpersonal psychologist, Ken Wilber (*Religion*). He is presently working on a monograph, *C. G. Jung, Numinous Experience and the Study of Mysticism*, for Routledge.

Robert A. Segal (PhD) is Chair in Religious Studies, University of Aberdeen. Previously he was Professor of Theories of Religion, University of Lancaster. He is author of *The Poimandres as Myth: Scholarly Theory and Gnostic Meaning* (1986); *Joseph Campbell: An Introduction* (1990); *The Gnostic Jung* (1992); *The Allure of Gnosticism* (1995); *The Myth and Ritual Theory* (1998); *Jung on Mythology* (1998); *Theorizing About Myth* (1999); *Hero Myths: A Reader* (2003); *Myth: A Very Short Introduction* (2004), and *The Blackwell Companion to the Study of Religion* (2006).

Ann Shearer is a Jungian analyst working in London. She lectures widely and recently spent four years as a visiting supervisor for the International Association for Analytical Psychology training in St Petersburg. From 2001–3 she was also the Royal Literary Fund Writing Fellow at Imperial College, London. Previously, she was a journalist and a writer and international consultant on aspects of social welfare. Her books include *Athene: Image and Energy* (Viking/Penguin, 1996/1998) and (as co-editor), *When a Princess Dies* (Harvest Books, 1998).

David Tacey (PhD) is Associate Professor and Reader in the School of Critical Enquiry, La Trobe University, Australia. He is author of eight books and over 100 articles. His most recent books are: *How to Read Jung* (Granta, 2006); *The Spirituality Revolution* (Routledge, 2004); and *Jung and the New Age* (Routledge, 2001).

Acknowledgements

This rich collection of essays found their original form and expression as papers of 'Psyche and Imagination', the first conference of the *International Association of Jungian Studies* (IAJS: http://www.jungianstudies.org), at the University of Greenwich, UK, July 2006.

This landmark event brought together for the first time scholars of Jung and post-Jungian studies from across the world, to debate current academic research within a multidisciplinary framework. For this conference, I was fortunate to chair a particularly creative, astute and witty programme committee in Don Fredericksen, Leslie Gardner, Raya Jones, Susan Rowland (the then Chair of the IAJS) and David Tacey. Together we sought and found a diverse array of academic papers that explored and charted the imaginative depths of the psyche.

From out of the many representations of psyche and the imagination presented at the conference, a number of common themes inevitably emerged. I am grateful to Susan Rowland for highlighting two themes in particular, which have found their way to publication in two respective volumes: this book, on myth in the context of Jungian theory and practice and its companion book, *Psyche and the Arts: Jungian Perspectives in Painting, Art, Architecture and Poetry* (ed. Susan Rowland, London and New York: Routledge, forthcoming).

A number of people deserve recognition and praise for their direct and indirect contributions to this book. Most important, I wish to thank the authors of its chapters, who have not only made it what it is, but have put up with my fastidious comments in the process – I hope you enjoy the result of your efforts. I also thank them all for making the general editing of this book strangely entertaining.

I am especially thankful to David Tacey for the lengthy discussions (particularly those few occasions where we have disagreed) that have enabled the consolidation of my intuitions into thoughts for the shaping of this book. In a similar vein, a special thank you goes to Leslie Gardner and Susan Rowland for the frequent sessions of Pinot grigio and ice cream, which undoubtedly enabled the formation of these intuitions in the first place.

I am grateful for the editorial assistance of Jane Harris at Routledge, who was very efficient, helpful and friendly at every stage of the book's production.

The photograph of 'Apollo and Daphne' by Gian Lorenzo Bernini (sculpted between 1622–1625) is for David Tacey.

Note on the text

All references to the works of Jung are to paragraph number, not to page number, in accord with scholarly practice. References to the writings of Jung are indicated by the essay or chapter followed by *CW* (*Collected Works*) and the volume number. All references are to *The Collected Works of C.G. Jung*, translated by R.F.C. Hull, edited by H. Read, M. Fordham, G. Adler and William McGuire, and published in England by Routledge, London, and in America by Princeton University Press, Bollingen Series XX, 1953–1992. There are 20 volumes in the collected works and four supplementary volumes. The exceptions to this rule, where the page number is cited, are the following four works of Jung: *Memories Dreams Reflections*, *Modern Man in Search of a Soul*, *C.G. Jung Letters* (2 vols), *Visions: Notes of the Seminar Given in 1930–1934* (2 vols).

Chapter 1

Introduction: ordinarily mythical

Lucy Huskinson

> Not for a moment dare we succumb to the illusion that an archetype can be finally explained and disposed of. Even the best attempts at explanation are only more or less successful translations into another metaphorical language . . . The most we can do is to *dream the myth onwards* and give it a modern dress. And whatever explanation or interpretation does to it, we do to our own souls as well, with corresponding results for our own psychic well-being.
>
> (Jung 1951a: 271)

This is a collection of essays about myth. At a cursory glance, some essays may appear more closely linked to 'myth' than others. This is because I have extended the idea of myth beyond its common conception, which is, I believe, mistakenly reductive.

There are many theories and ideas about myth and I do not profess to give the definitive explanation here, far from it. To do so would be to inflate my own personal myth to the level of objectivity, thereby succumbing to the illusion Jung speaks of in the opening quotation. I do think it important, however, to outline my understanding of myth, not simply to shake myth free from common conception – which, as I shall show, it naturally eschews – but because it is the thread that binds the following chapters in sequence, enabling the book to be read as a coherent mythical story.

In this introduction, I delineate different aspects of myth as I envisage it. Close to the end of its writing, I became aware that my explanations are constellated in binary pairs, which is itself an expression of a collective myth of the West since Plato, which I have inherited. The reader of this book ought to bear in mind, therefore, that its conception is preconditioned by a particular mythological stance. The aspects of myth that I shall expound are (1) its personal and collective designations; (2) its dual function of describing an understanding of the world, and revealing how we might change this understanding; (3) its expression in different post-Jungian models as either one grand narrative (to which I give the name the *integrative* model) or multiple narratives (to which I give the name the *pluralist* model); and finally (4) its dynamic composition conceived as image and image-making process.

Roots of living myth

In my reading, myth is not merely an archaic story of human relationship (within the self, between each other, the gods or the natural world) that expresses universal truth of the human condition. Myth is also a living story that is developing within you, the reader, at this very moment. Myth refers as much to the extraordinary feats of embroidered characters as it does to the more familiar and subtle routines and patterns of our personal experiences. It is perhaps precisely because of their magnitude and extraordinariness that such epic stories have left a strong impression on us and have become known as the prototype of mythic adventure, while, the more mundane aspects of our personal lives become relegated – and even pitted in opposition to 'myth' – to the level of banality or to a disparaging notion of 'reality'. I am not suggesting that every moment of one's waking life comprises one's mythical ethos; such a position renders myth meaningless – for every experience is equalized, leaving no room for the imaginative and creative dialogue of contrary narratives, which is the prerequisite of psychological development. Rather, at the risk of being branded a primitive thinker, I want to reclaim aspects of our ordinary lives as the stuff of myth. The aspects to which I refer are those experiences that enable imaginative and creative dialogue within ourselves and from ourselves to others. Myth, as I see it, is a narrative that shapes and affects us, it is the order in which we make sense of ourselves and it reveals to us, through this ordering, how we might develop into something different.

Today we tend to lose sight of myth as an everyday phenomenon. We hold ourselves in poor regard, as unworthy loci of meaning. We thus search for meaning outside of ourselves, locating it, for example, within myths of the past, or in institutions of faith and materialism; or we try to alter ourselves artificially – through drug-induced states – to produce meaning and to enable its containment. This tendency of feeling out of place within ourselves exemplifies a lack of *rootedness* of being, a tendency that is frequently lamented in discourses of continental philosophy and also by Jung. Thus, Heidegger, who asserts that we have lost our home in the world, seeks *Bodenständigkeit* ['rootedness to earth'], by which he meant to convey (in addition to national affiliation and a regional sense of belonging) a metaphysical relation or profound attunement to the earth as a place of dwelling. *Bodenständigkeit* is a relationship to the earth that acknowledges its hidden and concealed dimension; only when we are rooted to the earth as the source and ground of our being, can we find meaning within ourselves. Nietzsche similarly calls for rootedness of being: 'Here we have our present age . . . bent on extermination of myth. Man today, stripped of myth, stands famished among all his pasts and must dig frantically for roots [*Wurzeln*], be it among the most remote antiquities' (1872: 136). Jung aligns himself to these ideas. In close parallel to Heidegger, Jung asserts: 'He who is rooted in the soil endures. Alienation from the unconscious and from its historical conditions spells rootlessness [. . . to the] earth ground of his being' (Jung 1927/1931: 103), and later, echoing Nietzsche – as he so often does – Jung contends: '[The] man who thinks he can live without myth, or outside it, like one uprooted, has no true link either with the past, or with the ancestral life which continues within him or yet with contemporary human society' (Jung 1951b: xxiv). Myth is that which sustains our rootedness to the world, and the vehicle through which we find meaning within ourselves. Our myths are the roots to our being and our relationship with the world.

Myth is not an ancient relic or closed narrative that applies only to days of yore; and neither, I contend, is myth merely a matter of our being affected by ancient narratives through their timeless applicability to human behaviour, though this of course is part of it. Myths are personal stories that are constantly evolving, and working themselves out through us. Myth is a narrative pattern that gives significance to our existence, and given that we are creatures of individuality and collectivity, 'myth' refers to both our collective and our personal stories. The boundaries of myth can be extended even further, beyond the collective realm, to include that of the transcendent, thereby suggesting that myth is autonomous and seeks conscious expression in us, through our stories. This latter speculation speaks of the ineffable, and could easily be considered a mythical story – one among many – of my psychological devising, rather than an a priori justification for the nature and origin of myth. Whether the transcendent is itself a myth or a source and composite of myth is, however, not a matter of dispute for Jungians, who readily accept its influence. The nature of the transcendent, however, is a matter for dispute for post-Jungians and later I shall address an implication of this disagreement for an understanding of the nature of myth.

Personal and collective myths

In my academic experience, myth as personal narrative is often eclipsed by analyses of traditional, epic stories of times long past. This tendency is reflected in Jung's work in terms of the numerous mythical stories examined throughout its corpus and the unremarkable, fleeting allusions to one's 'personal myth'. This is not to say that Jung values the personal myth any less; on the contrary, Jung maintains that, 'therapy only really begins after the investigation of that wholly personal story' (1961: 138). Furthermore, Jung took it on himself:

> [To] get to know 'my' myth, and I regarded this as the task of tasks, for – so I told myself – how could I, when treating my patients, make due

> allowance for the personal factor, for my personal equation, which is yet so necessary for a knowledge of the other person, if I was unconscious of it?
>
> (1951b: xxv)

It would seem that Jung was successful in his task of tasks, for later, at the age of 83, he decides it is time 'to tell my personal myth', '*my* fable, *my* truth'. Naturally, we find this proclamation in the prologue to his autobiography (*Memories, Dreams, Reflections*, 1961), which is by definition a narrative of life story and an attempt to communicate personal myth.

Strictly speaking 'personal myth' is a category error. The individual does not encounter a myth for himself or herself alone, which would be tantamount to him or her encountering a unique myth. To speak of a personal myth is to speak of an individual, original subjective colouring or variation of a myth that has been encountered before. Nihan Kaya expresses this point nicely in the following chapter, in citing Rollo May: 'No matter how many times Monet returned to paint the cathedral at Rouen, each canvas was a new painting expressing a new vision.' We are not so dissimilar from each other in our patterns of behaviour to warrant the discovery – individually or collectively – of a wholly new myth. Indeed, Jung argues that it is because we are all linked by a common ancestral life, which continues within each one of us, that a personal myth is not an individual matter: myth, for Jung, has 'sprung from the perennial rhizome beneath the earth'. In this sense, myth cannot be *created*; it is not a conscious or individual construct. What I refer to as 'personal myth' would in Jungian terms 'find itself in better accord with the truth if it took the existence of the rhizome into its calculations' (Jung 1951b: xxv). In this sense then, myth is a *discovery* of the collective within the individual. Myth is construed through imagery, but this imagery is not to be conceived as static narrative applicable for all time. Rather, it is dynamic, and is continually reshaped according to the living experiences and subjective orientation of its recipient – a point Susan Rowland encapsulates in her chapter with the words, 'a novel changes with every reading'. Myth is a story of human behaviour, which is continually retold in line with the developing behaviours of the human race, society, or individual personality with which it is concerned.

Myth is the story of your own life, which is itself rooted within a collective narrative of basic human behavioural patterns. Our mythical stories are personal narrations of our psychic situations. Our complexes, transferences and countertransferences, our childhood experiences and memories, our dreams and fantasies all provide fuel for the storylines and characters of our myth. One might go a step further, as did Freud, and maintain that the instincts – which constitute our psychic makeup – are themselves entities of myth (Freud 1933: 127). We could say that myth, as a narrative of the instincts, determines individuality. Indeed, while a Jungian might emphasize myth as the link between the individual and the collective (as that which roots us to our ancestral life and contemporary society), a Freudian might emphasize myth as a prerequisite of self-consciousness, as 'the step by which the individual emerges from group psychology' (Freud 1921: 136). Freud (and Jung would no doubt agree) sees the 'magnificence' of myths 'in their indefiniteness', which is to say that the value of myth lies in its subjective expression and dynamic nature, as opposed to abstract or closed stories of historical narrative. Myth as a narrative of instincts gives rise to new possibilities, new stories and situations, evolving in response to the old. Myth is thereby seen as a continuing life story, which is therapeutically valued in its capacity to heal and transform impotent, unworkable life experiences into ones that are productive and enriched. Myth is therapy insofar as it enables us to function according to new structures of meaning.

As an evolving account of human behaviour, myth narrates the past, present, and future experiences of psychological development. I take the past narrative of a person to comprise the facts of his or her past experiences, which are ungraspable and recorded accurately only in the unconscious. The present narrative, in contrast, describes the current psychic disposition of a person. This subsequently determines how a person understands and makes sense of his or her life, which is to say how he or she remembers and interprets his or her past experiences. This narrative is filtered through the complexes and transferences that have grown in response to these experiences. Finally, the future narrative describes the potential development of the psyche and how the person can learn to approach the world differently and reinterpret his or her place within it. While the present narrative is an interpretation of the past narrative, the future narrative is a potential redressing and compensation of the present narrative. The future narrative describes the movement away from old and defunct ways of understanding; it suggests a resolution – if only partial – of the complexes and transferences that influenced the present narrative and its understanding of the past. The future narrative is thus a new storyline, which can replenish and overcome the failure of the old. The future narrative is the promise of a greater understanding of one's life story, which is tantamount to the ego realizing that it is not the sole actor and narrator of the story. And this enables the many voices of the psyche their expression. The healing capacity of myth is harnessed when we recognize that myth is not wholly personal – ego centred or narcissistic and of personal construct – but is a narrative of the collective and is thus a discovery of the personal within the collective.

Regressive and progressive myths

I have schematized the nature of myth chronologically, in terms of a developing psychological life story of past, present and future narrative. Of course, one's life story cannot be dissected in so clear-cut a fashion as my depiction suggests – just as Jung's depiction of the 'life-stages' does not translate well into many people's experiences of life or, indeed, into their personal mythology. Myth is timeless in its applicability, and its nature cannot be pinned down and encapsulated by reason alone, for as I outline here, myth is a composite of reason and non-reason, of conscious and unconscious expression. My personal myth and my subsequent understanding of the dynamics of life will not be the same as yours and, indeed, I hope it isn't – for to reiterate Freud's remark: in the indefiniteness of myth we find its magnificence. Reason can, however, help to communicate abstract aspects of myth and in this introduction I wish to convey what I consider to be a dual aspect of myth, which is itself an expression of the therapeutic process of healing. That is, myth describes our understanding of life, and subsequently reveals how we might change this understanding. To further stress its twofold character, I turn to Rollo May, who defines myth in terms of its regressive and progressive functions:

> First the myth brings into awareness the repressed, unconscious, archaic urges, longings, dreads, and other psychic content. This is the *regressive* function of myths. But also, the myth reveals *new* goals, *new* ethical insights and possibilities. Myths are a breaking through of greater meaning which was not present before. The myth in this respect is the way of working out the problem on a higher level of integration. This is the *progressive* function of myths.
>
> (May 1991: 86)

May believes that classical psychoanalysis has focused on the regressive function of myths at the expense of the progressive function, so that myths are considered phenomena of the outside world – as '"projections" into ethical and other forms of meaning' (ibid.) – and not as an integrative function of the internal world. To conceive myth as a regressive function only is to reduce myth to historical narrative, where life is determined by past experience, of who we were and not who we could be, which, as Birgit Heuer's chapter suggests, is equivalent to evaluating the patient negatively through the lens of pathology – that is, according to his or her ambivalent attachment to an object that is appropriate to an earlier stage of development. These conceptions do not correspond to premises of the Jungian model of the psyche, which is essentially progressive and teleological.[1] The self-regulating aspect of the Jungian psyche anticipates the future narrative or appropriate psychic development by unconsciously redressing the imbalance and prejudices of the current ego orientation. The Jungian psyche therefore mediates past, present and future narratives. Myth, as a narrative of how we understand ourselves, must, from a Jungian perspective, include a sense of our future selves and must therefore incorporate the progressive aspect. As well as traversing time, the Jungian psyche traverses space, between the personal and collective, so that the deeper an understanding of one's personal myth, the deeper the connection and empathy would be for the collective myth of the human condition. (cf. Jung 1917/1926/1943: 74; 1921: 119; 1957: 540). May also regards myth as a bridge between personal and collective, which effectively leads to mental healing:

> By drawing out inner reality [myths] enable the person to experience greater reality in the outside world . . . They are roads to universals beyond one's concrete experience. It is only on the basis of such a faith that the individual can genuinely accept and overcome earlier infantile deprivations without continuing to harbour resentment all through one's life. In this sense myth helps us accept our past, and we then find it opens before us our future.
>
> (May 1991: 87)

Myth reveals the nature of our life journey; it charts the development of our neuroses and suggests how we might begin to resolve them. While May suggests a division in psychological perspectives in the value of the regressive and progressive functions of myth – which I take to mean that a typical Freudian is likely to favour the regressive aspect, while a typical Jungian is likely to favour the progressive aspect – I want to go a step further, and suggest a division in Jungian views over the progressive function itself.

The potential for psychic change or healing – which May calls the progressive function and which I have referred to as the future narrative – cannot be harnessed by the ego alone. Indeed, earlier I said that it is expressed or initiated by 'the many voices of the psyche'. Psychological change is a feat that transcends ego consciousness, and which finds motivation in the autonomy of the unconscious. How we conceptualize this transcendent motivation is disputed in post-Jungian circles: it either has a unified agenda or it does not. The astute reader of the chapters that follow will find both positions represented and the debate that takes place between the chapters animated, for in most cases it is the author's intention to extol the virtues of one position at the expense of the other. Those post-Jungians who contend that the transcendent has a hidden plan of unity, maintain that it sanctions values of wholeness or completeness of being. That is to say, they maintain that a person's psychological development is influenced by a transcendent ordering principle, the aspiration of which is to transform the ego with its one-sided prejudices into a whole Self of objective interest. I call this interpretation the *integrative* position. Those who reject this thesis, believing the transcendent to be without unifying intention, maintain that the ego is affected in its encounter with the transcendent as the recipient of a multitude of different – often contradictory – principles. Although patterns and connections emerge in this seeming disarray, the transcendent in this scenario favours 'dissolution' as much as it does integration.[2] I call this interpretation the *pluralist* position.

These two positions offer very different accounts for the understanding of one's life. We could therefore say that they express different myths – the integrative position advocates a myth of balance and harmony, while the pluralist position upholds a myth of multiplicity. We could go a step further in establishing these positions as expressions of collective myth through their amplification and affective appeal. This can be achieved through their personification as mythical figures of human form, thereby enabling us to converse with them more naturally or instinctively. Because my imagination is rooted in Western European tradition, it often finds shape and form in the mythological traditions of Christianity, ancient Greece and Rome. The monotheistic paradigm of Christianity lends appropriate representation to the integrative position, while the pantheon of the many gods of Greece and Rome exemplify the pluralist position, with specific personification in Hermes, the trickster god of changing roles, or Proteus, god of many forms. The two positions I expound are not bifurcated by these different mythological traditions of the West; these mythologies personify both positions. Thus, the Trinity and the many saints and martyrs of Christianity epitomize the pluralist position; and I am inclined to imagine the integrative position in light of Ann Shearer's chapter, as an expression of the Greek goddess Themis: the 'right order' and lawgiver of balance and justice.

The integrative and pluralist positions offer very different interpretations of the nature and dynamics of myth and, subsequently, of the many voices of the transcendent. As Themis brings the gods together in lawful governance and assembly, Hermes flutters between them as their messenger. To accept that the transcendent has an agenda of unity is to acknowledge that we are all embroiled in a master narrative or master myth, which is an understanding of the world according to the transcendent – an understanding of the world in itself, of objective reality. Likewise, our personal myths are but facets of this master myth: vehicles through which the transcendent communicates its cause. An implication of this is that, as we develop, we advance and evolve towards greater knowledge of the master myth and to a greater experience and comprehension of objective reality. The Self – Jung's mythological conception of the fully individuated ego – is his personification of the one who experiences all, through the integration of unconsciousness into consciousness. To reject the notion that the transcendent has an agenda of unity is to reject the hypothesis of a master narrative or master myth. There is no cohesive whole or embodied synergy of which the many myths are part; there are only the many myths, which may form meaningful relationships between themselves, but are not constellated in an a priori single organized structure or configuration.

The integrative and pluralist positions appear very differently from the perspective of the ego. Both positions demand a defeat for the ego (which is a prerequisite for psychological development and healing); but while the first scenario grants salvation to the ego by facilitating its rebirth in a more enriched form, the second leaves it at the mercy of the objective forces that it encounters. In the first scenario, the ego is an active participant in a hidden process, while, in the second, the ego experiences itself within its own boundaries, which are then pushed and pulled in its encounters with the many archetypal forces that remain outside it. It is easy to get carried away by describing these different conceptions of the interplay of ego and transcendent, and it is even easier to exaggerate their difference, making them appear crude. Nevertheless, I would like to draw attention to their different emphases, of a gradual and unseen process of integration, on the one hand, and an immediate encounter with many faces and voices, on the other. I want to do this in order to contrast the two post-Jungian positions further and to have them introduce two important facets of the composition of myth: myth as image and myth as process of image making. Although the different emphases of the two post-Jungian positions share similarities with these two facets of myth, they do not map directly on to them, as I shall show. These facets are not so much the expression of the different emphases of the post-Jungian positions, as they are connotations of the nature and function of the symbol, as conceived by Jung. (And yet we shall see that these different emphases are not unrelated to the different connotations of the symbol.) In its symbolic status, I see myth as an image and a process of image creation.

Symbol, image, process

Myth mediates between ego consciousness and transcendent Other, regardless of whether it finds itself a vehicle of integration and harmony. Myth reveals old and new patterns of thinking and self-reflection and while there is continuity between old and new, they can be experienced as wholly different in character and the transition between them is tantamount to dialoguing with the Other. As mediator of ego consciousness and the transcendent, myth is in liminal space and is symbolic in status. Myth is a conscious interpretation of unconscious communication and as such its nature is both rational and non-rational, archetypal image and ineffable, numinous 'content'. As symbols, myths are clothed with finite images that are subjectively defined by the ego according to its response to the transcendent and its own conscious attitude or orientation (Jung 1951c: 355). The image has a subjective power and can therefore be experienced as a symbol for one person and an ineffective sign for another. Likewise, from an objective standpoint, one mythic image is only as appropriate as the next. If a mythic image no longer affects ego consciousness it is demoted from the symbolic order to that of sign, and then, in accordance with Jung's premise of a teleological and self-regulating psyche, another mythic image –

potent and alive – will take its place. In this scheme we can see the two facets of myth at work: myth as an image and myth as a process of image making.

These two facets of myth are significant and I find them located within Jung's thesis. For instance, in the following passage, which is often cited in support of the idea that image is primary, Jung alludes to something more fundamental and a priori, which lends image its form:

> A dark impulse is the ultimate arbiter of the pattern, an unconscious *a priori* precipitates itself into plastic form . . . Over the whole procedure there seems to reign a dim foreknowledge not only of the pattern but of its meaning. Image and meaning are identical; and as the first takes shape, so the latter becomes clear. Actually the pattern needs no interpretation: it portrays its own meaning.
>
> (1931: 402)

Admittedly, Jung implies here that, strictly speaking, this more fundamental impulse is not 'meaningful'; however, it is useful as it functions as a transcendental postulate of the objective origins of the symbolic image (in contradistinction to the subjective origin in its recipient). Although the mythic image is all that we can comprehend, Jung seems to posit the existence of an authority that oversees the development of the image. I have further speculated that this is an ineffable manifestation of energy that replaces obsolete signs with living symbols.[3] Of the two post-Jungian positions I mention, only the integrative position would regard the image-making process and the sequence of its images as having a preordained symmetry and wholeness. Although the pluralist position is unlikely to regard the manifestation of images as arbitrary and unrelated to each other and would admit an *a priori* constellation of images in small groupings (such as the archetypal dyads of hero/villain and parent/child), it would not go so far as to consider these images snapshots of divine harmony or of one primary constellation seeking conscious expression.

The pluralist position may still accept a purposive process underlying the manifestation of mythic images, so long as the images of its production are equivalent, which is to say that a more recent image is not an 'improvement' on previous ones. Both positions value the images in themselves and they would look between the images to try to discover the underlying meaning of which they are sequential, descriptive narratives.[4]

The image of myth and its underlying creative process are two interpretations of the way in which myth configures an understanding of the world. Although they may lead to very different conclusions, they do so according to a common premise: that meaning is transitory (as an evolutionary process of development or flux of multiple values). I understand myth as a dynamic composition, which mediates between self and other, thereby facilitating creative dialogue and psychological development. Myth is a healing narrative, but only insofar as it is located within the self. To find myth outside of oneself is to become famished and isolated from creative interplay with the other; to find myth within is to harness the communications of the transcendent and subsequently to encounter narratives different from that of the current ego orientation, thereby encouraging its change and potential enrichment. Our myths change as we do; they continually regenerate within us. The theory that I extol here is part of my myth and it may become empty for me as I develop and encounter its different parts. The myth of Jungian theory is no less in transition: its structures must be revised and updated to incorporate changes in our collective values or meanings. *Dreaming the Myth Onwards: New Directions in Jungian Therapy and Thought* is precisely about the changing faces of the Jungian model. Whether these chapters exemplify *progress* and advancement or just another set of viewpoints is left for the reader to decide.

The chapters

By outlining my understanding of myth on the pretext that it binds the following chapters in sequence, lending coherence to the book as a whole, I have upheld the *integrative* position. I wish also to advocate the *pluralist* position by letting the chapters speak for themselves. To this end, I offer only their brief summary and introduction.

The book is divided into four parts. The first part, Directing Onwards, which comprises one chapter, describes further how we might conceptualize the underlying conditions that enable myth and therapy. In other words, how might myth be dreamt onwards and in what conditions can new directions of Jungian thought and therapy be conceived? Myth and therapy are expressions of creative play and Nihan Kaya in her chapter examines how creativity transforms aspects of the ordinary into experiences of art. In Kaya's chapter, the mythic and therapeutic concern becomes the existential motivation of the artist. Myth and therapy are achieved through the vision of the artist, who is compelled to create. Kaya argues that the artist is a 'non-conformist', found outside the norms and boundaries of tradition and the consensus of collective consciousness. This has important implications for the transition of myth and the generation of new meaning, for it suggests that the seeds of progress are found in marginalized structures: in the overlooked minority we find the new visionaries (a point taken up later by David Tacey and Susan Rowland).

The second part, Changing Faces of Myth, comprises six chapters, which examine the contemporary relevance of myth by assessing its utility as a general approach to life and by locating its position in the context of Jungian thought. The questions raised in this part express the ambiguity of this thing we call myth. It is elusive in its transcendence and yet it is within our reach. Vincenzo Sanguineti and Ann Shearer begin this part by grasping myth in the here and now, as an effective tool of examination and integration.

Sanguineti elaborates the epigraph of this introduction to argue that myth is a narrative of many voices, which translate an ineffable truth into metaphor. Sanguineti analyses the myth of Psyche from the perspectives of modern physics, neuroscience, psychology, art, poetry and artificial intelligence (computer science) to argue for the universal applicability of the meaning of myth. While Sanguineti utilizes disparate concepts to illustrate the general significance of myth, Shearer utilizes a particular myth to illustrate the significance of the multifaceted concept of the Jungian Self. Shearer argues that the personification of the Self in the goddess Themis enables us to explain the unconscious dynamic that underlies the healing of the splits and traumas of modernity. To illustrate her argument, she explains how the opposites of victim and perpetrator find resolution in their integration through systems and models of restorative justice.

David Tacey and Susan Rowland continue Shearer's quest to expound a cure for modernity's ills through the discourse of myth, and likewise find in Jungian narrative an appropriate resource. Tacey identifies modernity's illness as the promotion of rational discourse at the expense of the non-rational, while Rowland's diagnosis is of an imbalance in the complementary discourses of separation and relationship (and, perhaps we could also conceive this as an imbalance in the promotion of the pluralist and integrative positions).

Tacey argues for the constancy of the transcendent despite its apparent recent disappearance in modern collective consciousness. Through a comparative analysis of the thought of Jung and Derrida, Tacey argues that its disappearance is an expression of a deconstructive phase, which is necessary to unravel old meanings in order to evoke the new. We are thus living in a liminal time – at the brink of a new collective myth – when a new more imaginative discourse will emerge from the now tired discourses of reason, and the transcendent will be perceived as having re-awoken from its slumber.

Rowland, by using theories of Foucault and Bakhtin to link Jung's writings to notions of dialogics and science, shows how Jung powerfully unites the seemingly disparate functions and practices of myth and discourse. Rowland argues that the content and stylistic manner of Jung's writings express both an underlying unity and a plurality of voices, which suggests that Jung strove for a rational coherence that is continually interrupted by a diversity of representation.

While Tacey and Rowland assert Jung's writings as myth, Michael Vannoy Adams and Robert Segal separate this identification to question the compatibility of mythological thinking with Jungian thought, asking at the same time whether myth is an appropriate contemporary approach for life.

Adams argues that myth still has an essential function in Jungian studies. In contrast to Wolfgang Giegerich, who asserts that at this stage in the history of consciousness myth no longer has any psychological function because the modern situation is so radically different from the ancient situation as to be incommensurable with it, Adams contends that myth remains vitally relevant. To demonstrate how the 'gods' and 'goddesses' are not dead but are alive and well, Adams discusses how the image of Aphrodite manifests itself as a metaphor in the lives of contemporary men and women.

Segal surveys the historical role of myth in relation to natural science and examines the conditions for its relevance in the twenty-first century and to Jungian psychology in particular. Segal asks whether myth can provide insight into the physical world as well as remaining compatible with natural science; and the Jungian answer, he argues, is problematic and ambiguous. Thus, on the one hand, Jung regards myth as a narrative of the mind and not the physical world, so that myth functions to encounter, not to explain, the mind. On the other hand, Jung develops a theory of synchronicity, which links the mind to the world, but in a way that sidesteps the traditional scientific issue of causality. Segal seeks resolution to this ambiguity by asking whether a myth tied to synchronicity is in fact about the world and not just the mind.

The third part, Myths at Play, examines the phenomena of active imagination, transference and countertransference as psychodynamic processes of myth, and illustrates how these mythic phenomena give meaning to Jungian theory and therapeutic experience. Active imagination is a 'dreaming with eyes open', whereby the image of myth is brought into greater conscious awareness, thereby enabling one to engage directly with the immensity of mythical image or, as Leon Schlamm explains through the words of Gerhard Adler, 'it enables one to talk *with* God, rather than *about* him'. In his chapter, Schlamm examines Jung's *Answer to Job* as both a paradigmatic illustration of the meditative practice of active imagination and as independent confirmation of the efficacy and value of its practice.

Transference and countertransference lends expression to the liminal space of myth as typically placed within the mythological figure of the analyst: the person who embodies both the real and the illusory, the object of both inner and outer worlds. Through transference the analyst becomes an active figure in the personal myth of the analysand. Joy Schaverein explains transference as a journey taken by both analyst and analysand in a time machine, a journey of imagination that travels through narratives of past, present and future. By returning to the personal imaginal realm of the past, Schaverien argues that the analysand can anticipate the future. Countertransference, by contrast, inhibits progress of the healing journey, as Schaverein reveals it is a form of active imagination or 'enchantment', which causes the analyst to become temporarily transfixed by the personal, mythical narrative of the analysand. Konoyu Nakamura continues to explore the *fascinans* of transference and the therapeutic implications of working within this liminal space of myth. Nakamura evokes the affective and transformative power of transference as the carrier of mythological image, as she recalls the time when the image of *Mahavairocana-tatha-gata* – the principal deity of esoteric Buddhism – appeared to her in response to a critical moment in her analysis of a patient.

The fourth and final part, Psychic Revisions: Towards a New Mythology, showcases fresh readings of Jungian concepts that are central to his model, updated in accordance with shifts and changes in the cultural and epistemological concerns of contemporary Western consciousness. The first three chapters in this part focus on changes in cultural connotations of gender and age – of femininity, masculinity and childhood respectively – and the implications of this for the Jungian model: either as a tool for making sense of these changes, or for pointing out how the Jungian model must adapt to accommodate these changes. Thus, Phil Goss explains how the concept 'animus' has come to be associated with unhealthy taboo, which infects its expression and utility not only in the 'consulting room', but also in our wider dialogues around gender. Goss draws on clinical example, folklore and mythological narrative on animus to explain how the negative animus can be valued as a bridge to intra-psychic development and fuller interpersonal relations. Frances Gray similarly calls for a revised interpretation of the anima and its role within psychological development. Gray argues for this through a comparative analysis of the feminine soul as propounded by Plato and Jung. Gray criticizes the emphasis they place on the anima's propensity to disorder, non-reason, and apparent 'immorality'. By utilizing the ideas of Luce Irigaray, Gray attempts to reinvest the anima with positive and 'morally' acceptable meaning. Shiho Main asks us to re-imagine the adult's image of the child and asks how Jungians can challenge and advance the prevailing social frameworks for understanding childhood issues. She focuses her argument on controversies over international legislation on children's rights, with particular reference to current debates about the United Nations Convention on the Rights of the Child.

The final two chapters seek to incorporate Jungian ideas into the narrative of scientific myth. Science, as an understanding of the world, is after all mythical narrative. As Freud asserts in a letter to Einstein:

> It may perhaps seem to you as though our theories are a kind of mythology . . . but does not every science come in the end to a kind of mythology like this? Cannot the same be said today of your Physical Sciences?
>
> (September 1932; cited in Nathan and Norden 1960: 199)

I am wary of the dangerous desire to rationalize the non-rational and of the scientific premise of making myth mundane, rather than, as I seek, of finding myth in the mundane. However, if Jungian discourse is to step out of the sidelines and have its visionary voice integrated more fully into collective consciousness, it would do well to enter into dialogue with other, widely accepted, 'scientific' disciplines; and this is what Birgit Heuer and Honor Griffith attempt valiantly, at the risk of controversy. Heuer rethinks the way in which clinical theory conceptualizes therapeutic process, by resituating the dynamics of psychotherapeutic healing in a more positive and integrative perspective, one that links quantum field theory and research, mystical experience and psychotherapy. Griffith argues that a new paradigm for understanding and treating psychopathology is emerging out of the convergence of research in the fields of neurobiology, attachment theory and in the effects of trauma. Griffith applies this new paradigm to Jung's theory of the complex and argues for a new method that can animate the embodied image at the core of the complex and subsequently facilitate healing. Implicit in both Heuer's and Griffith's chapters is the controversial idea that one can manipulate the transcendent, either by visualizing it a certain way and thereby making it so (i.e. by wishing the patient into health) or by increasing its capacity for communication (i.e. by speeding up the therapeutic process, thereby anticipating the potential for short-term psychoanalysis – but not its desirability).

I end the introduction to this book with Apollo and Daphne, who animate its (paperback) cover in mutual struggle. In their relationship we find the dynamic of mythical narrative, as I have presented it: the changing image, which maintains appropriate relations between reason and imagination and a subsequent transition of meaning.

Apollo (embodiment of reason) is in inappropriate pursuit of Daphne (an anima figure) as a result of having been pierced through the heart with the arrow of resentful Eros. Daphne, fearful of Apollo's desire for her, flees from him, leaving his romantic plea to her half uttered. As Apollo gains on his prey, Daphne calls on her father, Peneus the river god, to change her form from that which has brought her into such danger. Daphne is subsequently changed into a laurel tree. Apollo stands amazed, embracing her branches and declares the tree to be his evergreen and splendid representative – in contradistinction to an object of his possession. Daphne, in her tree form, bows her head in grateful acknowledgement.

There is no relationship or dialogue between Apollo and Daphne in her human (nymph) form. In this scenario, reason desires to possess the imagination, seeking to reduce the non-rational to its rational terms (which is expressed by Apollo in response to Daphne's windswept hair: 'If so charming in disorder, what would it be if arranged'). To counteract this, Daphne is transformed into a different form – a laurel tree, which is a Self-symbol according to Jung (1950: 582) – which enables her to face the reasoning of Apollo: to acknowledge and accept his words, which now affirm her nature, rather than her idealized image. In this scenario, reason finds grounding in nature: a rootedness to the earth.

I thank David Tacey for our discussions over the general themes presented here, and Arthur David Smith for helping me to comprehend the philosophical implications of teleology through a process of dissolution.

Notes

1 Of course, the Jungian psyche has both a positive and a negative current (Jung 1925: 26). Nevertheless, to accentuate the contrast between the regressive psychoanalytic understanding of myth and its more progressive stance in Jung, we would do well to cite the clinical concept of 'personal myth', first expounded by Ernst Kris (1956). By 'personal myth', Kris refers to an autobiographical set of memories that are distorted and recalled as screen memories. These are constructed in order to repress a traumatic memory associated with Oedipal conflict. The autobiographical self-image subsequently takes the place of repressed fantasy from which it derives. A personal myth in this case is a pathological extreme in a particular kind of obsessional personality – one that clings to a distorted version of its personal history, both resisting any exploration of it and incapable of identifying any significant events within it. 'Personal myth' in its clinical psychoanalytic usage is a narrow concept of a particular kind of personality *disorder*, which is in stark contradistinction to the wider usage I expound in this introduction – of a general *ordering* of life experience. It is a function that conceals rather than reveals, a manifestation of unconscious conflict rather than of conscious and unconscious creative dialogue, a compromise formation rather than a mediation to more enriched functioning.

2 This is not to say that the integrative position avoids dissolution. Dissolution is an inevitable process of psychological development. My point is that while the integrative position regards dissolution as a process second in significance to integration (that is, things dissolve in order to facilitate a greater integration later on), the pluralist position regards the two processes as having equal status.

3 The transcendent symbolic unfolding of the image-making process of myth is equivalent to Jung's concept of the transcendent function – where new symbolic content and impetus is established to overcome the inertia of outmoded content. According to Jung, the transcendent function is 'a natural process, a manifestation of the energy that springs from the tension of opposites, and it consists in a series of fantasy-occurrences which appear spontaneously' (Jung 1917/1926/1943: 121). It is 'a process not of dissolution but of construction, in which thesis and antithesis both play their part. In this way it becomes a new content that governs the whole attitude, putting an end to the division and forcing the energy of the opposite into a common channel. The standstill is overcome and life can flow on with renewed power towards new goals' (Jung 1921: 827). The transcendent function is a third living thing that is grown from the tension of opposites. Likewise, myth is the mediation point between the mystery of life and the ego's struggle to make sense of it.

4 In differentiating between myth as image and image-making process, we arrive at two different approaches to understanding the world. To illustrate the significance

of these contrasting approaches, I shall outline how they might respond to the question of God's existence.

The prevailing tendency of postmodern times is to value the mythic image and disregard the meta-narrative of the image-making process, even if it is divested of purpose and does not point to divine agency. In this case, the image is regarded in isolation and as having contingent value; likewise, images are not sequential but appear in random flux. The postmodern position can proclaim the death of God because the traditional God-image is no longer an affective symbol of modern consciousness. God has been demoted to mere sign for the majority of educated people and another (more potent) image takes its place as a representation of meaning (such as humanism, deconstructionism, or materialism). While mythic images come and go to replace one another, the underlying creative process of image making is constant. If God were identified with this creative process, then God would be very much alive and the God image (or images) would be in transition. In this scenario God would not be conceived as one image in isolation – potent as a living symbol or impotent as a dead symbol or sign depending on the recipient. Instead God would be identified with the underlying process of image making, or as the totality of images in dynamic transition. God is kept alive only if God's image is allowed to evolve. This explains why the Christian image of God is dying and doomed to stagnation for Jung: 'Christianity slumbers and has neglected to develop its myth further in the course of the centuries . . . [consequently, this] myth has become mute, and gives no answers' (Jung 1961: 364). God can be interpreted as the source of the renewal of images, and not an image. In this sense, God is the living symbol – God is alive when meaning is formed and where there is a change or transition in meaning. God is, likewise, that which *roots* our being, for God is the capacity that enables us to make sense of our lives, a capacity that we discover working within us and not an image external to us.

References

Freud, S. (1921) 'Group Psychology and the Analysis of the Ego', trans J. Strachey, London: The Hogarth Press and The Institute of Psychoanalysis, *Standard Edition* 18: 69–143.

—— (1933) 'New Introductory Lectures on Psychoanalysis', The Penguin Freud Library, vol. 2, Angela Richards (ed.), London: Penguin Books.

Jung, C.G. (1917/1926/1943) 'On the Psychology of the Unconscious', *CW* 17, 1954/1970: 1–201.

—— (1921) *Psychological Types*, *CW* 6, 1971.

—— (1925) *Analytical Psychology: Notes on the Seminar Given in 1925*, ed. W. McGuire, Princeton: Princeton University Press, 1989.

—— (1927/1931) 'Mind and Earth', *CW* 10, 1964/1970: 49–103.

—— (1931) 'On the Nature of the Psyche', *CW* 8, 1960: 343–442.

—— (1950) 'A Study in the Process of Individuation', *CW* 9i, 1959/1968: 525–626.

—— (1951a) 'The Psychology of the Child Archetype', *CW* 9i, 1959/1968: 259–305.

—— (1951b) 'Foreword to the Fourth (Swiss) Edition', *Symbols of Transformation*, *CW* 5, 1956: xxiii–vi.

—— (1951c) *Aion: Researches into the Phenomenology of the Self*, *CW* 9ii, 1959/1968.

—— (1957) 'The Undiscovered Self (Present and Future)', *CW* 10, 1964/1970: 488–588.

—— (1961) *Memories, Dreams, Reflections*, London: Fontana Press, 1995.

Kris, E. (1956) 'The Personal Myth' in *The Selected Papers of Ernst Kris*, New Haven: Yale University Press, 1975: 272–300.

May, R. (1991) *The Cry for Myth*, New York: Dell Publishing.

Nathan, O. and Norden, H. (eds) (1960) *Einstein on Peace*, New York: Schocken Books.

Nietzsche, F. (1872) *The Birth of Tragedy*, trans. W. Kaufmann, New York: Vintage, 1967.

Part 1

Directing onwards

Chapter 2

Compelled to create: the courage to go beyond

Nihan Kaya

Creativity is defined as 'the ability to bring something *new* into existence' (Barron 1965: 3; italics mine). Likewise, all artistic products are characterized as being new, authentic and highly subjective. Indeed, this characteristic is the essential core of any artistic piece. A piece is considered to have no artistic value if it is simply a copy of something else that exists. When a painter depicts a tree in nature, the painting is no longer a portrayal of the tree in nature; it becomes another, unique and original tree *beyond* that which it portrays. This *beyondness* is what makes a work of art rather than a commonplace perception of reality; it is the motivation of the artist; it is our sense of artistic pleasure; and it is the ground that enables the artist's communication of his or her inner world in the objective outer world. The artwork is produced by elements that are brought together, which in themselves reveal a self-expression; but art itself begins at the point where the piece goes *beyond* its elements. A novel is more than its composition of plot, language and story. It may be considered a bad novel by literary criteria, even if its different elements or components are considered to be very good. Artistic energy generates charge in a synthesis of elements, but it is not to be identified with these elements; it goes *beyond* their combination. Art lies beyond its elements, which appear ordinary. Rollo May illustrates the point, 'No matter how many times Monet returned to paint the cathedral at Rouen, each canvas was a new painting expressing a new vision' (May 1975: 90).

I uphold Ayn Rand's definition of art, as '*a selective recreation of reality according to an artist's metaphysical value-judgments*' (Rand 1969: 19). Art is a new interpretation of that which is already created. The created work destroys the prevailing forms of existence, while offering a new form of its own instead. As Picasso remarked, 'Every act of creation is first of all an act of destruction.' The work of art deconstructs the conventional, the official and the standardized, in order to replace it with the individual, authentic substitute that it reconstructs. Jung calls this 'creative destruction' (1934: 119). Jung writes:

> Far from his work being an expression of the destruction of personality, the modern artist finds the unity of his artistic personality in destructiveness. The Mephistophelian perversion of sense into nonsense, of beauty into ugliness – in such an exasperating way that nonsense almost makes sense and ugliness has a provocative beauty – is a creative achievement that has never been pushed to such extremes in the history of human culture.
>
> (Jung 1934: 118)

With reference to *Ulysses*, Jung continues to say that art finds 'wonder' in destruction:

> In its destruction of the criteria of beauty and meaning that have held till today, *Ulysses* accomplishes wonders. It insults all our conventional feelings, it brutally disappoints our expectations of sense and content, it thumbs its nose at all synthesis.
>
> (ibid.)

The artist uses his or her tools, such as paint, images, stones and musical notes, which are common and familiar to all; but the keynote of his or her art is concealed within the nuances through which he or she uses these differently to others. The poet takes words that are communal and which function in their communality; and then, through clipping, intertwining and distorting their conventional meaning and usage, he or she transcends their ordinariness, working them into a new network of language, out of which the art of poetry is born. A peculiar language is created from out of the ordinary one, which provides the medium for this creative process. It is impossible to speak of any artistic stir when everything conforms to the established order. The established is a standstill. Art, by the same token, is perceived as a stir, either when it *stir*s the mind of the artist, causing him or her to produce it or when it reaches out to those who are able to be *move*d by it. The creative action is essentially non-conformist. Anthony Storr writes:

> Most authorities who have studied creative people agree that one of their most notable characteristic is independence. This shows itself particularly in the fact that they are much more influenced by their own, inner standards than by those of the society . . . Another interesting aspect of this trait of independence is the fact that the highly creative belong to fewer organizations and social groups than do their less creative contemporaries.
>
> (Storr 1972: 189)

It is my personal conviction, without any academic ground, that artists feel compelled to produce works because they don't know of any other way to *exist*. It is crucial that the concepts 'to be' and 'to create' go hand in hand. In the preface of his book *Courage to Create* (the title of which is derived from Paul Tillich's *The Courage to Be*), Rollo May says that 'Creativity is a necessary sequel to being'. The individual cannot really exist if he or she is fully integrated into his or her already existing environment (cf. Winnicott 1962: 61).

'It is only the true self that can be creative': Winnicott and Jung

This 'false existence' through full compliance or integration is similar to the 'false-self' in Winnicott. According to Winnicott, every person is divided into a false and a true self in some ratio or other. Furthermore, he argues that 'Only the True Self can be creative' (Winnicott 1960: 148), and 'the False Self, however well set up, lacks something, and that something is the essential central element of creative originality' (ibid.: 152). Winnicott defines psychotherapy as the search for the (true) self, meaning the search for the sense of feeling *real* inside (Winnicott 1971b), and this is achieved through creativity: 'it is only in being creative that the individual discovers the self' (Winnicott 1971a: 54).

Winnicott describes the false self as a polite or socialized self that each person develops to help him or her adapt to his or her environment. The false self is thought to correspond to Jung's understanding of the *persona* (see Abram 1996: 282). This term derives from the Latin word for 'mask', which was a prop worn by actors in classical times and which indicated the character role they played. Jung defines persona thus:

> A mask of the collective psyche, a mask that *feigns individuality*, making others and oneself believe that one is individual, whereas one is simply acting a role through which the collective psyche speaks . . . [it is] a compromise between individual and society as to what a man should appear to be.
>
> (Jung 1928: 157–8)

In his autobiography *Memories, Dreams, Reflections* (1963), Jung refers to his own persona as the 'No.1 personality', which, he says, is overshadowed by his creative, skeptical and mystical No.2 personality. Like Winnicott, Jung agrees that every person has these two, divided personalities. Furthermore, Jung says that his No.2 personality or true self is 'Other' and doesn't abide by the demands of society, and subsequently has to be hidden from others.

Because of its reformist nature, creativity has always been perceived as a threat to the collective consciousness. Gardner writes:

> Gruber reminds us of the difficulty and loneliness of any creative undertaking. Despite the pleasure that individuals obtain from their

> work, they are typically embarked on a solitary voyage, where chances of failure are high. To pursue the risky tack, they must be courageous and willing to deviate from the pack, to go off on their own, to face shame or even outright rejection. It requires a strong constitution to go it alone in creative motives, and most innovative people at times experience a strong need for personal, communal, or religious support.
>
> (Gardner 1982: 355)

The created product resembles the child archetype, as it 'represents the strongest, the most ineluctable urge in every being, namely the urge to realize itself' (Jung 1951: 170). Jung continues, 'Nothing in all the world welcomes this new birth, although it is the most precious fruit of Mother Nature herself, the most pregnant with the future, signifying *a higher stage of self-realization*' (Jung 1951: 168; italics mine).

Jung and Winnicott discuss the interplay between the false self or persona and the true self. They both talk about the various degrees to which a person may develop a false self or persona and point to the danger of identification with it (Jung 1950: 123; Winnicott 1960: 150).

Of course, it is practically impossible for the individual to deny all aspects of the false self or persona and identify completely with the true self, while living in a society. I am not referring here to socially unintegrated beings, like babies or psychotics; but, by the same token, isn't this precisely the reason why we consider them as incomplete or undeveloped persons?

Do we feel complete when we live a false self as if it were our whole self? Maybe this feeling of completeness is no more than an introjection of established systems of existence. Maybe we feel complete, when we become *one* with the prevailing standards and forms of life. If it is the *system* which suggests an idea of completeness, where does our own completeness lie?

Jung states that:

> For the purpose of individuation, or self-realization it is essential for a man to distinguish between what he is and how he appears to himself and to others, so it is also necessary for the same purpose that he should become conscious of his invisible system of relations to the unconscious.
>
> (Jung 1928: 195)

Individuation, according to Jung, is the process through which one becomes what one really is. This means becoming individual, an indivisible 'whole' within society. The individual retains his or her unique and separate self *in spite of* the community that he or she is still a part. Paul Tillich, in support of this claim says, 'The self is a part of the world which it has as its world. The world would not be what it is without *this* individual self' (1952: 88). Therefore, an individual 'can meet the demands of outer necessity in an ideal way only if he is also adapted to his own inner world, that is, if he is in harmony with himself' (Jung 1948: 39).

Individuation aims to divest the false wrappings of the persona that functions to hide the inner essence of the individual, the true self. It should be noted that artists are known for having an unusual access to the inner realm of the psyche, which is, as Storr sets forth, essential for the creative work (see Storr 1972: 214). Jung writes that any form of 'ism' that promotes the collective consciousness first of all victimizes those 'who have the least access to their interior selves' (Jung 1954: 116).

Knowing begins with knowledge of one's own self. The individual cannot acknowledge the collective environment that surrounds us without knowledge of his or her unique self. Becoming aware of one's self also means becoming aware of a surrounding environment from which the self is distinguished.

The process of becoming aware is based on a deconstruction. According to Winnicott, the newly born infant does not realize the existence of its own self since it perceives itself to be one with its environment. Realization of the self begins with the negation of this idea. In order to become aware of something, we have to strip it bare from all collective values and primordial images first and then re-dress with our own values. The more we are able to negate, the more self-conscious we become. The individual must first deconstruct ideas before he or she can reconstruct them in his or her inner world, even if the same set of values become reconstructed as a consequence. Without personal deconstruction we would have, what Jung calls, 'the mass psyche', which destroys the meaning of individuality and culture. Jung says, 'The bigger the organization, the more unavoidable is its immorality and blind stupidity' (1928: 153).

Creativity and individuality

Jung writes:

> An advance always begins with individuation, that is to say with the individual, conscious of his isolation, cutting a new path through hitherto untrodden territory. To do this he must first return to the fundamental facts of his own being, irrespective of all authority and tradition, and allow himself to become conscious of his distinctiveness. If he succeeds in giving collective validity to his widened consciousness, he creates a tension of opposites that provides the stimulation which culture needs for its further progress.
>
> (Jung 1948: 59)

The history of humanity is also the history of the individual (Jung 1917: 50). Just as any progress within the individual takes place after the point that the person goes beyond the self that he or she has acknowledged so far, any significant achievement that contributes to humanity is performed by an *individual* against the status quo of his or her society. Jung therefore says: 'There is no cure and no improving of the world that does not begin with the individual himself' (1928: 226; cf.: 152–3). Founders of all religions (including Jesus, Muhammad, the Buddha or other respectable figures, such as Joan of Arc, Socrates, Galileo and Copernicus) were ostracized as rebels by society and punished for what we owe to them today. These individuals, with idiosyncratic potential, were not only ahead of their time and venue, but also *beyond* them.

Going 'beyond' is a state that emerges out of the clash between being 'with' and going 'against'. To go beyond a tradition one must interact with it and then act against it. The creative act is mainly constructive: it *deconstructs* in order to *reconstruct*. In fact, the idea of reconstruction is so intertwined with deconstruction in the creative process that some theorists claim that reconstruction is prior to deconstruction in creation (see Storr 1972). Genuine contributions to the arts and humanities are forms that contain the opposites of 'being with' and 'going against'. Any of such contributors has re-formed his or her subject area and has therefore gone beyond it. This is a lonely experience, as Jung writes: 'Higher consciousness, or knowledge going beyond our present-day consciousness, is equivalent to being *all alone in the world*' (1951: 169). And:

> Peoples and times, like individuals, have their own characteristic tendencies and attitudes. The very word 'attitude' betrays the necessary bias that every marked tendency entails. Direction implies exclusion, and exclusion means that very many psychic elements that could play their part in life are denied the right to exist because they are incompatible with the general attitude. The normal man can follow the general trend without injury to himself; but the man who takes to the back streets and alleys because he cannot endure the broad highway will be the first to discover the psychic elements that are waiting to play their part in the life of the collective. The artist's relative lack of adaptation turns out to his advantage; it enables him to follow his own yearnings far from the beaten path, and to discover what it is that would meet the unconscious needs of his age. Thus, just as the one-sidedness of the individual's conscious attitude is corrected by reactions from the unconscious, so art represents a process of self-regulation in the life of nations and epochs.
>
> (Jung 1931: 83)

Creativity stands between the opposites

For Jung, 'everything is a phenomenon of energy' (1917: 75) and 'there is no energy unless there is a tension of opposites' (ibid.: 53). Everything exists with its opposite, as 'a being without opposites is completely unthinkable, as it would be impossible to establish its existence' (Jung 1954: 122). 'The greater the tension between the pairs of opposites, the greater will be the energy that comes from them; and the greater the energy, the stronger will be its constellating, attracting power' (Jung 1948: 26). The pairs are not derived from one another, do not fight with one another, but make the other relative and make a 'whole' when they are reconciled. Jung says, '*Union of opposites through the middle path* . . . is at once the most individual fact and the most universal, the most legitimate fulfilment of the meaning of the individual's life' (1928: 205). The transcendent function, which is 'synonymous with progressive development towards a new attitude' (Jung 1917: 99), is born of the union of opposites.

The creative energy results from the dialectical tension between opposites – such as discipline and inspiration, form and spontaneity, order and chaos, Eros and Logos, the internal and the external, stasis and kinesis, unconscious and conscious – even if it is just one term of these pairs, which gives the creative act its essential characteristic. Storr says that 'creative people are distinguished by an exceptional degree of division between opposites and also by an exceptional awareness of this distinction' (Storr 1972: 196). He continues: 'The divisions within him recurrently impel the use of his imagination to make new synthesis' (ibid.: 240). The process of creation lies parallel to the process of individuation. Storr defines individuation as 'coming to terms with oneself by means of reconciling the opposing factors within' by Storr (ibid.: 230; also see Huskinson, 2004).

This motivating force of creation does not destroy for the sake of destruction and neither does it conform to any notion of non-conformity. The nature of creativity is not *un*-conformist, but *non*-conformist; is not irrational, but supra-rational; is not random, but meaningful; is not anarchic, but self-regulative and transcendent. This view is supported by May:

> When I use the word *rebel* for the artist, I do not refer to revolutionary or to such things as taking over the dean's office; that is a different matter. Artists are generally soft-spoken persons who are concerned with their inner visions and images. But that is precisely what makes them feared by any coercive society. For they are the bearers of the human being's age-old capacity to be insurgent. They love to immerse themselves in chaos in order to put it into form, just as God created form out of chaos in Genesis. Forever unsatisfied with the mundane, the apathetic, the conventional, they always push on to newer worlds. Thus are they the creators of the 'uncreated conscience of the race'.
>
> (May 1975: 28)

Creativity seeks the 'whole' in its peculiarity; similarly, individuation 'does not shut one out from the world, but gathers the world to oneself'

(Jung 1954: 136). This is because the individual gets closer to the universe when he or she gets closer to his or her own self. Tillich writes:

> The bearer of this creative process is the individual who, as an individual, is a unique representative of the universe. Most important is the creative individual, the genius, in whom, as Kant later formulated it, the unconscious creativity of nature breaks into the consciousness of man. Men like Pico della Mirandola, Leonardo da Vinci, Giordano Bruno, Shaftesbury, Goethe, Schelling were inspired by this idea of a participation in the creative process of the universe. In these men enthusiasm and rationality were united. Their courage was both the courage to be as oneself and the courage to be as a part. The doctrine of the individual as the microcosmic participant in the creative process of the macrocosm presented them with the possibility of this synthesis.
> (Tillich 1952: 105)

Even if the motive force of the creative act is originally the true self, the created product stands in between the false and the true self. This is because, once the artwork is produced, it becomes public. The created piece provides a bridge between the artist's true self and society. This bridge, which functions as compromise between the true self and the persona, is where Jung and Winnicott place the healthy individual.

Art gradually evolves through time. Art becomes institutionalized when it is considered of a particular era. New forms of art can appear, but only if they transcend this established pattern. As Winston Churchill put it: 'Without tradition, art is a flock of sheep without a shepherd. Without innovation, it is a corpse' (1954). Through their negation, established systems, not only in art but also in all ways of life, provide criteria for the creative individual to transcend. Would Jung have been provoked to ponder on the archetypal inner experience of religion, which allows for creative developments within the psyche, if he weren't dissatisfied with the official Church-ianity of his father? (for the term 'Church-ianity', see Haughey, 2004) Would he have been inspired to found his own psychology under the separate title of 'analytical psychology', if there had been no psychoanalysis of Freud before him?

Art should be handled in accordance with concepts like religion, myth or the transcendent function, when considering Jung's writings on art and the general structure of his theory.

I shall end this chapter with two quotations from Jung:

> Every individual needs revolution, inner division, overthrow of the existing order, and renewal, but not by forcing them upon his neighbours under the hypocritical cloak of Christian love or the sense of social responsibility or any of the other beautiful euphemisms for

unconscious urges to personal power. Individual self-reflection, return of the individual to the ground of human nature, to his own deepest being with its individual and social destiny – here is the beginning of a cure for that blindness which reigns at the present hour.

(1917: 5)

The man who is pauper or parasite will never solve the social question.

(1928: 226)

References

Abram, J. (1996) *The Language of Winnicott: A Dictionary of Winnicott's Use of Words*, London: Karnac Books.

Barron, F. (1965) 'The Psychology of Creation', *New Directions in Psychology II*, London: Holt, Rinehart & Winston.

Churchill, W. (1954) 'Address to Royal Academy of Arts', *Time*, New York, 11 May 1954.

Gardner, H. (1982) *Art, Mind and Brain: A Cognitive Approach to Creativity*, New York: Basic Books.

Haughey, J.C. (2004) 'Church-ianity and Christ-ianity', *America*, 190, 18, 24 May 2004.

Huskinson, L. (2004) *Nietzsche and Jung: The Whole Self in the Union of Opposites*, Hove and New York: Brunner-Routledge.

Jung, C.G. (1917) 'On the Psychology of the Unconscious', *CW* 7, 1953/1966: 1–201.

—— (1928) 'The Relations Between the Ego and the Unconscious', *CW* 7, 1953/1966: 202–406.

—— (1931) 'On the Relation of Analytical Psychology to Poetry', *CW* 15, 1966: 97–132.

—— (1934) '"Ulysses": A Monologue', *CW* 15, 1966: 163–203.

—— (1948) 'On Psychic Energy', *CW* 8, 1960: 1973: 1–130.

—— (1950) 'Concerning Rebirth', *CW* 9i, 1959/1968: 199–258.

—— (1951) 'The Psychology of the Child Archetype', *CW* 9i, 1959/1968: 259–305.

—— (1954) 'On The Nature of the Psyche', *CW* 8, 1960: 343–442.

—— (1963) *Memories, Dreams, Reflections*, trans. R. and C. Winston, London: Fontana Press, 1995.

May, R. (1975) *Courage to Create*, New York: Bantam Books, 1978.

Rand, A. (1969) *The Romantic Manifesto: A Philosophy of Literature*, New York: New American Library, 1971.

Storr, A. (1972) *The Dynamics of Creation*, New York: Atheneum.

Tillich, P. (1952) *Courage To Be*, New Haven, CT: Yale University Press, 1961.

Winnicott, D.W. (1960) 'Ego Distortion in Terms of True and False Self', *The Maturational Processes and the Facilitating Environment: Studies in the Theory of Emotional Development*, London: Hogarth Press and the Institute of Psycho-Analysis, 1965.

—— (1962) 'Ego Integration in Child Development', *The Maturational Processes*

and the Facilitating Environment: Studies in the Theory of Emotional Development, London: Hogarth Press and the Institute of Psycho-Analysis, 1965.
—— (1971a) 'Creativity and Its Origins', *Playing and Reality*, London: Tavistock, 1971.
—— (1971b) 'Playing: Creating Activity and the Search for the Self', *Playing and Reality*, London: Tavistock, 1971.

Part 2

Changing faces of myth

Chapter 3

Exploring the mythical realities of Psyche

Vincenzo Sanguineti

From poems and paintings to mathematical formulas and diagrams, through time different systems of metaphors have represented the attempt of the human brain to communicate the workings occurring in its depth. When dealing with pre-symbolic realities, the communications of the human brain are expressed in imaginal form – to the Self as well as to other minds.

The different metaphorical translations of any specific aspect of the universe are languages that often appear unrelated to each other. Yet, the diverse symbolic expressions of human imagination may indeed reveal an impressive concordance in their ultimate meaning, and in their descriptions of the underlying reality. They may actually offer complementary substance and confirmation of one another.

This chapter explores the ability of the mind in its capacity to create different metaphorical descriptions of reality, which are ultimately correlated, in spite of the remarkable diversity in their imaginal expression. More specifically, it explores whether mythical reality – where humanity encounters the collective, evolutionary themes of the species, vested with a 'universality' that since the dawn of Man has imbued each encounter with immanence, numinosity, 'spirit' – carries an intrinsic, original truth, rather than it simply representing a 'cloak of validating antiquity' for the idiosyncratic use of modern 'mythologists'.

Mythical reality, once it left the realm of the divine, became, fundamentally, a reality of humanity, which defines particular concepts according to universal ones. It is a structure gravid with timeless significance and always susceptible to recurrence (Snell 1986: 96). Therefore, if myth holds some truth, such truth should be present also in other metaphors that deal with the same content. The languages used may differ but, as with the famous Rosetta Stone, they should be translatable into one another, and, subsequently, expand our understanding of the phenomenon. With this objective in mind, this chapter draws a path of correlations: beginning with the mythical realm, and proceeding through the different but complementary approaches of modern physics, neuroscience, psychology, artificial intelligence (computer) science, (and poetry, as a counterpoint).

The chosen myth of Psyche has been looked at in many ways, not always accurately – a not infrequent phenomenon in Jungian mythology. M.L. Von Franz in, *The Golden Ass of Apuleius* (1992), exemplifies the misuse of mythical material. In this work, Von Franz revisits the myth of Apuleius with the intent of making a detailed analysis of Apuleius' personal relationship with his feminine side. To build her case, Von Franz reports that Eros, before leaving Psyche, tells her about the child in her womb: 'If you had not broken the secret it would have been a boy, but because of what you *have done* you will not lose the child, but will give birth to a girl' (Von Franz 1992: 110; emphasis added). This, however, is a complete fabrication of the mythical story: nowhere, in Eros' rather brief and distressed parting comment to Psyche – after he flew away, and unwillingly dragged her for a distance – does he mention the pregnancy. But he does say, *long before* the disastrous light-shedding episode: 'Adhuc infantilis uterus gestat nobis infantem alium, si texeris nostra secreta silentio, divinum, si profanaveris, mortalem' (Your infantile uterus bears another child for us, who will be divine if you guard our secret in silence, but mortal if you profane it. (Apuleius 1989: V-11). And this statement closely reflects the pivotal message of the myth: if too much (logical) light is poured on feelings, they will vanish, leaving behind an empty container, like an Ego that has lost its numinosity and is now merely 'mortal'.[1]

Dr. Von Franz's custom-made 'translation' sacrifices the mythical message in favor of a fictitious meaning, which has been distorted to support the author's idiosyncratic misuse of the myth. Such misuse, and the entire distorted misinterpretation built on it, is then communicated to the readers, who, appropriately, are inclined to trust the scholar's ostensible accuracy.

In this chapter, I will approach the myth from a more literal viewpoint, staying close to the original text. In his work, Apuleius – lecturer, philosopher and serious humanist – wrote about Psyche apparently on the template of an older Greek myth. From this perspective, the metaphor is the oldest and most detailed extant description of the human mind, written in the first-person language. It captures, with astonishing metaphorical precision, the pre-symbolic essence and mystery of a living mind. And it describes the vicissitudes of the complex relationship between Logos and Eros: the 'human', very appealing but ultimately sterile, rational ego (Psyche); and the 'numinous', danger-ridden, but also rich in creative potential, world of affects (Eros and Aphrodite).

As I described earlier, I will revisit the myth of Psyche, seeking correspondence between components that are described by Apuleius in the *subjective language* and those that are described in the *objective language* – such as neuroscience, computer science, mathematics and physics.

The selection of these sources is motivated: there are significant benefits to approaching these languages with healthy curiosity, rather than with neurotic diffidence. Unable to cope with the subjective domain, neuroscience lateralized 'psyche' to a simplified behavioral epiphenomenon; likewise psychology, unable to cope with the objective landscape, lateralized the brain to a simplified neuroanatomical epiphenomenon. This dichotomy has carried a devastating effect on the understanding of the dynamic human mind, and it needs to be abandoned. In order to fill the gap, all interested parties will benefit by becoming conversant with one another.[2]

I will now briefly outline the vision of a few selected 'mythologists' from the disciplines of neuroscience, computer science, mathematics and physics, so that I can then demonstrate how the myth of Psyche is at work within each of them:

A Nobel Prize winner, Dr. Gerald Edelman, in his search for the organization of consciousness, has probed into neural dynamics for several decades. In his 'Neurodarwinism' model, he demonstrated how embryonic, genetically induced developmental selection is superseded by the more extensive and individualized experiential selection. Furthermore, he demonstrated how the phenomenon, which he calls 'reentrant mapping', re-proposes endlessly the uniqueness of each brain, and mind; and how (individual) value systems are crucial in the ongoing recategorization of reality. His main focus is Cartesian reason and ego consciousness (what he calls the state of being 'conscious of being conscious'). He has purposely avoided, in a programmatic way, the issues of a dynamic unconscious and of subjective utterances, because he considers them as not fit for scientific investigation. Most of his experiments, which apply micro- and macro-neurophysiology to the study of consciousness, have used virtual robotic models of increasing complexity that are ultimately supplied with 'self-learning' programs.

B Antonio Damasio – neurologist and neuroscientist – used his decades of experience of 'real' individual brains and minds to analyze the physiology and pathology of conscious states. His conclusions describe the major role played by emotions and correlated states in directing our understanding of, and adaptation to, life. Damasio is a strong proponent of the claim that an immense unconscious wisdom exists within the brain and mind, and he enumerates the extent of this 'unconscious consciousness'. (Is this what we would call self-consciousness?)

C David Gelernter – artificial intelligence (AI), 'computer' scientist, and serious scholar of ancient Jewish texts – is an international leader in the field of parallel computing. His position is that the mind operates on two bands of thinking: the high-focus band (characteristic of rational thinking: logical, penetrating, and emotionally numb), and the low-focus band (characteristic of analogical constructs, driven by affect links). In the former, two mental acts predominate: honing in and suppressing individual idiosyncrasies in favor of common features. AI is capable of this mode of thinking. In the latter, 'the stream of thoughts aren't random; they are thematic, but their themes are emotional themes' (Gelernter 1994: 32). AI cannot operate in this low band.

D Alwyn Scott – neuroscientist and mathematician – anchors the operations of the brain and mind to nonlinear classical physics. The tenet of the entire nonlinear emergence process that he expounds is that *the total is always greater than the sum of its parts*. Within such context Scott demonstrates the following: (i) reductionism is impossible, when confronted with the scale and the complexity inherent to the biological and cognitive domains; (ii) causality is bidirectional, in opposition to the unidirectional path of linear classical physics; (iii) a series of increasingly complex, higher level outcomes emerge from the dynamics of lower level systems; (iv) happenstance events are a basic factor in outcome generation.

In a broad sense, the myth of Psyche is structured in two sections. In the first section, Apuleius describes – by a brilliant progression from the superficial and visible to the complex and invisible – the organization of the psyche and the gradual discovery of its stunning intricacy. And the second section describes the 'healing journey' that Psyche has to undertake in order to mend her splintered selfhood. While the last section offers further examples of Apuleius' insight into psychic dynamics, I will limit the discussion to the first section, and will give close attention to several specific elements. For each of these areas, the meaning hidden in the metaphor is explored in some detail to document the impressive correspondence that can be found among studies and different disciplines that span almost three millennia. These focal areas of comparison are:

1 The necessary prerequisite of a dimmed consciousness to allow for the emergence of affectivity, and for its vital role in the unfolding of true creativity.[3] The corresponding elements of sleep and darkness that are found in the myth of Psyche are also significantly represented in the disciplines outlined above. For instance, they are crucial to the work of computer scientist Gelernter; they constitute a well-established fact for all psychological schools; and they are a recurring theme in the work of neuroscientist Damasio.
2 The astonishing complexity of the biological structure of the mind, inspiring the image of the 'Divine Castle' of the myth, finds correspondence in the extent of the dynamic connectivity of the brain (see, for example, Edelman's system of neural Darwinism; Elsasser's (1998) and Scott's immense numbers;[4] and Dickinson's (1924) poetry 'The Brain').
3 The collective immensity of Psyche's exclusive possessions correlates with Scott's 'phase space' of creativity; Damasio's extent of hidden

knowledge; Edelman's global maps and dynamic core images; the findings of depth psychology, and those of evolutionary sciences.

4 The power and wisdom of unconscious directives upon consciousness (Psyche's 'invisible servants') reappear in nonlinear science as 'emergence' phenomena; in Gelernter's AI, as 'intuition'; in Edelman's dynamic core (also called a 'functional cluster'), from which consciousness emerges; in Damasio, as the path to the 'autobiographical self'; in all major schools and practices of psychology; and in the organization of a poem (or any other work of art).

5 The role of affectivity – facilitated by a shift in conscious focus, and represented by the marriage between Psyche and Eros – finds correspondence in the role of Edelman's value systems; in Damasio's remarks about feelings; and in Gelernter's analysis of the limitations of AI.

In the first section of the myth, all these areas are described sequentially. I will identify each segment in the sequence with an explicatory heading, and explore it accordingly

The myth of Psyche

The myth starts with a description of Psyche as the most beautiful virgin woman on Earth, looking for a husband. She is so attractive that people flock to see and worship her, as the temples of Aphrodite stand deserted, fostering the anger of the goddess. She is described as a perfectly polished statue. Actually, Apuleius uses the term *simulacrum*, which is more enigmatic than 'statue': it is a term that indicates something is a representation of something else – a symbol rather than a sign.

In spite of this attractiveness, Psyche will have to be cast away, because ultimately 'no one, neither king or prince or even commoner, desired to marry her' (Apuleius 1989: IV-32) Her 'visible' and polished perfection may indeed attract, but it also conveys the sense that something crucial is lacking: her essence is ultimately empty of affective potential.[5] I would suggest that in this very appealing but 'incomplete' early version of Psyche (as compared to the final version that evolves out of the mythical journey), Apuleius describes with impressive insight the visible ego psyche, gifted with logical reasoning but without any significant affective identity.

Despite the young woman's glaring lack of 'eroticism', Aphrodite – perhaps the ultimate symbol of eroticism without reason? – continues to be very jealous; she calls on her son Eros, to command him to dispose of the rival. In the meantime, Psyche is left by her family on the top of a cliff, at the mercy of some horrible monster (a relatively common destiny in ancient times for young Greek daughters of displeased king-fathers).

Shift in conscious awareness

While weeping on her fate, Psyche is carried by the wind god, Zephyrus, to the bottom of the cliff, where she *falls asleep*. This is a major transition, a turning event in Psyche's life (a similar but deeper shift in consciousness will prelude the second, and permanent, reunion with Eros). A lowering of ego presence has been long recognized as a necessary prerequisite to access the dynamic unconscious. Historically, such recognition was implied in the weight given to dreams by 'archaic man'; it is the center of all meditative schools;[6] and a given in all depth psychologies from Freud onwards.

It is also an essential theme in Gelernter's work. This scientist convincingly describes how the mind is able to reach a level of creative, analogical thinking only by lowering the focus of conscious awareness and focused attention. At this lower level 'unexpected associations and transitions, and leaps in the thinking process' emerge (Gelernter 1994: 6). These changes are due to an affective correlation between overtly disparate thoughts and images. AI is not creative because it lacks affectivity and the related analogical ability. Edelman introduces his position concerning the unconscious by affirming that 'unconscious aspects of mental activity, such as . . . so-called unconscious memories, intentions, and expectations play a fundamental role in shaping and directing our conscious experience' (Edelman and Tononi 2000: 176). He also states that dreams 'can be as informative as conscious events (and) can be used as sources of inspiration and insight' (ibid.: 33). However, he does not discuss the difference between the awake and the dream state, and he does not appear to appreciate any substantial *causal* difference between dream imagery (or dream consciousness) and the images produced in conscious awake states; therefore his brief comments on dreams are not that informative.

Level of structural complexity

When Psyche wakes up she sees in front of her a magnificent palace, the like of which she has never seen before. It appears to have been constructed not with human hands but by divine skills. Profoundly surprised by what is being revealed to her, she walks inside and finds it to hold an endless multitude of staterooms; it is definitely a concrete, physical structure; and yet it is also immense and boundless. Apuleius' description of the structure of this palace of Eros is dimly perceived by the psychological sciences, but its complexity is impressively represented in the objective neurosciences. For instance, Edelman illustrates the immense connectivity of the brain (the 'structure' within which the mind resides), supported by 20 billion neurons in the cerebral cortex (plus another, approximately, 80 billion in the rest of the brain), with each neuron having approximately 50 thousand points of connection with other neurons. Scott elaborates further on the data, by claiming that, given that there are 1 million billion connections in the brain, the number of possible neural circuits (which parallel the palace staterooms) that can be constructed through such connective potential, is hyperastronomical (i.e. 10 followed by millions of zeros, while the number of particles in the universe is equal to 10 followed by a puny 80 zeros). It follows that the brain is by far the most complicated known physical structure in the entire universe. The extent of the structural complexity is further illustrated by the concept of *phase space* (a system of coordinates representing all the variables required to allow all possible outcomes for a specific process). In the case of the human mind, this space would have to include not only the ideas that have been thought (and that can be viewed as real objects), but also all those thoughts that may emerge at any instant as recursive loops with, among others, the upper levels of social order and culture of the cognitive hierarchy, as follows:

> Human culture
> Phase sequence
> Complex assemblies
> Assemblies of assemblies of assemblies
> Assemblies of assemblies
> Assemblies of neurons
> Neurons
> Nerve impulses
> Nerve membranes
> Membrane proteins
> Molecules
>
> (Scott 2002: 305)

Scott defines this phase space as the *dimension of creativity*. One finds a strong echo of this portrayal in Damasio's independent, but almost identical, description of an *image space*, which contains every image that has actually happened, and a *dispositional space*, which contains the knowledge, out of which images are constructed.[7]

Uniqueness of the subjective experience

As the mythical story unfolds, Psyche is told by an invisible voice that she should not be surprised, given that all that lies around her is her own property; her exclusive property. As she can see, there is no need for locks or doors or guards because *no one else but Psyche* could access the treasure.[8] The ultimate uniqueness and privacy of the subject finds confirmation in the findings of Edelman. He claims that the microscopic variability within each brain and between brains is immense; no two brains are identical, even in identical twins. Furthermore, to this structural uniqueness one has to add the uniqueness of each person's life experience, which keeps remodeling the connectivity and the operations of the neuronal organization. Scott's mathematical conclusions are equally compelling. He argues that the number of possible minds is hyperastronomical; the entire life of the universe will be too short for the emergence of all possible minds; the combination of complexity and bidirectional causality makes mental duplication impossible.

Extent of knowledge and unconscious consciousness

Psyche comes to realize that the castle contains 'omnis mundi thesaurus' [the treasure of the entire world]. Actually, Apuleius goes even further, with a somewhat cryptic statement: 'Nec est quicquam quod ibi non est' (Nothing exists that is not there) (Apuleius 1989: V-2). It seems, from this statement, that the only things that are excluded are those that do not exist yet. The only boundary to the content of the psyche is the future itself. All that has happened along life's evolution is part – in one form or another – of Psyche's inheritance.

In parallel to this narrative, Damasio lists the knowledge contained in the unconscious: (1) all fully formed images to which we do not attend; (2) all neural patterns that never become images; (3) all dispositions that lie dormant and never become neural patterns; (4) all quiet remodeling and renetworking of those dispositions; (5) all the hidden wisdom that nature embodied in innate dispositions. He concludes: 'Amazing, indeed, how little we (consciously) ever know' (Damasio 1999: 228). Likewise, Scott, as we have seen, classifies all the information concerning the cognitive hierarchy that is required to organize the phase space of creativity, and this is constantly linked by self-sustaining *causal loops* among all levels of hierarchy, from molecules to culture.[9] Furthermore, Edelman describes how the entire brain continuously recategorizes all data made available by evolution and by learning – and how this entire set is organized below the separator of consciousness (in the unconscious). Edelman illustrates how neuronal recruiting (for a specific task) proceeds from local, circumscribed neuronal maps (assemblies of neurons), to global maps (assemblies of assemblies), and eventually to a 'dynamic core', formed by the temporally coherent integration of the neuronal maps, and involving most of the brain (phase space). Consciousness – he sustains – is the product of the activated dynamics of the core.

All of this unconscious dynamic knowledge, and its emerging outcomes, are delightfully illustrated by the 'invisible servants' of the myth – the directives and messages reaching ego consciousness from the unconscious – who seem to pop out from nowhere and continue to anticipate every single one of Psyche's needs; they bathe her and feed her and entertain her. Eventually they bring her to her bedchamber and prepare her for the night.

Imagination and creativity: Logos and Eros

Predictably, in the middle of the night, Psyche is joined by a male presence. He takes her and he tells her he will be her husband, provided she agrees to receive him only under the cover of darkness, without her trying to shed direct light on his face. Should she have a clear look at him, he will then have to leave her forever. Psyche is willing to go along with this and she actually begins to enjoy her husband. The myth describes how she cherished him, and gradually fell in love with the smell of cinnamon in his hair, the taste and texture of his skin, the way he touched her, and the way he made love to her. Actually, Apuleius has her call him 'tuae Psychae dulcis anima' (sweet soul of your Psyche) (Apuleius 1989: V-6); in Apuleius' perception it seems that Eros represents the numinous, transformative, soul-like aspect of the psyche. And we are left to wonder whether he was suggesting discrimination between psyche and soul.

While in this enhanced emotional state – reached primarily through 'sensations', or feelings – Psyche becomes fully creative, which is symbolized in her becoming pregnant, in the generation of her own 'creation'. Apuleius' message that the 'polished simulacrum' of the visible Psyche (Logos) becomes creative ('pregnant') only by interacting with Eros (and that the interaction requires a dimming of ego consciousness) is confirmed by the modern metaphors.

Edelman demonstrates how the complex neuroanatomical 'value systems as well as emotions are essential to the *selectional workings* of the brain that underlie consciousness' (Edelman and Tononi 2000: 218). He asserts that these systems are crucial to our categorization of reality, clearly implying the primary role of the emotional domain in our understanding of reality. He also states that, 'metaphorical products, while ambiguous, can be richly creative. Logic is not creative but it can tame excesses. It can prove theorems but it cannot choose axioms' (Edelman 2004: xx). Damasio goes even further by promoting the concept that the affective domain assists the organism in *maintaining life.*

We have seen how Gelernter considers low focus streams of thought as being not random, but emotionally thematic. In low focus, unexpected transitions based on affect linking emerge, and these are ground for metaphorical, analogic thinking and creativity. This emerging material may appear to be not consequential or of any use, but 'it always contains a truth' (Gelernter 1994: 100). He concludes that, 'Creativity can only emerge . . . as a byproduct of affect linking in low-focus thought, and no existing computer program has ever grappled with low-focus thought. Without computer models of the low focus it is not possible to build a truly convincing fake mind' (ibid.: 191).

At this point in the myth, things got complicated. Psyche tried to shed light on Eros' face, lost the meaning of being alive, and had to go through her personal journey of reintegration, which included a descent into Hell and a phase of profound unconscious depth. A truly 'Stygian sleep' invaded her, and she collapsed on the path where she stood, like a sleeping corpse until the returning Eros wiped the sleep off and woke her with a *harmless* prick of his arrow. However, I will not follow our heroine in her journey, but I will remain at the door of the castle: that early source of neuropsychological understanding.

All the different images presented in this chapter are simply different metaphors that emerge from the creative phase space of specific human minds. As I mentioned in my opening lines, the metaphorical expressions can be as varied as the disciplines involved: from the construction of gods to mathematical equations and electrochemical diagrams. But if they convey some truth – and many of them do – this truth will become selectively illuminated, and recognized, as it bounces from one metaphor to the next one.

As a final example of the power imbedded in creative thinking I submit the opening verse from Emily Dickinson's poem 'The Brain':[10]

> The brain – is wider than the sky –
> For – put them side by side –
> The one the other will contain
> With ease – and you – beside.

In 1862 Ms. Dickinson turned her attention to the brain – not the mind, which would have constituted a more appropriate subject for a poetic image! – a time when neurophysiology was very rudimentary at best. The voices of Sherrington, Freud, and William James were not yet known. Yet, the poet captured the hyperimmense quality of the brain as poignantly as the scientific models introduced earlier.

Behind the façade of a poetic metaphor, a deeper level of intuitive knowledge percolates upward. This intuitive knowledge – and the actual workings of a creative mind in organizing such knowledge – should represent a fundamental subject of scientific research, and it justifies Scott's suggestion that biological science in general, including neuroscience, has to undergo a paradigmatic shift: the *linear* (reductive, causally unidirectional) scientific paradigm of the twentieth century – the Machine – has to be abandoned for the Poem to take its place, as the new *nonlinear* paradigm. The emergence of a poem is, in fact, a highly compelling example of the workings of the brain along nonlinear and emergentist directions, where the dynamics grasp and elaborate a specific theme within the phase space of creativity. *The visible outcome is always quite different from the linear sum of its parts.*

Conclusion

The vignettes I have provided demonstrate how a certain kind of knowledge was captured and illustrated by different scholarly minds, through different sets of metaphor. All of these serious scholars, who speak not out of territorial pressure but out of primary fascination with the mystery of the human mind and with its unraveling, expand our phase space by adding different and enriching coordinates.

Evidently, this chapter does not have the pretension of having elucidated the works of these other 'mythologists'. It suffices that it provides an example of how a multidimensional approach gives a different perspective and depth to the material under investigation, and to the specific method of investigation: in this case the human psyche and the mythical language. Hopefully, it will also raise curiosity, and ease the process of breaking the boundaries among disciplines. A crucial key to the understanding of mind is the shedding of some light on the divide between mental images and neural patterns, between matter and imagination – across, what Damasio calls, 'the explanatory gap' (Damasio 1999: 322). Crossing the divide will require, as a bridge, mutual understanding and communication between neural and mental, psychology and neurology, top-down and bottom-up, subjective and objective: all these inputs being – when 'honest'– *equally* important and *equally* enriching.

As a related point, it is crucial for Jungian scholars to use myth with due respect and, whenever possible, to keep an ongoing reference to the original text and story. Too liberal rearrangements – even if not to the point of full fabrications as the one described earlier on – weaken the Jungian message, because the skeptic or critic infers from them that the Jungian approach to knowledge is questionable, approximate at best, and all too often self-serving. One has just to consider the prolonged and rather complicated effort of Von Franz to make a daemon out of Psyche, and in the process we see Psyche identified with almost every goddess and divine feminine figure in the Western and Eastern pantheons. In fact, the text of the myth – the major source of detailed information that we have about this figure – consistently identifies Psyche as fully human (and fully mortal!) until, at the very end of her saga, Zeus gives her a cup of ambrosia, the drink of immortality (which does not necessarily mean divinity). With that, the integrated psyche described by Apuleius – the Psyche–Eros system – becomes part of the collective inheritance of humanity, of the hidden wisdom and know-how that nature imbued into the human brain.

Notes

1 The sex of Psyche's child is identified only twice in the entire myth. Aphrodite, when Psyche finally comes to her, says: 'In the flower of my youth I shall be called grandmother, and the *son* of a cheap servant will be known as my

grandson' (Apuleius VI-9, emphasis added). And, the last sentence of the myth reads, 'And, when her time was come, a *daughter* was born to them, whom we call by the name Pleasure' (Apuleius VI-25, emphasis added).

2 Repudiation of non-psychological sciences with the excuse that they are used defensively, and that Jungians do not need such defense, is in my opinion a *defensive* argument that only limits the breath of human knowledge.

3 I use the term 'affectivity' in a technical sense to define a family of psychic states and events, for which a 'feeling' characteristic represents a primary attribute of each state. It accommodates emotional constructs, affects, instincts, values, meanings, intentional states, and qualia.

4 Mathematically, an immense number is any finite number greater than 10^{100}, which represents the number of protons in the universe multiplied by the age of the universe in picoseconds.

5 Interestingly, in our modern Western culture, we observe how Cartesian reason and the linear logic of scientific materialism have reached a de facto dogmatic and quasi-religious status. However, and differing from the ancient Greeks, modern man has married logic as the only truth, even when faced with blatantly discordant data from the emotional domain.

6 'When, through meditation . . . the identification with the Ego of the individual self ceases, then the radical subjectivity . . . of the "I" of the Self shines forth' (D.R. Hawkins, MD – Director, Institute for Advanced Spiritual Research, Sedona, AZ – op. cit. Sanguineti 2007: xix).

7 This cognitive partition finds its anatomical correspondence in a partition of the brain between neural pattern maps (defining the image space) and convergence zones (defining the dispositional space).

8 Does Apuleius imply that in an integrated psyche the affective domain provides the containment and the organization of the 'treasure' (Damasio's collective and individual knowledge), and puts it at the disposal of the subject?

9 Scott (1995) acknowledges that, in strictly scientific terms, this space is too intricate to be represented with any accuracy, and, he defines it, mathematically, as *hyperimmense*.

10 This verse of the poem has attracted the attention of Dr. Edelman repeatedly, and may have played a significant role in this scholar's recent shift in attitude with regard to 'poetic utterances', and to the importance of the subjective position in experiencing *and studying* consciousness.

References

Apuleius Madaurensis (1989) *Metamorphoseon*, Books IV–VI, ed. and trans. J.A. Hanson, Cambridge, MA: Harvard University Press.

Damasio, A. (1999) *The Feeling of What Happens: Body and Emotion in the Making of Consciousness*, New York: Harcourt Brace.

Dickinson, E. (1924) *The Complete Poems*, Boston: Little Brown.

Edelman, G.M. (2004) *Wider than the Sky: The Phenomenal Gift of Consciousness*, New Haven, CT: Yale University Press.

Edelman, G.M. and Tononi, G. (2000) *A Universe of Consciousness: How Matter Becomes Imagination*, New York: Basic Books.

Elsasser, W.M. (1998) *Reflections on a Theory of Organism: Holism in Biology*, Baltimore, MA: Johns Hopkins University Press.

Gelernter, D. (1994) *The Muse in the Machine: Computerizing the Poetry of Human Thought*, New York: Free Press.

Sanguineti, V. (2007) *The Rosetta Stone of the Human Mind*, New York: Springer-Verlag.

Scott, A. (1995) *Stairway to the Mind: The Controversial New Science of Consciousness*, New York: Springer-Verlag.

Scott, A. (2002) *Neuroscience: A Mathematical Primer*, New York: Springer-Verlag.

Snell, B. (1986) *The Discovery of the Mind in Greek Philosophy and Literature*, New York: Dover Publications.

Von Franz, M.L. (1992) *The Golden Ass of Apuleius: The Liberation of the Feminine in Man*, Boston, MA: Shambhala.

Chapter 4

The myth of Themis and Jung's concept of the Self[1]

Ann Shearer

The idea of the Self was both central to and encompassing of Jung's map of psyche, just as it was for him the centre and circumference of psyche itself. Yet of all his concepts, this may be the one that now causes commentators most difficulty. Is the Self an idea of psychic totality or an archetype within that totality? Is it pre-existent or emergent? Is it goal or process – or both? Does it exist at all, or is it simply a remnant of the Protestant monotheism in which Jung was reared? And, if it does exist, is it written with an upper or lower case 'S'?

These are just some of the questions about the Self that have preoccupied commentators over the past two decades. At the start of them, a *Journal of Analytical Psychology* symposium devoted to the implications of that initial 'S' began from a shared assumption that the entity existed (Hubback 1985).[2] At the end, one observer was pointing out that this was the most difficult of Jung's concepts to find a parallel for in attachment theory and cognitive neuroscience, and suggesting that it was Fordham's model rather than Jung's to which research evidence gave support (Knox 2004).

In between and alongside, Jung's dictum that 'the goal of life is the realisation of the self' (1951: 25) has been explored and amplified, together with his idea of the Self as empirical natural process (1949: 529). Warren Colman has elaborated the idea of Self not as goal but as process, as 'neither myself nor the experience of myself, but the very possibility of my having self-experience'. For him, the self is both totality *and* archetype, 'both organising principle and that which is organised'; 'the psyche is self-structuring and the name for that process is the self' (Colman 2000: 14, 15). In a further amplification, he links this process with the appearance of archetypal forms as 'emergent properties' (2006: 170). Sherry Salman also sees the Self as a symbol of process, which expresses and accompanies 'the emergence of evolving psychological ground'. For her, an emergent Self is 'less like a knowing, definitive, prophetic voice of truth . . . less identified with a redemptive god-imago, and more like a still, small voice of unknowing, whose whisperings are barely discernable but are always there' (Salman 1999: 75).

This understanding seems far from Jung's awesome experience of the Self as a *diras necessitas* rather than a *summum bonum* (1949: 529), as an image of the transcendent (1948: 487) and as a constant, painful and often humiliating challenge to the ego (1937: 392; 1963a: 778). Lucy Huskinson's evocation of the Self as 'violent Other' and her emphasis on ego's numinous experience of its energy seems nearer to Jung's own; 'the self is "violent" because it is experienced as an overwhelming force that violates the self-containment of the ego, and forces the ego, often against its will, into a new identity' (Huskinson 2002: 438).

For Jung himself, the concept of the Self first emerged in numinous certainty. As he recalled it at the end of his life, the 'Liverpool' dream could hardly have been more important:

> This dream brought with it a sense of finality. I saw here that the goal had been revealed. One could not go beyond the centre. The centre is the goal and everything is directed towards that centre. Through this dream I understood that the self is the principle and archetype of orientation and meaning. Therein lies its healing function . . . Out of [this insight] emerged a first inkling of my personal myth. After this dream I gave up drawing or painting mandalas. The dream depicted the climax of the whole process of the development of consciousness.
>
> (Jung 1963b: 224)

Despite this retrospective certainty, however, the Self, as is its inevitable nature, remained beyond the power of consciousness to grasp or describe. 'So far', Jung told Miguel Serrano 30 years after his dream, 'I have found no stable or definite centre in the unconscious and I don't believe such a centre exists. I believe that the thing I call the self is a dream of totality' (Serrano 1966: 50; quoted in Salman 1999). Yet dreams remain a vital part of psychic reality, and Jung's dream is far from his alone. He borrows his definition of the Self as 'centre and circumference' from the thirteenth century St. Bonaventure's description of God as 'an intelligible sphere whose centre is everywhere and circumference is nowhere' (Jung 1963a: 41). And Jung quoted too the seventeenth century Polish mystic Angelus Silesius: 'God is my centre when I close him in;/And my circumference when I melt in him' (ibid.: 132n). Though Jung's preoccupation was above all with Christian symbology of the Self, he knew well that such imagery had appeared across place as well as time. In his scheme of things, this insistent similarity was sure indication of underlying archetypal reality: 'The self is a living person and has always been there. It is an insight upon which Hindu philosophy (the equivalent of Western theology), Buddhism. Taoism, mystical Islamic sects and Christianity are all agreed. My psychology is a modest contribution to this illustrious assemblage' (Jung 1952: 84).

This assemblage has included countless others, by no means all of them psychologists, in their own attempt to express the inexpressible which they nevertheless know to be there. Eliot's 'still centre of the turning world', without which there would be no dance; Hopkins's kingfishers catching fire among the whole creation of mortal things that 'deal out that being indoors each one dwells'; Yeats's falcon spiralling out of containment when 'the centre cannot hold': these images speak to the same intuited reality (Eliot 1959: 11; Hopkins 1995: 115; Yeats 1990: 184). The 'idea' that Jung called the Self won't, it seems, let go. To take just one further example of its insistence, James Hillman has long been critical of its 'old monotheistic senex structure of unity and centering' (1983: 83). But he too has a Self of his own: an animistic 'interiorisation of community' which is a psychic field shared with buildings, animals and trees just as much as other human beings, without which 'I am not' (Hillman and Ventura 1993: 40).

'Image and meaning', said Jung, 'are identical and as the first takes shape, so the latter becomes clear' (1947: 402). That was how the concept of the Self emerged, from the shaping of images – of a sooty city on a dark winter night, an alleyway of death, a broad square, a round pool, an island blazing with light and a red magnolia (Jung 1963b: 223). I want to evoke another set of images, from a very different time and place, that nevertheless seem to speak directly of the qualities and energy of Jung's Self and so, I hope, amplify again its nature.

They say that Zeus let fly two eagles, one from his right hand and one from his left, and declared the place where the two met to be the centre of the world, which he marked by the great *omphalos*, the navel stone. That place was Delphi, which became the most famous and wealthy temple of Apollo and the place of his greatest oracle, to which for centuries pilgrims and seekers flocked from all over Greece and beyond (Pendazos and Sarla 1984). Yet Apollo was not the first oracular voice of Delphi. That was Mother Earth herself, and the second was her daughter, Themis, one of the race of Titans. She was the oracle for some 2000 years until she was vanquished by Apollo, who violently slew her protective serpent:

> The lord Apollo
> who works from afar,
> let fly at her his strong arrow.
> Then heavily, she lay there,
> racked with bitter pain,
> gasping for breath
> and rolling about on the ground.
> An unspeakable scream
> came into being,
> a more than mortal sound.
> All over the wood

she writhed incessantly,
now here, now there,
and then
life left her,
breathing out blood.
(Cashford 2003: 46)[3]

That 'unspeakable scream' of the vanquished feminine marked an usurpation of the ancient order by the sky gods which was no less significant for the development of Western consciousness than was Marduk's slaying of the great she-dragon Tiamet (Baring and Cashford 1991 explore the latter tale).

After that defeat, Themis became somewhat hidden. Her name is not included on the rollcall of Olympians who have figured so significantly in Jungian attempts to amplify archetypal energies. Yet Themis remained of crucial and lasting importance. Her name means 'right order'; she represents the divine and natural law that governs relations between gods and humans. Significantly, she is one of only two Titans to survive the war between her people and the incoming Olympians. More than that, she is greatly honoured: when her golden horses drew near the hallowed staircase to Olympus, the gods and goddesses rejoiced. There seemed something as necessary and inescapable as nature itself about her arrival: some say that she was brought there by the Fates, those three workwomen who between them spin, weave and cut the thread of human life. She is celebrated as the first wife of Zeus: she sits next to him, their heads leaning intimately towards each other as they converse wisely together. Their three daughters are Eunomia, Eirene and Dike (Order, Peace and Justice) – an indication of just how important their union is to the world. Themis has also a very particular role: she calls the gods together in council and presides over their feasts (Cashford 2003: 128; Hesiod 1989a: 30, 52; Homer 1990: 366; Pindar 1997 (2): 232–3).

So immediately in the imagery and attributes of Themis there is much that Jung attributes to the Self. As a Titan, she 'predates' the consciousness which the Olympians represent, and offers an image of a deeper, perhaps more instinctual, psychic ordering. As personification of the divine law, the goddess governs the relations between gods and humans – or in Jung's terms, the archetypes and the ego. As the Delphic oracle, she draws humans from the circumference of the known world to its very centre, to go beyond their own ego knowledge and desires to learn what the gods will of them. She brings together not only humans and gods but the gods themselves. Her unique relationship with Zeus offers a powerful image of balance between the 'masculine' and 'feminine' orders: in those wise conversations, she was neither swallowed up like her niece Metis, nor locked in power struggle as was Hera; neither was she, as so many others, pursued, impregnated and abandoned by that abundantly procreative energy. And when Themis calls together the gods and orders their feasts, she gives an image of the function which is central to Jung's concept of the Self as 'primarily the regulator and orderer of chaotic states, giving the personality the greatest possible unity and wholeness' (Jung 1959: 622).

These stories and images of Themis suggest an inherent psychological energy, which encompasses and contains the consciousness the Olympians represent, and fosters a relationship between them which promises good order, peace and justice as its fruits. This sounds very like the Self as it works in individual psychology, as explored by Jung and some later commentators. Yet the realm and remit of Themis runs far wider than the ordering of individual lives. So it is on the possible *collective* implications of this energy that I also want to focus.

It is not just the gods that Themis calls together in assembly; she does the same among humans. The classicist Jane Harrison, her great admirer, calls her the very spirit of the *agora*, the marketplace, which was also the place of government. In a definition of the goddess that touches on Jung's idea of the Self at many points, Harrison sees Themis as the energy that binds people together, the collective conscience, the social sanction which underlies concepts of law and justice, and the source of religion itself (Harrison 1927: 485). This power to summon and bind together is not confined to official assemblies, but can work wherever humans honour the goddess in their need to come together in peace. The people of the great trading centre of Aegina, for instance, turned to Themis above all deities to protect and foster their dealings with the many strangers who came to their shores (Pindar 1997 (1): 139).

As then, so now. Paradoxically, this hidden Olympian is today the most widely seen of them all. Themis became the very figure and image of Justice, and she still presides over civic halls and law courts across the Western world and beyond.

The longing to come together in the name of justice seems to be built into human beings, however often and horribly the yearning is betrayed. They say that when the human race entered its final degradation, lapsed from the glories of the Golden Age through the Silver and Bronze Ages into the lies and betrayal, suffering and warfare of the Age of Iron, Justice was the last of the deities to leave the blood-soaked earth. She can still be seen as the constellation Virgo, a reminder of what the world has lost and a focus for its longing for her return. (Hesiod 1989b: 62–5; Kerenyi 1974: 102–3; Ovid 1955: 53). In an important sense, though, Justice has never left, for the one who flew away was not Themis but her daughter, Dike. This ancient story encapsulates the distinction between the idea and its manifestation, between justice and law. In Jung's terms, this is the distinction between the archetypal, timeless idea carried by Themis, and its manifestation in human times and affairs. And for him, this is also the realm of the Self. In his discussion of conscience, for instance, he distinguishes between moralities, which change in time and place, and the deeper inner ethical authority, which transcends the ego (Jung 1958: 856). Elsewhere he says roundly: 'The superego is a necessary and unavoidable substitute for the experience of the self' (1937: 394).

This might seem far from the realities of the courtroom, where for all that Themis may preside, the conventions of adversarial justice do little to bring people together, and may more likely, by fixing them in their persona as victim or perpetrator, drive them further apart. Yet the adversarial approach is not the only one. For the past 30 years, the practice of restorative justice has affected the lives of thousands of people in different countries, and it seems to draw on many of the attributes that I have associated with Themis and Jung's concept of the Self.

Restorative justice has been called 'one of the most important developments in contemporary crime policy – a vibrant international campaign' (Johnstone 2002: ix). Research can show that it works, both in terms of decreased reoffending rates and a sense of healing for victims that is rarely found through conventional systems. Although it has mostly been applied to young offenders, its potential seems valuable enough for the United Nations to have urged its introduction at every stage of criminal justice procedure (ibid.: 477–88).

Although the administration of restorative justice schemes, their *dike*, varies, the fundamental approach, the *themis*, does not.[4] This aims to bring together the people whom the adversarial system splits apart. Victims and perpetrators meet with community representatives, with the express objective of restoring the balance between all three. The very words associated with the approach – re-store, re-pair – suggest that something lost is being rediscovered, that there is a pre-existent right order between individuals in their communities which can be re-established. Advocates of restorative justice have reached back into history to argue that European justice before the rise of state power in the twelfth century operated on just these principles. The old law, says the historian Harold Burman, was based on 'a sense of the wholeness of life, of the interrelatedness of law and all the other aspects of life, a sense that legal institutions and legal processes as well as legal norms and legal decisions are all integrated in the harmony of the universe' (Burman 2002: 108).

This sense is so far from contemporary European justice and other systems based on it that it might seem a Golden Age indeed. But from the start, restorative justice schemes have drawn inspiration from the still living practices of traditional societies, seeking to re-establish their essential feature: the reintegration of offenders with their community rather than, as so often in adversarial systems, their segregation from it. The first thoroughgoing approach was in New Zealand, whose 1989 youth and family justice act introduced the 'family group conference', which has been widely influential since. This was modelled on the traditional Maori justice of the *marae* or community centre, itself fuelled by the spiritual energy of Papatuanuku, or Earthmother. The *marae* has parallels with community meetings among the native people of North America, which have inspired many other schemes. (As a president of the American Bar Association once said: 'Our Navajo peers could teach us a thing or two about conflict resolution.')

Critics of restorative justice accuse its advocates of romanticizing traditional approaches. They are concerned that this voluntary system can offer less protection of rights than a court of law, as well as imposing both harsher punishments for some offences and more lenient ones when the victims are women. They question the contemporary relevance of justice models that draw on a worldview in which the needs of the individual are subservient to those of the community, and individuals are contained in an unquestioned collective belief system (Johnstone 2003).

Yet against this are the many stories – and statistics too – of the reconciliations that can be effected, and the lives changed, when people are brought together in the assurance that all, whether victim or perpetrator, will have the chance to tell their story. When crime is seen not as violation of a law or 'the state', but of one *person* by another and when 'justice' is seen as the restoration of right relationship between them, then there seems to be a coming together of individual and collective, in which both aspects are honoured. This process seems to express that deeper ethic that Jung identified as the Self.

Some critics say that only a minority of victims and perpetrators can ever be reached by a system that depends on the willingness of both parties to participate. But this is to discount the possible cumulative effect that the many individual experiences and different small schemes may have. Already there is one extraordinary example of a nationwide act of restorative justice, whose implications have reverberated across the world.

By the turn of the twenty-first century, there had been over 20 'truth commissions'; in the wake of the bloodiest century yet known, they had become a crucial tool of 'transitional justice'. But among them all, the South African Truth and Reconciliation Commission stands out. The seven volumes of its 1 million-word report are a hugely moving testimony to the suffering imposed by apartheid, the extraordinary resilience of the human spirit and its humbling capacity to move beyond anger and bitterness. It would take a great deal more space than there is here to begin to do justice to this; what follows can only outline some of its essential aspects.[5]

Unusually for a truth commission, this one sought maximum publicity: 'Truth Hurts, But Silence Kills', said its advertisements. In more than 70 public hearings, victims of apartheid told their stories and these were broadcast daily in the country's 11 languages. For the first time, the black majority had a public voice and the white minority heard it. In this bringing together of hitherto bitter opposites, a shared history began, a basis for the commission's work of reconciliation. The country's new interim constitution had set its unique tone: 'There is a need for understanding but not for vengeance, a need for reparation but not retaliation, a need for *ubuntu* [the recognition of common humanity] but not for victimisation.'

The commission offered a methodology for reconciliation, through a process which was also its goal. It sought no instant transformations in those who came before it: its approach from the start was as realistic as it was ideological. Its unique and contentious power to grant amnesty to perpetrators included no demand for expressions of remorse, but was extended to all those who told the truth and could show that their actions had pursued political aims. Its invitation to victims to tell their stories held no expectation that they should also show forgiveness. Yet by the end of the hearings, there had been some extraordinary individual expressions of forgiveness among the 21,000 victims' testimonies and of remorse among the 7000 applications for amnesty. Familiar dictionary definitions of 'reconciliation' are concerned with 'conversion from a state of hostility or distrust' and 'the promotion of goodwill by kind and considerate measures'. But older usages of the word give some idea of what else may be involved: reconciliation has also meant 'confession', 'making atonement' and purification of sacred objects after desecration or pollution. All these meanings are there in the commission's work. So it can be seen as a powerful expression of the energy that not only brings together disparate and warring psychological states, but contains them so that each can be heard and honoured and through this process works to rediscover a healing 'right order' and a shared sense of justice.

In South Africa this energy is associated with the concept of *ubuntu*, which means, in the words of the isiZulu and isiXhosa proverb, 'a person is a person because of, through, other people'. This simple statement has huge implications. As Archbishop Desmond Tutu, Chairman of the Truth and Reconciliation Commission, has put it: a person with *ubuntu* 'has a proper self-assurance that comes from knowing he or she belongs in a greater whole and is diminished when others are humiliated or diminished, when others are tortured or oppressed, or are treated as if they were less than who they are' (Tutu 1999: 35). This seems to be very much the energy that also runs through traditional methods of restorative justice, and is imaged in the West by Themis, and by Jung in his concept of the Self. In her own study of *ubuntu*, Astrid Berg points to its universality. She suggests that a universal and basic attitude that ensured the species' survival may have originated with the first humans in Africa, and is still alive there today as a reminder to other cultures of what they have forgotten (Berg 2004).

There is nothing easy about wresting a remembrance, any more than there is in understanding and living with Jung's idea of the Self or the relationship between it and the ego. The Truth and Reconciliation Commission showed that dramatically: the emotional and physical cost to its members, and to many others involved, was huge. And as Berg has emphasized, individuals can find the expectations of *ubuntu*, just as of traditional justice systems, oppressive as well as embracing. The commission achieved the extraordinary when it held together a society that had been so horrendously split and created an enduring container for the potential meeting of opposites. But it never earned the cooperation it sought from the white community, or from sections of the black. This 'Kleenex Commission' has also been dismissed as too sentimental, too Christian and ineffective. Despite its urgings, compensation for victims of apartheid still lags sadly behind the instant amnesty granted for some perpetrators, while others have still not been brought to trial. In the muted commemorations that marked the commission's 10th anniversary, Tutu lamented this reality and President Thabo Mbeki wondered whether black and white South Africans were 'even pretending at times that the other does not exist' (Mbeki 2005: 18).

In its containing of opposites, the Self, that *diras necessitas*, cannot but appear both bright and dark, both 'good' and 'evil' (Jung 1952: 53; 1959: 640). Yet Jung also saw in this concept a great hope for humankind: 'The self plays the chief role in uniting apparently irreconcilable opposites and is therefore the best suited to compensate the split-mindedness of our age' (1959: 622). This hope seems no less relevant among today's painfully warring opposites, when there is so great a need for a containing energy that offers individuals and collectivities the chance to become more conscious of their shared humanity.

The prospect of such containment may seem unattainably distant and the road towards it bafflingly obscure. Jung himself, after all, was able to find no evidence of a 'stable or definite' centre in the human psyche. But his 'dream of totality' remains an insistent theme in human perceptions of their own nature and that of their world; the yearning for a pre-existent 'right order' and for a return to its state of justice, permeates religious, political and psychological thought across time and space. In Jung's terms – and as Astrid Berg's reading of *ubuntu* suggests – these themes seem to be archetypal. So however distant, even fanciful, their promise may seem to rational consciousness, they are nevertheless part of the human psychological makeup. They are expressions of an archetypal pattern that is, by its very nature, a 'system of readiness for action' (Jung 1931: 53), a potential theoretically as available to human consciousness as its opposite.

As Jung insisted, the archetypes are unknowable in themselves. But through their images and the psychological energy that these mediate to consciousness, archetypal potential may come nearer to conscious realisation; 'image and meaning are identical, and as the first takes shape, so the latter becomes clear' (1947: 402). This is the psychological value of spending time with the old myths and the personified archetypal energies that make up their pantheons and players: these stories of the relationships between gods and humans can help imagination make more ample the notion of what constitutes human beings in their rational and irrational, and individual and collective, nature. This chapter has been about just one of these stories – Jung's 'dream of totality', of the archetypal function that contains and orders psychic energies. This finds an image in Themis, personification of the 'right order' between gods and humans, the one who calls together and contains the myriad expressions of psyche. The stories of the goddess and intimations of this energy at play in the world carry an archetypal promise: they offer one way to greater imagining, and through that greater understanding, of the process and goal of reconciliation which for Jung was also the work of the Self.

The author would like to acknowledge Jules Cashford's generous permission to quote from her translation of the *Homeric Hymn to Apollo*.

Notes

1 This chapter draws on a much longer work written with Jungian analyst Pamela Donleavy (*Themis* to be published by Routledge in 2008). She was the one who first saw Themis at Delphi as an image of the Self and made the link with restorative justice. Since then we have amplified these and other themes around Themis, both together and – as here – separately.

2 The vexed question of upper or lower case 'S' is not resolved here; I favour the first, but have retained the second where it is used in quotations.

3 Special thanks are due to Jules Cashford for her generous permission to quote from her translation of *The Homeric Hymn to Apollo*.

4 Unless specified, information on restorative justice comes from articles in Johnstone (ed.) (2002), *A Restorative Justice Reader*; articles in Zehr and Toews (eds) (2004), *Critical Issues in Restorative Justice*; and Johnstone (ed.) (2003), *Restorative Justice: Ideas, Values, Debates*. Other resources online: www.restorativejustice.org and www.restorativejustice.org.uk (the British Restorative Justice Consortium includes international summaries of research on the positive effects on re-offending rates). Accessed May 2007.

5 Unless specified, information on the Truth and Reconciliation Commission comes from the seven volumes of its own reports; Boraine (2001), *A Country Unmasked*; Krog (1998), *Country of my Skull*; Rotberg and Thompson (2000), *Truth v. Justice;* and Tutu (1999), *No Future Without Forgiveness.*

References

Baring, A. and Cashford, J. (1991) *The Myth of the Goddess*, London: Viking Press.

Berg, A. (2004) '*Ubuntu* – Civilisation of the Universal', in T. Singer and S.L. Kimbles (eds) *The Cultural Complex*, Hove: Brunner-Routledge.

Boraine, A. (2001) *A Country Unmasked: Inside the South African Truth and Reconciliation Commission*, Oxford: Oxford University Press.

Burman, H. (2002) 'The Background of the Western Legal Tradition', in G. Johnstone (ed.) *A Restorative Justice Reader*, Cullompton, Devon: Willan.

Cashford, J. (2003) *The Homeric Hymns*, London: Penguin Books.

Colman, W. (2000) 'Models of the Self' in E. Christopher and H. McFarland Solomon (eds) *Jungian Thought in the Modern World*, London: Free Association Books.

—— (2006) 'The Self' in R.K. Papadopoulos (ed.) *The Handbook of Jungian Psychology*, London and New York: Routledge.

Eliot, T.S. (1959) 'Burnt Norton' in *Four Quartets*, London: Faber & Faber.

Harrison, J.E. (1927) *Themis: A Study of the Social Origins of Greek Religion*, Cambridge: Cambridge University Press.

Hesiod (1989a) *Theogony*, in *Hesiod and Theogonis*, trans. D. Wender, London: Penguin Books.

—— (1989b) *Work and Days*, in *Hesiod and Theogonis*, trans. D. Wender, London: Penguin Books.

Hillman, J. (1983) *Inter Views*, New York: Harper & Row.

Hillman, J. and Ventura, M. (1993) *We've Had a Hundred Years of Psychotherapy and the World's Getting Worse*, San Francisco: HarperSanFrancisco.

Homer (1990) *The Odyssey*, trans. R. Fagles. New York: Penguin Books.

Hopkins, G.M. (1995) 'As Kingfishers Catch Fire', in C. Phillips (ed.) *Gerald Manley Hopkins: Oxford Poetry Library*, Oxford: Oxford University Press.

Hubback, J. (1985) 'Concepts of the Self: The self or the Self?' *Journal of Analytical Psychology*, 30, 229-71.

Huskinson, L. (2002) 'The Self as Violent Other: The Problem of Defining the Self', *Journal of Analytical Psychology*, 47, 437–58.

Johnstone, G. (ed.) (2002) *A Restorative Justice Reader*, Cullompton, Devon: Willan.

—— (ed.) (2003) *Restorative Justice: Ideas, Values, Debate*, Cullompton, Devon: Willan.

Jung, C.G. (1931) 'Mind and Earth', *CW* 10, 1964/1970: 49–103.

—— (1937) 'Transformation Symbolism in the Mass', *CW* 11, 1958/1969: 296–308.

—— (1947) 'On the Nature of the Psyche', *CW* 8, 1960: 343–442.

—— (1948) in G. Adler (ed.) *Letters*, vol. 1, London: Routledge & Kegan Paul, 1973.

—— (1949) in G. Adler (ed.) *Letters*, vol. 1, London: Routledge & Kegan Paul, 1973.

—— (1951) in G. Adler (ed.) *Letters*, vol. 2, London: Routledge & Kegan Paul, 1976.

—— (1952) in G. Adler (ed.) *Letters*, vol. 2, London: Routledge & Kegan Paul, 1976.

—— (1958) 'A Psychological View of Conscience', *CW* 10, 1964/1970: 825–57.

—— (1959) 'Flying Saucers: A Modern Myth', *CW* 10, 1964/1970: 589–824.

—— (1963a) 'Mysterium *Coniunctionis*', *CW* 14, 1963/1970.

—— (1963b) *Memories, Dreams, Reflections*, London: Collins and Routledge & Kegan Paul.

Kerenyi, K. (1974) *The Gods of the Greeks*, London: Thames & Hudson.

Knox, J. (2004) 'Developmental Aspects of Analytical Psychology' in J. Cambray and L. Carter (eds) *Analytical Psychology: Contemporary Perspectives in Jungian Analysis*, Hove and New York: Brunner-Routledge.

Krog, A. (1998) *Country of My Skull*, Johannesburg: Random House.

Mbeki, T. (2005) quoted in 'Tutu bemoans failure to bring rights abusers to justice', *The Guardian*, 17 December 2005.

Ovid (1955) *Metamorphoses*, trans. M. Innes, London: Penguin Books.

Pendazos, V. and Sarla, M. (1984) *Delphi*, Athens: Yiannikos-Kaldis.

Pindar (1997) *Olympian Odes, Pythian Odes, Nemean Odes, Isthonian Odes, Fragments*, 2 vols, ed. and trans. W.H. Race, Cambridge, MA: Harvard University Press.

Rotberg, R. and Thompson, D. (eds) (2000) *Truth v. Justice: The Morality of Truth Commissions*, Princeton, NJ: Princeton University Press.

Salman, S. (1999) 'Dissociation and the Self in the Magical Pre-Oedipal Field', *Journal of Analytical Psychology*, 44, 69–85.

Serrano, M. (1966) *C. G. Jung and Herman Hesse: A Record of Two Friendships*, New York: Schocken.

Tutu, D. (1999) *No Future Without Forgiveness*, London: Rider.

Yeats, W.B. (1990) 'The Second Coming', in A. Martin (ed.) *W.B. Yeats: Collected Poems*, London: Vintage.

Zehr, H. and Toews, B. (2004) *Critical Issues in Restorative Justice*, Mousey, NJ: Criminal Justice Press.

Chapter 5

Imagining transcendence at the end of modernity: Jung and Derrida

David Tacey

I would like to explore the 'return of transcendence' at the end of modernity and consider how this process is linked to a reappraisal of the role of myth and imagination. I will briefly track the fate of the transcendent in Jungian depth psychology and Derridean deconstructive philosophy.[1]

At first glance, the situation of the transcendent looks dire: the master narratives that expressed the transcendent in former times have been attacked and deconstructed (Ward 1997). In contemporary post-structuralism, the sacred narratives have been exposed as mere patterns of discourse, not necessarily pointing to anything real (Tracy 1999). The old metaphysics has been collapsed by modern philosophy and 'God is dead' (Pelz and Pelz 1968). However, this is a very superficial outline of the spiritual landscape, and one that, though popular, does little justice to the complex situation of the spirit in contemporary times.

Since the advent of the postmodern movement in the late 1960s, philosophers have suspected that the contemporary mind is not only post-modern, but post-secular as well (Caputo 2001). Just as the educated public had become familiar with the idea of the 'death of God', along came the new idea of the 'death of the death of God'. This was an inevitable consequence of the overcoming of certain 'modern' assumptions that had been surpassed by postmodernity. As Gianni Vattimo, a close colleague of Derrida, has said:

> The 'end of modernity', or in any case its crisis, has brought about the dissolution of the main philosophical theories that claimed to have done away with religion: positivist scientism and Hegelian-Marxist historicism. Today there are no good philosophical reasons to be an atheist, or in any case, to dismiss religion.
>
> (Vattimo 2003: 29)

The general community, including a large portion of its 'educated' membership, seems to have developed the impression that 'postmodernity' is the latest fad in an ongoing saga of atheism and disbelief. Nothing could be further from the truth, if we care to examine the writings of late Derrida, late Foucault, Vattimo, Gadamer, Trias, Marion, Caputo, Hart and Taylor, to name but a few of the key names in postmodernity (Berry and Wernick 1992). It could be that the postmodern movement has been ruled by the archetypal figure of Hermes the trickster, because, while it seems that this movement has advanced atheism, in fact, the reverse has taken place (Neville 1992). Those who have not been attentive to the tricksterish pattern of the spirit of the times have got the wrong impression, and in the mind of university culture, for instance, it seems that this impression has suited prevailing atheistic prejudices; this is why it has stuck.

In Eastern meditation practice, we hear the famous chant: first there is a mountain, then there is no mountain, then there is. The same can be said of the transcendent in recent times: first it is expressed in master narratives, metaphysics, onto-theology, religion, high culture. Then the transcendent is torn down and eradicated, refuted, dismantled. So that's it, we say to ourselves. That's the end of the transcendent and its vision splendid. It would seem that the ugly, the banal, the flat, has won the day. At this point we hover at the edge of the abyss, at the brink of nihilism. There is *only* language, culture, history, discourse, and a lot of empty signifiers pointing to nothing in particular and perhaps pointing only to one another.

But the transcendent reappears in a completely new guise, in new places, with a new logic and a different rationale. Something rises up from the void, from nothingness, to announce itself. Then we realize we have to start all over again, to figure everything out anew, with a new philosophy, a new science and reason. Why does the transcendent keep returning in this way? I believe the answer is because it exists and it is real. Reason and rationality can never encompass the transcendent, never nail it down. We are on a rocky road where at one moment we think we have engaged with the meaning of reality, and at the next it all comes unstuck: 'Things fall apart, the centre cannot hold' (Yeats 1920: 124). In times of disintegration, such as our own, we see that our former certainties were over-confident, and our cultural expressions of the transcendent asserted too much and went beyond their legitimate domain. If we are unable to maintain a degree of *humility* in our religious assertions, the religious enterprise has to be *humiliated*, before we can begin again to reflect on the nature of the infinite.

When high culture and religion become hubristic, the historical process moves into a deconstructive phase, where all that was certain vanishes into air. It is healthy for civilizations to realize from time to time that their sacred icons are fashioned by human hands and made of wood and stone. It is healthy to be delivered over to anxiety and loss of belief because absolute reality must constantly elude us, since it is infinite and we are finite. Our thought, in particular, is finite and limited, although our imagination is a different story. It stretches further toward the mysterious depths of reality, which is why the arts, music and the humanities are important carriers of spirit, especially in times when religion has been forced to its knees because of its hubris. But acknowledging the limits of our thought, our philosophy, our reason is a liberating enterprise, as Derrida and others have found. As soon as we acknowledge our limits, the transcendent, the 'impossible', becomes available again, and we are able to use imagination and reason to encompass the larger dimensions of reality.

Jung offers an interesting account of the modern condition in his essay, 'The Spiritual Problem of Modern Man':

> The modern man is solitary and the ways of [the past] have begun to pall upon him . . . An honest admission of modernity means voluntarily declaring oneself bankrupt, taking the vows of poverty and chastity in a new sense, and, what is more painful, renouncing the halo of sanctity which history bestows.
>
> (1928/31: 152)

The deconstructive philosophers 'voluntarily' declared themselves bankrupt, that is, devoid of the master narratives of Western civilization. They took 'the vows of poverty and chastity in a new sense', subscribing to a lean, scrubbed-down and illusion-free view of the world. In the course of this process, they won the support of the academic establishment, at least, in literary and cultural studies, if not in philosophy, which remained skeptical. Literary and cultural studies was keen to jump on board, because deconstruction appeared to be dispelling myths, breaking illusions, and attacking the idea of transcendence. But then something happened which was scandalous to the followers of the nihilistic interpretation of deconstruction, but inspirational for those who were looking for alternative visions of the deconstructive movement.

At the point of near total nihilism and silence, mystery began to reassert itself. The nothingness that Derrida and his postmodern associates designated is not a common nothingness, but a Buddhist-like void from which the numinous reasserts itself:

> The modern man . . . is completely modern only when he has come to the very edge of the world, leaving behind him all that has been discarded and outgrown, and acknowledging that he stands before the Nothing out of which All may grow.
>
> (1928/31: 150)

Jung is quoting Goethe: 'In this, your Nothing, I may find my All!', from *Faust, Part Two*. In his writings, Jung expresses the sentiment that the 'growing impoverishment of religious symbols has a meaning' (1934/54: 28). That meaning, we discover, is to collapse the thought forms of the past and to experience anew the living spirit, the living God. 'Since the stars have fallen from heaven and our highest symbols have paled, a secret life holds sway in the unconscious. Our unconscious hides living water, spirit that has become nature, and that is why it is disturbed' (1934/54: 50).

We live in a time of the death and rebirth of the gods, but today we are more conscious of the death of the old than the birth of the new. We are engaged in mourning, loss, grieving, because, writes Jung, 'the sacred images have crumbled away . . . they became dubious, for they conflicted with awakening reason' (1934/54: 22). But a secret life holds sway, and we do not yet know what this life will look like, how it will take form. We live between and betwixt the times. But standing at the abyss, as Romanyshyn has said (1997), is a holy place to be, because we stand without illusions, without the protection of culture and the armory of religion, and in our nakedness we know that something is present, even though we cannot speak its name. The religion of *kataphasis* (that is, expressed through revelation and scripture) has been mortally wounded, but the religion of *apophasis* (the intimation of the Unknown God, beyond words and creeds) has a new opportunity to develop and unfold. Apophasis gives rise to the *via negativa*, negative theology, and the emergence of faith through not knowing.

Something has sprung to life in postmodern and deconstructive philosophy. After about 1989, there was a turning away from the abyss and a new affirmative spirit took hold of the leading postmodern philosophers. It is hard to know what triggered this turnaround. Some believe it was the influence of Emmanuel Levinas on Derrida and his deconstructive school (Hart 1998). Others argue that the collapse of the Berlin Wall, and the sudden turn to religion in the countries of the former Soviet Union and the Eastern bloc, impressed a number of deconstructive philosophers with its urgency and meaning, its cry for spiritual sustenance (Trias 1998). Suddenly the most important of continental philosophers, including Derrida and Vattimo, Gadamer and Trias, were gathering in 1994 on the Isle of Capri to talk about 'the return of the religious' (Derrida and Vattimo 1998).

Derrida was, apparently, an atheist, but he talked increasingly of God. In his major work, *Circumfession*, he confessed that 'the constancy of God in my life is called by other names' (1993: 156). Jung made similar statements in his autobiography. In *Memories, Dreams, Reflections* he wrote: 'I prefer the term 'the unconscious', knowing that I might equally well speak of God or daimon if I wished to express myself in mythic language' (1961: 369). Both Derrida and Jung were engaged in 'other-speaking' about the sacred, not because they were being deliberately difficult, but because the old ways were blocked, and new avenues had to be found. The religious spirit had to be revived, but it could not be revived using the 'same old' language.

In his book *Religion*, Derrida wrote: 'Whatever side one takes in this debate about the "return of the religious" . . . one still must respond. And without waiting. Without waiting too long' (Derrida and Vattimo 1998: 38). Gianni Vattimo was even more explicit: 'In spirit, something that we had thought irrevocably forgotten is made present again, a dormant trace is reawakened, a wound re-opened, the repressed returns and what we took to be an overcoming is no more than a long convalescence' (Derrida and Vattimo 1998: 79). Elsewhere, in discussion with Derrida, Vattimo said:

> While religions, in accordance with the Enlightenment and positivist view, were seen for decades as residual forms of experience, destined to diminish with the imposition of modern forms of life, now they appear once again as possible guides for the future. By now, all of us are used to the fact that disenchantment with the world has generated a radical disenchantment with the very idea of disenchantment. In other words, demythologization has finally turned against itself, thereby acknowledging that the ideal of the elimination of myth is a myth too.
>
> (Vattimo 2003: 29–30)

This is one way of looking at the problem, which would have excited Jung. Modernity felt that the religious spirit was being destroyed and exposed as a 'superstition'. However what had been declared null and void has been 'reawakened', and this, for rational culture and the humanist tradition, is 'a wound re-opened'. Enlightenment reason is revealed as limited, as serving a form of rationalist ideology. The 'repressed returns', not as sexual libido (Freud), but as spiritual concern (Jung). Spirit has not died but has been dormant. This could mean that Jung, not Freud, is the key to our immediate cultural future.

Derrida's career presents a perfect example of Jung's major theme: that the modern mind *must* push away received religion, rejecting its concern with 'belief' for the more compelling arena of direct human experience. As Jung writes: 'We moderns are faced with the necessity of rediscovering the life of the spirit; we must experience it anew for ourselves' (1929: 780). When everything is stripped away, the heart of religion, *spirit*, will return and command attention. 'Spirit returns', writes Derrida, '[and] the word 'spirit' starts to become acceptable again' (1989: 23).

Derrida dedicated the last 15 years of his life to this topic, and he entered a state of mind that could be described as mystical, or at least poetic–lyrical and receptive to mystery. The author of late modern nihilism experienced a profound shift of attitude, and discovered that deconstruction led not to nihilism, but to a new hunger for mystery. Yet the vast throng and industry of postmodern academics has been unable to follow Derrida's lead, since it remains committed to 'disenchantment' rather than *re-enchantment* (Tacey 2000). Many of Derrida's followers were stuck at the abyss, while the charismatic and hermetic leader had moved on. They were not true followers, but they were wedded to an earlier stage in his thought and could not depart from it. Derrida complained that he had 'been read less and less well over almost twenty years, like my religion about which nobody understands anything' (Caputo 1997: xvi). His interest in Jewish mysticism, he said, 'is what my readers won't have known about me' (Caputo 1997: xvii). There is a hidden Derrida, an unknown Derrida, that has been buried by the Derrida industry, and that Jungians are well disposed to make known.

Derrida's deconstruction of the master narratives of culture exposed him directly to the *meaningfulness* of religion. Ironically, the very thing that Derrida once despised had returned in his mind to such prominence that it occupied primary place at the end of his career. He called spirit by various names, but among his favorite were the *gift*, the *messianic*, and the *impossible*. Jung's collective unconscious, so incredible earlier in the century, was now in the same street as Derrida's impossible, Vattimo's spirit, Gadamer's something. With the forms taken away, we were not left with nothing, but with something. This was the conclusion reached by Hans-Georg Gadamer at the Capri dialogues: 'Philosophy' he says, 'has been unable to answer the fundamental question as to why there is something rather than nothing' (Derrida and Vattimo 1998: 211).

This is the theme of Derrida's classic, *Of Spirit*. This book discusses Heidegger's philosophy and the legacy of that philosophy in the postmodern context. In 1927 Heidegger announced that there were some words that he was keen to avoid, and should be set aside in the interests of clear thought. Among them was spirit (*Geist*). But by 1953, in his essay on *Trakl*, Heidegger began to break his own rules. Derrida writes: 'Heidegger often spoke not only of the word "spirit" but, sometimes yielding to the emphatic mode, in the name of spirit' (1989: 1–2). Derrida admits that his and Heidegger's interest in *spirit* must seem 'anachronistic' and 'provocatively retro' to many readers, and especially to academics. Derrida does not apologize for the way spirit has intruded into philosophy; on the contrary, he blasts the academic establishment for its systematic avoidance of this theme:

> Is it not remarkable that this theme, spirit, occupying a major and obvious place in Heidegger's line of thought, should have been disinherited? No one wants anything to do with it any more, in the entire family of Heideggerians, be they the orthodox or the heretical, the neo-Heideggerians or the para-Heideggerians, the disciples or the experts. No one ever speaks of spirit in Heidegger. Not only this, even the anti-Heideggerian specialists take no interest in this thematics of spirit, not even to denounce it. Why? What is going on? What is being avoided by this?
>
> (Derrida 1989: 3)

As this philosopher entered late career, he sounded much like old-man Jung in his phase as misunderstood mystic. He was, like Jung, the prophetic bearer of a new spirit that was not understood by his academic discipline.

Like Jung (1930), the late Derrida took to criticizing the intellectual elites and the academic establishment for their apathy and inertia, their resistance to spirit, their lack of imagination, their inability to see mystery in the symbolic forms of culture. Derrida found himself in a very Jungian place at the end of his career: at odds with traditional religion, yet affirming the religious spirit in a new way. Caputo calls it 'religion without religion' (1997).

The philosophy that Jung longed to dialogue with had arrived, but in a postmodern form, using a deconstructive critique. In his own time, Jung longed for a meaningful conversation with philosophy and theology. Theology tended to snub him, or to go part of the way, as with Victor White and Martin Buber, and withdraw in horror from his vision. Theologians did not appreciate his view of evil, and many thought he was reducing the transcendent to psychology. But philosophy was not interested in dialogue either; it found Jung's ideas ungainly and unsophisticated. Jung said he was Kantian, but scholars said he did not understand Kant (Clarke 1991; Huskinson 2004; Voogd: 1977). Jung claimed to be a phenomenologist, or to use a phenomenological method, but the phenomenologists did not agree (Wulff 1991).

But a link with Jung's vision has been established, a bridge has been created between the deconstructionists and Jung's gnostic spirit. That link is clearly through the *via negativa*. The life of the infinite is not affirmed through revelation or tradition, through the richness of dogma or the security of belief, but through the radical insecurity of not knowing, of not believing, of renunciation. The way to mystery today is similar to John Keats's favored 'negative capability', that is, through a sensitive attunement to the depths of reality without any irritable reaching after fact or reason. It is a negative state that religion has frowned upon as morbid and shadowy, a pathway to confusion and doubt (Tacey 2004). But it seems to be the 'royal road' to the recovery of transcendence in our time. Jung predicted that philosophy would make this breakthrough, away from atheistic materialism: 'Whether we will or no, philosophy keeps breaking through, because the psyche seeks an expression that will embrace its total nature' (1917/26/43: 201).

I would like now to turn to my last point, which relates to the importance of myth and imagination as carriers of transcendent values. As I have argued, the recovery of spirit is not a regression to spirit in its old forms. It is not a return to dogma, onto-theology or metaphysics. The sacred returns in a more humble form; it is no longer in the certain strains of metaphysics or affirmations of a supernatural order. We continue to carry the dark cloud of atheism about us, as Gadamer reminds Derrida: 'No matter to what extent we recognize the urgency of religion, and even after the breakdown of the Marxist doctrine of ideological self-deception promulgated by a dogmatic atheism, there can be no return to the doctrines of the church' (1998: 207).

The return of the religious has nothing to do with the reactionary reassertion of religious truth and doctrine. Fundamentalism is not what the deconstructive philosophers, or what Jung or Hillman, have in mind. The trend toward fundamentalism is a parody of the spirit of the time, a defense against listening to what is new.

If Derrida, Gadamer and Vattimo had access to Jung's language, which they did not, they would concede that the 'return' is not to religious systems or ideologies, rather, it is a return to *mythos* as a mode of perception, as a way of being in the world. Jung distinguished between *religions* per se and the *religious attitude*, and the postmodernists were looking – in their own way – for precisely this distinction. Derrida exclaimed, sounding again like Jung: 'For us today, the word 'religion' is inadequate' (1989: 36).

Jung argues that the sacred, once it has deserted its dwelling place, will no longer be found in the old abode: 'The myth says [the God] will not be found where his body was laid' (1938/1940: 149). After the collapse of master narratives, where do we find transcendence? Poet Matthew Arnold, at the end of the nineteenth century, hinted at its new place of dwelling: After religion, poetry, he said (1880). Imagination is a place where the spirit can be reborn. Imagination as a faculty of soul, as the way the psyche thinks about the world and imagines itself.

At the height of modernity, imagination and fantasy were given short shrift, and viewed as inferior to science and fact, on the one hand, and to religion and theology, on the other. Modernist science overlooked the reality of the imaginal realm through its exclusive concern with external or 'objective' knowledge, and modernist religion ignored the sacred potentials of imagination through its focus on external or revealed truth. The sacred depths of the psyche, with its own 'objectivity' hidden in the folds of our subjectivity, was of little interest to a science claiming to be rational and empirical, or to a religion claiming to be based on a revelation independent of the productions of psyche.

Freudian analysis was 'at one' with the modernist project of stripping the psyche of its religious dimension, and refused to consider the psyche as the locus of spiritual truth. Freud and Jung parted company on this point, and in their rupture we witness the separation of the ways, the epochal differentiation between modernist and non-modernist approaches to psyche and imagination. Jung's non-modernist project seemed *backward* and out of date in his time, but today it can be regarded as offering ground and inspiration for a postmodern recovery of our relationship with the sacred after the collapse of positivistic science and after loss of belief in theistic religion and absolute truth.

The impact of postmodernism has not been a descent into nihilism and despair, as was feared by humanists and by British–American analytic philosophers who resisted the influence of continental postmodernism. The impact of postmodernism has been felt not in a slide into moral panic, but in the restoration of the pivotal role of imagination, play, theatre, and the symbolic mode in life, art and culture. The thoughts of Vattimo are instructive:

> In today's culture, mythological figures and metaphors are used widely, taken for granted, and implicitly justified by the fact that the relation of philosophy with poetry is no longer conceived in antagonistic terms, or by the destruction of the boundary between metaphor and its 'proper meaning', which seems to be the main consequence of the end of metaphysics announced by Heidegger. At the very end, the introduction of mystic and religious terms in philosophy, without any explicit theoretical elaboration, seems justified by the new relationship that philosophy (especially after Heidegger) claims to establish with poetry, and with aesthetic experience more generally.
>
> (2003: 31)

In this important essay, Vattimo makes a comment that should awaken all Jungians and post-Jungians from their intellectual slumber, from their inherent resistance to the *postmodern* as an authentic and valuable *experiment* in consciousness:

> Today continental philosophers speak increasingly, and without providing explicit justification, about angels, redemption, and various mythological figures. This is a practice that, as far as classical mythology is concerned, is clearly promoted by psychoanalysis. Jungian psychoanalysis, in particular, speaks explicitly of a new polytheism; but even in classical Freudian theory, the relation with mythological figures cannot be conceived merely as a recourse to metaphors that must be reduced finally to their 'proper meaning'.
>
> (2003: 30–1)

It is rare for a postmodern philosopher in the tradition of Derrida and Heidegger to make such approving comments about Jungian thought. This indicates that there is a real possibility of finding common ground between Jung's analytical psychology and postmodern deconstructive philosophy, provided that Jungians do not take their own terms and concepts so literally, but regard them in a metaphorical or playful light. Jungians and postmodernists agree that the creativity of the imagination, the spontaneous and 'ephemeral' productions of the imaginal realm, the apparently 'inconsequential' works of myth and dream, of metaphor and fantasy, are all we have *left* after the collapse of established traditions, after the wreckage of absolute religious truths, on the one hand, and empirical and positivistic science, on the other.

The postmodern has been scathing toward all systems that abrogate to themselves grand or mighty ideas and meanings. But elements of discourse that are humble and less strident have escaped the blast of deconstructive philosophy, and have been elevated to a new status. This is scriptural in its sense of dramatic reversal: the high and mighty have been laid low, whereas the meek in spirit have been elevated, and may even be seen as the carriers of meaning in a relativistic and skeptical time. The imagination, dream, myth and fantasy, enjoy considerable status today, because much else is suspect. The humble carriers of transcendence are able to pass muster, because they are not proud, not certain of themselves, not triumphant.

Note

1 In discussing Jung and Derrida – strange bedfellows, perhaps – I am aware of earlier work in this area by Michael Adams (1989), Edward Casey (1990), David Miller (1990) and Susan Rowland (2006).

References

Adams, M.V. (1989) 'Deconstructive Philosophy and Imaginal Psychology: Comparative Perspectives on Jacques Derrida and James Hillman', in Rajnath (ed.) *Deconstruction: A Critique*, London: Macmillan. Reprinted (1992) in Sugg, R.P. (ed.) *Jungian Literary Criticism*, Evanston, IL: Northwestern University Press.

Arnold, M. (1880) 'The Study of Poetry', in *Essays in Criticism*, London: Dent, 1964.

Berry, P. and Wernick, A. (eds) (1992) *Shadow of Spirit: Postmodernism and Religion*, London and New York: Routledge.

Caputo, J. (1997) *The Prayers and Tears of Jacques Derrida: Religion without Religion*, Bloomington, IN: Indiana University Press.

—— (2001) *On Religion*, London and New York: Routledge.

Casey, E.S. (1990) 'Jung and the Postmodern Condition', in K. Barnaby and P. D'Acierno (eds) *C. G. Jung and the Humanities*, Princeton, NJ: Princeton University Press.

Clarke, J.J. (1991) *In Search of Jung*, London and New York: Routledge.

Derrida, J. (1989) *Of Spirit: Heidegger and the Question*, Chicago: University of Chicago Press.

—— (1993) *Circumfession: Fifty-Nine Periods and Periphrases*, in G. Bennington and J. Derrida, *Jacques Derrida*, Chicago: Chicago University Press.

Derrida, J. and Vattimo, G. (eds) (1998) *Religion*, Stanford, CA: Stanford University Press.

Gadamer, H.-G. (1998) 'Afterword', in J. Derrida and G. Vattimo (eds) *Religion*, Stanford, CA: Stanford University Press.

Hart, K. (1998) 'Jacques Derrida: The God Effect', in P. Blond (ed.) *Post-Secular*

Philosophy: Between Philosophy and Theology, London and New York: Routledge.

Huskinson, L. (2004) *Nietzsche and Jung: The Whole Self in the Union of Opposites*, Hove and New York: Brunner-Routledge.

Jung, C.G. (1917/1926/1943) 'On the Psychology of the Unconscious', *CW* 7, 1953/1966: 1–201.

—— (1928/1931) 'The Spiritual Problem of Modern Man', *CW* 10, 1964/1970: 148–96.

—— (1929) 'Commentary on *The Secret of the Golden Flower*', *CW* 13, 1968: 1–84.

—— (1930) 'Richard Wilhelm: In Memoriam', *CW* 15, 1966: 74–96.

—— (1934/1954) 'Archetypes of the Collective Unconscious', *CW* 9, part 1, 1959/1968: 1–86.

—— (1938/1940) 'Psychology and Religion', *CW* 11, 1958/1969: 1–168.

—— (1961) *Memories, Dreams, Reflections*, London: Fontana Press, 1995.

Miller, D. (1990) 'An Other Jung and An Other', in K. Barnaby and P. D'Acierno (eds) *C. G. Jung and the Humanities*, Princeton, NJ: Princeton University Press.

Neville, B. (1992) 'The Charm of Hermes: Hillman, Lyotard and the Postmodern Condition', *Journal of Analytical Psychology*, 37, 2, 337–53.

Pelz, W. and Pelz, L. (1968) *God is No More*, Harmondsworth: Penguin Books.

Romanyshyn, R. (1997) *The Soul in Grief*, Berkeley, CA: North Atlantic Books.

Rowland, S. (2006) 'Jung and Derrida: The Numinous, Deconstruction and Myth', in A. Casement and D. Tacey (eds) *The Idea of the Numinous: Contemporary Jungian and Psychoanalytic Perspectives*, London and New York: Routledge.

Tacey, D. (2000) *Re-Enchantment*, Sydney: HarperCollins.

—— (2004) 'Post-Religion: The Return to Beginnings', in *The Spirituality Revolution: The Emergence of Contemporary Spirituality*, London and New York: Routledge.

Tracy, D. (1999) 'The Spiritual Situation of Our Times', in J. Caputo and M. Scanlon (eds) *God, the Gift, and Postmodernism*, Bloomington, IN: Indiana University Press.

Trias, E. (1998) 'Thinking Religion: The Symbol and the Sacred', in J. Derrida and G. Vattimo (eds) *Religion*, Stanford, CA: Stanford University Press.

Vattimo, G. (2003) 'After Onto-Theology: Philosophy between Science and Religion', in M. Wrathnall (ed.) *Religion After Metaphysics*, Cambridge: Cambridge University Press.

Voogd, S. De (1977) 'C. G. Jung, Psychologist of the Future, "Philosopher" of the Past', *Spring Journal* (Dallas) 22, 152–82.

Ward, G. (ed.) (1997) *The Postmodern God*, Oxford: Basil Blackwell.

Wulff, D.M. (1991) *Psychology of Religion: Classic and Contemporary Views*, New York: Wiley.

Yeats, W.B. (1920) 'The Second Coming', in T. Webb (ed.) *W. B. Yeats: Selected Poetry*, Harmondsworth: Penguin Books, 1991.

Chapter 6

Jung as a writer of myth, discourse and the healing of modernity

Susan Rowland

> What or who, indeed, is this all-powerful matter? It is once more man's picture of a creative god, stripped this time of his anthropomorphic traits and taking the form of a universal concept whose meaning everyone presumes to understand. Consciousness today has grown enormously in breadth and extent, but unfortunately only in spatial dimensions; its temporal reach has not increased, for were that the case we should have a much more living sense of history.
>
> (Jung 1931/1933: 180–1)

Introduction

C.G. Jung lived and worked as an explorer of the whole psyche. He believed that by seeking out the mind's margins, and the mysteries of the unconscious, not only the individual, but also culture could be healed. It is therefore unsurprising that Jung as a writer aims to be the scribe of irrational, creative and numinous dimensions of being.[1] *The Collected Works* are a record of a lifelong descent into the depths. They are a harvest of compositions reflecting the diversity of archetypal imprints. While Jung's writings describe a coherent psychology, they are also the harbour for many spectral voices. To this tension between oneness of meaning and a plurality of possibilities, I will return.

However, Jung's writing is far more than personal therapy. Part of its narrative experimentation, as I shall show, is an attempt to weave the individual into the collective. Such a challenge to the solitary self is in the interests of ameliorating modernity's disastrous (to Jung) overemphasis on rationality to the exclusion of 'other' aspects of the psyche. One of Jung's main tools for such a task is the kind of narrative he called 'myth', by which he meant a collective story capable of facilitating exchanges between conscious and unconscious parts of the mind.

It is my contention that Jung draws on the existing repository of myths in order to reframe them creatively so they imbue his own writing with psychic potency. That potency stems from his belief that myths and religious tropes are a culture's method of structuring subjectivity. In effect, Jung's writing becomes myth itself, offering a healing narrative, or healing fiction, to the reader (1931/1933: 230–1). To put it another way, Jung's writing is a deliberate intervention into cultural discourses: it is an attempt to improve the health of cultural consciousness by repositioning what is marginal to modernity. And the relationship between the notion of discourse and Jung's myth is a good place to start this chapter.

Discourse, Jung's myth and M.M. Bakhtin[2]

Cultural theory after Foucault has made central the notion of discourse. Stemming from Karl Marx's groundbreaking contention that it is not the consciousness of men that makes the conditions of the world, but the material conditions that make consciousness, 'discourse' is the notion that society is made up of material practices and languages that structure subjectivity, often imperceptibly to the individual (Marx 1846: 656). Foucault revised classical Marxism by insisting that the social world consists of multiple discourses, rather than a few broad class divisions. Some discourses are more effective than others and they are productive of power, subjectivity and cultural forms:

> Indeed, it is in discourse that power and knowledge are joined together . . . Discourses are not once and for all subservient to power or raised up against it, any more than silences are. Discourse transmits and produces power; it reinforces it, but also undermines and exposes it, renders it fragile and makes it possible to thwart it.
>
> (Foucault 1976: 100–1)

It is precisely in this multiple quality of discourse that the subject is fashioned by being caught up in it. Such a mutable flickering quality of discourse should be productively compared to Jung's myths: the indispensable stage between conscious and unconscious cognition, as he tells us (1931/1933: 335).

There is far more to Foucault's ideas of social power, but it is his multiplicity of discourses and their mutability that is significant in the context of Jung.

During the 1930s both Jung and Bakhtin, unknown to one another, produced a series of lectures with very similar core theories. Jung was writing papers that became *Psychology and Alchemy*, an extended exposition of archetypal images as part of myths in a culture removed from his own. Bakhtin was working out his theory of cultural dialogics in texts that became *The Dialogic Imagination*, not published in English until 1981.

Bakhtin's dialogics relies on a metaphysical notion of an underlying dichotomy in language, culture and even the human mind. The divide is between centripetal, unifying forces that exist always in tension with centrifugal energies of dispersal and plurality. This means that any society is made up of languages with always more than one type of energy. These multiple energies are the operations of social power. A society will have languages of superior power, unitary languages, yet they can never be manifested absolutely as pure centripetal energy. Why? Because they exist in the social realm, in relation to the forces of plurality. Centrifugal plurality produces a diversity of representations that Bakhtin called 'heteroglossia'.

For example, a church may have a pure language of liturgy, but in *actual social use* different emphases, accents, maybe even dialect words, creep in. So Bakhtin firmly asserts that pure unitary language only exists as an ideal; it can never be completely incarnated in social life. Once a language is in social use it is always *in dialogue* with the forces of social diversity and embodiment, producing heteroglossia.

Similarly, the many forms of language of the poor and the marginalized are in a dialogical relationship with centripetal, unitary languages, lest their diversity become unintelligibility. Furthermore, Bakhtin offers another contribution to the analysis of cultural functioning: the chronotope. Simply denoting 'time–space', the chronotope is the idea that a culture (and a language), is made up of forms that structure space and time in relation to each other. So a ubiquitous example of a chronotope is a 'meeting', a social or work event, in a particular space and at a particular time.

These tools for reading culture suggestively resemble key ideas of Jung. Despite the title of *The Dialogical Imagination*, Bakhtin does not consider the implications of his theories of language, dialogics and chronotopes for the psyche. One could argue that Jung supplies this deficiency. For the relationship of archetypes and archetypal images is dialogical. As Jung frequently insisted, archetypes are not inherited images; rather they are inherited potentials for certain sorts of images and meaning. Therefore archetypes are irrepresentable in themselves. They only ever appear as archetypal images, in which case they are coloured by their context in an individual's personal history and culture. In effect, archetypal images result from a dialogue between the centripetal forces of the archetype (aspiring to irrepresentable purity) and the centrifugal forces of plurality and dispersal in actual everyday experience. Jung's is the dialogical imagination.

Moreover, the patterns that archetypal images produce look suspiciously like chronotopes. If we take an archetype such as 'mother', at first glance it may seem unlike Bakhtin's most banal example of 'a meeting'. However, given that the human body is inevitable chronotopic, taking up both space and time simultaneously, 'mother' is a *particular* mode of spatial–temporal experiencing. 'Mother' is a social role, a practice, a location for multiple psychic images and fantasies, a discourse.

So we see here, in the similarities between chronotopes and archetypes manifesting as a pattern of images organizing our perception of time and space, how far Jung emphasizes the *image* dimension of the archetype. 'Mother's images operate as a practice, a narrative over time. It is time to take a closer look at Jung's images and narrative.

First of all, though, it is worth noting the three portrayals of 'discourse', the particular languages and practices of a society, that have been alluded to so far in this chapter. The Foucauldian–Marxist discourse is one of materialism as the sculptor of subjectivity. Bakhtin has a dialogical portrayal of discourse and power, stressing its social expression, while Jung could be said to explore the psychological implications of Bakhtin's dialogics. Jung's 'discourses', social and collective modes of signifying, are the cultural functioning of archetypes in images-forming-collective-narratives. So Jung's discourses are not only patterns of images: they are also collective narratives and social practices.

Jung, discourse and the framing work of myth

As a psychologist, Jung was naturally most interested in those discourses especially active in the making of the modern person. He was also profoundly historical in his approach, believing, conservatively, that those discourses (mainly religious) that had previously worked to regulate the psyche, still had a part to play in a revised modernity. As the quotation at the head of this chapter shows, Jung held that an historical understanding of the entwinement of religion and science would usefully decentre rational science from its dominant position for the modern person. When Jung rewrites discourse in the cause of marginalized archetypal creativity, he is subversive of modernity in the interests of its ultimate stability. Indeed, he aims to restore science, in the form of his psychology, by reframing it as myth. Where Bakhtin gloried in the revolutionary proletarian energies of the heteroglossia, Jung values the centralizing power of the archetype. His politics of discourse are a revolutionary conservatism.

The politics spills into the *matter* of the writing. Preference for the irrepresentable archetype, both as a psychologist and as a cultural critic, may be the reason Jung focuses so much on archetypal images at the expense of narrative. Paying direct attention to narrative would inevitably lead to considering social ideas; it would risk disconnection from the individual psyche. Indeed, this is precisely the problem that Jung discerns. To him myths are: 'the natural and indispensable stage between unconscious and conscious cognition' (Jung 1963: 335). He believes that modernity has lost these myths, these technologies of the soul, which are more than individual as they bind the psyche into the collective consciousness as well as unconscious. So what is the relationship between archetypal images and mythic narrative?

Jung offers a crucial example of these two aspects of his writing as his contribution to the theory of discourse in his short essay, 'On the Psychology of the Trickster Figure' (1954). In this essay, which I will return to, he ruminates on a mythic narrative, the Native American Trickster, and a psychological image, the shadow. Speculating on a helpful similarity between the two phenomena, he sees the growing difference between them as an aspect of modernity's sickness. Where the trickster myth keeps inferiority before the society so that it can be consciously criticized, the mythless, storyless individual shadow lacks that vital collective mobilization. In other words, a trickster myth helps shape a healthy society. Conversely, the individual shadow lacks the vital link to structures beyond the individual. So myths act as social discourse. That shadow alone cannot take on this role for it lacks the symbolic narrative properties of a myth. Only when animated as part of a greater individuation story can the shadow discursively intervene in culture.

A myth, we understand, is not just any narrative, but one capable of 'framing', making *collectively meaningful* individual archetypal images, just as a picture frame defines and encodes as artistically meaningful the elements within the work of art. Powerful collective narratives frame images and so the psychic *work* of the two together constitutes a myth, to Jung. These myths structure social as well as psychological meaning: the two are not separable; they are discourses. If there is no narrative frame then the archetypal images may remain unrealized. Jung gives a powerful modern example of a soldier, who is without ethics because his shadow is psychologically atrophied:

> How, under these circumstances can one expect a soldier to subject an order received from a superior to ethical scrutiny? He has not yet made the discovery that he might be capable of spontaneous ethical impulses, and of performing them – even when no one is looking.
>
> (Jung 1954: 479)

So where myth is an active social phenomenon (powerful discourse), it is a form by which the individual psyche is dialogically engaged with the collective. Such a dialogical relationship develops collective consciousness by its very participation in the collective unconscious. Mythical narrative without the internal image would appear uninvolving and meaningless. Meaning is creative and is found in the interaction between the inner image and outer narrative. Myths 'frame' and make intelligible inner contents through dialogical relationship. This suggests that Jung's concentration on archetypal images at the expense of framing narrative is a problem. If there is a comparative lack of effective myth in modernity, then, what is his strategy? Can Jung be a provider of myth for his own time?

Jung writing myth, creating discourses

> The medieval carnivals . . . were abolished relatively early . . . Our solution, however, has served to throw the gates of hell wide open.
>
> (Jung 1936: 182)

As a typical conservative, Jung believes that the European culture of the past possessed better psychic health than his own world. Europe *worked* as a social organism, he believed, when it inhabited collective symbols, narratives and practices (discourse) that facilitated individual and collective relationship with the unconscious. So not only the contemplative images of religion, but also its stories and traditions such as carnivals, were a functioning part of its psychological regulation of culture.

Unfortunately, European Christianity has lost much of its psychological efficacy, Jung suggested. Its images were no longer true symbols by which he meant that they did not work as 'bridges thrown out towards an unseen shore' (Jung 1931: 116). Once symbols lose their ability to evoke the numinosity of the unconscious, they become mere signs standing for knowable quantities. Then their framing narrative is no longer a myth, a technology for developing the soul through relating to the unconscious.

If modern science has succeeded religion as a culturally dominant practice, then to Jung, the conventional language of science is also no solution:

> We have to break down life and events, which are self-contained processes, into meanings, images, concepts, well knowing that in doing so we are getting further away from the living mystery . . . In this way we meet the demands of science.
>
> (Jung 1931: 121)

Like myth, science is a language that 'frames'. Science is a framework that *produces* scientific meaning: it does not merely transmit it from a pre-existing reality. For psychology at least, science *creates* itself by a particular practice of language. Science is a way of thinking and writing that transforms psychic phenomena into an 'object' of knowledge. It is the making of rational meaning by a collective discursive practice that omits much that Jung regarded as native to the psyche.

So if Jung had confined himself to logical language, his psychology would inevitably be partial. Modernity's standard discourse of science perverts psychic wholeness. There is no neutral, 'objective', descriptive language because we are always implicated in what we are observing. A discourse limiting science to rational expression is itself an act of repression. The discursive elevation of rational science is cultural marginalization, as Foucault, in his works on sexuality, madness and civilization, would agree

(1976: 10, 95–7). And what is repressed turns dark. Here Jung on a man's psychic feminine, the anima, defends his 'creative' writing:

> It is possible to describe [the anima] in rational, scientific language, but in this way one entirely fails to express its living character. Therefore, in describing the living processes of the psyche, I deliberately and consciously give preference to a dramatic, mythological way of thinking and speaking, because this is not only more expressive but also more exact than an abstract scientific terminology.
>
> (Jung 1951a: 25)

So, if his writing is to express the whole psyche, Jung needs a different kind of frame for his psychic material to one that relies solely on rational science. If this frame is to adequately express the psyche, it must be true to its unknowable, unfathomable depths; and such a framing narrative is what Jung calls myth. Moreover, this narrative must function as a myth for the reader (otherwise, the numinous qualities will have failed to be communicated). In effect, Jung seeks to extend the domain of science into religion so that scientific argument can become psychological myth. Jung is not primarily a writer *about* myth. He is a writer *of* myth, as he traces his own framing narrative around his archetypal images. Jungian psychology is science *as* myth in Jung's definition of myth as a story (with words and images), which promotes conscious and unconscious exchanges.

One prominent example of this peculiar aesthetic science is the relationship between two of Jung's works: *Answer to Job* (1952) and *Memories, Dreams, Reflections* (1963). *Answer to Job* traces the turbulent passions of the Judaeo-Christian God as his dawning relationship with 'man' makes possible a growth in self-consciousness. In retelling the stories of the bible, *Answer to Job* ends in the present with the horrific possibilities of weapons of mass destruction 'framed', or put into the context of, the apocalyptic narrative of the *Book of Revelation*.

The task for modern man is clear: is it possible to change the frame and subsequently alter the myth? Can a myth of apocalypse be diverted by unconscious creativity into a new beginning? By rewinding the biblical frame around psychic images, Jung generates out of his reading of the bible another narrative of creation; he provides a story of self-creation, which is creation by the God-Self. Jungian individuation is cast by *Job* into a mythic context: a narrative of the numinous that is less a psychological argument than itself a *way*. The story itself is a method, a technology for dealing with man's unconscious dark powers.

This new myth for collective culture is then reframed from the individual's point of view in *Memories, Dreams, Reflections*. This so-called autobiography is a sequel to *Answer to Job* and also its spatial companion. Both works offer the same myth: the narrative frame taken from Christian and scientific culture, which is then reinvigorated as a myth of 'being', as Jungian psychology. Yet the same myth is focused from different perspectives: the eccentric characterization of God in *Job* is Jung's attempt to write from the expanses of the Self's wayward command of the archetypes. *Memories*, meanwhile, is rooted in autobiographical realism. It is Jungian individuation from the ego's perspective.

In these two works, Jung uses religious tropes to generate his scientific myth. More usually in *The Collected Works*, he draws on history. To return briefly to the 'Trickster' essay, what Jung finds from a description of the phenomena is a Native American *myth* and a European *image* of the shadow. 'Trickster' is no longer an operational discourse in Jung's Europe: the myth is defunct. What functioned in Native American societies to remind people of their inferior selves and the past has been absent from Europe since the church gave up carnival and the feast of fools. Its remnant is the shadow, an individual's psychic image of inferiority. Unfortunately, without collective mobilization via a narrative (turning image into myth), the shadow trickster cannot assume its cultural role as a social discourse of (a)morality. So Jung takes up the task of 'framing' the shadow in the discourse where his public image is still to be found, in history:

> Outwardly people are more or less civilized, but inwardly they are still primitives . . . This contradiction was once brought home to me in the most drastic manner when I was watching a 'strudel' (a sort of local witch-doctor) taking the spell off a stable. The stable was situated immediately beside the Gotthard railway line, and several international expresses sped past during the ceremony.
>
> (Jung 1954: 482)

Jung regards the psyche as a spatial and temporal organ: it is chronotopic. To be healthy, modern consciousness needs spatial and temporal orienting through myth. Here above we see 'history' as 'other' in spatial form. The European witchdoctor, whom Jung takes to be an aspect of European medieval culture, is signalled as 'other', in the context of the twentieth century location and by the term 'witchdoctor', which is more often used in the context of 'other' lands. Through a complex weaving of temporal references into spatial tropes, Jung aims to rescue what has been marginalized in modern consciousness.

Myth here is first of all the property of the 'other', the Native Americans. Then it is reconstructed in Europe, through the excavation of the marginalized trickster of medieval culture – found alive and well in rural folk culture – which is now surviving alongside and against 'high-speed' technology. So medieval practices, banished from dominant discourses of modernity, survive as spatially proximate to them in the grounds of the modern soul. Through noting the social health of the Native Americans, because they have kept their myth, Jung provides a gradual increase of intimacy with this trickster-other. The trickster is first a discourse/myth of Native Americans, then medieval clown, then a Swiss 'witchdoctor', and then the shadow in spiritually impoverished modern man.

The final paragraphs of 'trickster' blend the shadow figure into Jung's typical individuation sequence. The shadow gives way to the anima and ultimately to the wise old man. In this particular essay, of cultural encounters and liminal boundaries, the individuation story of inner self-realization takes on the characteristics of a collective discourse; individuation seizes the trickster narratives and makes them a spatial framing of history with its many cultures. In effect, in the textual space of the essay, Jung expands his psychology trope of individuation to figure a complex relation to cultural otherness – the Native Americans – as both inside and outside this space. Jung thereby transforms his psyche logos, words about psyche, into an historically located myth. Indeed, one of the things that shows Jung's myth working as a discourse is its very cultural and historical location.

As a third and last example I will look at *Aion*, which concentrates on the temporal dimension of Jung's scientific myth.

Aion: novel and myth

It is worthwhile recalling Bakhtin in order to consider the structure of *Aion*. Bakhtin, with his dialogical language, held the novel to be the most significant form of literature. This is because the novel, above all other literary genres, feeds the diversity of the heteroglossia. The novel has many voices and evokes many social practices. No intrusive author, narrator, or major character can extinguish, or establish complete dominance over the many languages of the novel. Consequently, the novel will make a dialogical relationship with the reader. It follows that the dialogical engagement will affect a reader's consciousness differently every time it is read. A novel changes with every reading *into a new work*.

Conventional written history, by way of contrast, despite its population of characters, tends to be too abstract to liberate the reader's imagination, Bakhtin believed. Fortunately, literature has come up with the form of the historical novel, which aims to overcome the limitation of 'straight' narrative history by bringing all the multiplicity and dialogics of the novel into the discourse of history. In Jung's terms the historical novel converts history into (psychic) myth.

Aion is the history of the European psyche in its religious and scientific discourses. In this work Jung shows how today's scientific 'truisms' develop out of, and narratively resemble, gnostic, alchemical and Christian ideas. Jung writes:

> It is significant that Gnostic philosophy found its continuation in alchemy. 'Mater Alchemia' is one of the mothers of modern science, and modern science has given us an unparalleled knowledge of the 'dark' side of matter. It has also penetrated into the secrets of physiology and evolution, and made the very roots of life itself an object of investigation. In this way the human mind has sunk deep into the sublunary world of matter, thus repeating the Gnostic myth of the Nous, who, beholding his reflection in the depths below, plunged down and was swallowed in the embrace of Physis.
>
> (Jung 1951b: 368)

The achievement of *Aion* is its use of symbol and mythic narrative in order to twist together discourses into Jung's scientific myth. It attempts to restore the health-giving properties of European past culture by *restorying* them. Explicitly the words of Jungian psychology *are* themselves myth because they are designed to heal. The psychology is not only *about* healing the psyche; its words *are* healing in Jungian terms. They reconnect the individual psyche to culture, to history and to the cosmos. Jungian ideas occupy a particular time and space, a chronotope and make up a myth in relation to previous doctrines. As Jung says:

> The problems which the integration of the unconscious sets modern doctors and psychologists can only be solved along the lines traced out by history, and the upshot will be a new assimilation of the traditional myth.
>
> (Jung 1951c: 282)

So far I have been saying that Jung's notion of myth is close to cultural theory's description of discourse, minus the belief in material power as the major originating and shaping cause. For Jung the cultural mindscape of social discourse or myth is dialogical. No origin can be definitively ascribed to either the inner archetypal psyche or the outer world where its images are shaped by history. So Jung's myth/discourse is dialogical because it arises from a dialogue between inner image-producing archetypes, which are irrepresentable in pure form and outer material conditions. Like Bakhtin's discourses, Jung's myths function as a tension between an impossible oneness and purity of meaning and the forces of diversity and plurality in heteroglossia.

Jung writes novels in the Bakhtinian sense. Jung's myth discourse is a novelistic discourse because it liberates a plurality of voices rather than repressing them. True, Jung's writing also demonstrates the pull to oneness and unitary language in the principles of Jungian psychology. Yet this drive for rational coherence is always interrupted by the plurality of the heteroglossia that is Jung's psyche. *Aion* is an historical novel. It re-inscribes Jung's science as a myth for modernity.

Endnote: the larger frame

It is worth ending by remembering the larger frame to both Jung and Bakhtin's dialogics. The pull towards a centralization of meaning and power is an organ of monotheism. Here transcendence of meaning is a trope borrowed from the conception of a transcendent God. By contrast, the urge for diversity in the opposite pole has a number of antecedents in animism, paganism, polytheism and the Earth Mother Goddess. The idea that the living Earth is sacred in herself (as opposed to being merely the creation of a Sky Father God, who stands back from what he has made,) is a vision of reality caught up in a great and multifaceted web of being. In a Western culture suffering the dominance of discourses of rationality built on separation from all that is 'other' (as feminine, matter, body, indigenous, racially different etc.), both Jung and Bakhtin, in very different moods, aim to strengthen the signifying potential of the sacred Earth.

One diagnosis of modernity's ills rests on the contention that modern consciousness needs both Sky Father discourses of separation and Earth Mother myths of relationship to be healthily and dialogically aligned in the psyche (Baring and Cashford 1991). After several centuries of psychic imbalance, the modern self is fragile.

Jung casts his discourses as myths, myths of connection that take Sky Father logocentric science and translate it into Earth Mother myth. In wanting to transform the dominant discourses of his world into myths, he sought to save modernity from its own darkness. By seeking to replace a myth of apocalypse with a myth of self-creation, he wanted a new creation: a new heaven and a new earth.

Notes

1 A longer study of the varieties of Jung's writing is to be found in my book, *Jung as a Writer*.

2 Raya Jones was the first to connect Bakhtin with Jung. I am very grateful to her work.

References and further reading

Bakhtin, M.M. (1981) *The Dialogic Imagination: Four Essays*, ed. M. Holquist, trans. C. Emerson and M. Holquist, Austin, TX: University of Texas Press.

Baring, A. and Cashford, J. (1991) *The Myth of the Goddess: Evolution of an Image*, London and New York: Penguin Arkana.

Foucault, M. (1976) *The Will to Knowledge: The History of Sexuality: 1*, trans. R. Hurley, London: Penguin Books.

Jones, R.A. (2002) 'The Necessity of the Unconscious', *Journal for the Theory of Social Behaviour*, 32, 345–66.

—— (2003) 'Mixed Metaphors and Narrative Shifts: Archetypes', *Theory & Psychology* 13, 5, 651–72.

Jung, C.G. (1931) 'On the Relation of Analytical Psychology to Poetry', *CW* 15, 1966: 97–132.

—— (1931/1933) 'Basic Postulates of Analytical Psychology', *Modern Man in Search of a Soul*, London and New York: Routledge, 2005.

—— (1936) 'Individual Dream Symbolism in Relation to Alchemy', *CW* 12, 1953: 44–331.

—— (1951a) 'The Szygy: Anima and Animus', *CW* 9ii, 1959/1968: 20–42.

—— (1951b) 'The Structure and Dynamics of the Self', *CW* 9ii, 1959/1968: 347–421.

—— (1951c) 'The Psychology of Christian Alchemical Symbolism', *CW* 9ii, 1959/1968: 267–86.

—— (1952) *Answer to Job*, *CW* 11, 1958/1969: 553–758.

—— (1954) 'On Psychology of Trickster Figure', *CW* 9i, 1959/1968: 456–88.

—— (1963/1983) *Memories, Dreams, Reflections*, London: Fontana.

Marx, K. (1846) *The German Ideology*, extract in *Literary Theory: An Anthology*, ed. J. Rivkin and M. Ryan, Oxford: Blackwell, 1998/2004.

Rowland, S. (2005) *Jung as a Writer*, London: Routledge.

Chapter 7

Does myth (still) have a function in Jungian studies? Modernity, metaphor, and psycho-mythology

Michael Vannoy Adams

One of the most important novelists of the twentieth century declares that he has no interest in Freudians. 'Let the credulous and vulgar continue to believe that all mental woes can be cured by a daily application of old Greek myths to their private parts', Vladimir Nabokov says. 'I really do not care' (1973: 66). Jungians may not apply old Greek myths to their private parts as Freudians so notoriously do, but they do apply old myths – among them, Greek myths – in an attempt to cure mental woes. Jungians continue to believe that myth has a function.

If I did not believe that myth still has a function, I would never have written my book, *The Mythological Unconscious* (Adams 2001), and I would never have written the chapter 'Mythological Knowledge: Just How Important is It in Jungian (and Freudian) Analysis?' in my book *The Fantasy Principle: Psychoanalysis of the Imagination* (Adams 2004). Nor would I continue to teach my courses, 'Psychoanalyzing Greek and Roman Mythology' and 'Psychoanalyzing Jewish, Christian, and Islamic Mythology' at the New School in New York. Not only Jung but also Jungians like James Hillman – and not only Freud and Freudians like Wilfred Bion – also believe that myth has a function. What, however, *is* that function?

In a book that includes the word 'functions' in the subtitle, G.S. Kirk criticizes the proposition that 'all myths are about gods' (1970: 9). For example, he says that 'the heroes, who play so large a part in Greek myths, are obviously not gods' (ibid.: 10). I would say that most, if not all, myths are about gods. Even when myths are about heroes, like that favorite Freudian hero Oedipus, they are about those heroes in relation to gods. Kirk notes that myth has many functions. For Jung and Jungians, the basic function of myth is psychological.

Recently, one Jungian, Wolfgang Giegerich, has argued that, at this stage in the history of consciousness, myth no longer has any psychological function. Giegerich asserts that it is a fallacy to resort to 'any ancient mythological figures' in an attempt to account for the modern situation. Ancient mythological figures, he contends, 'do not suffice'. They are insufficient because, he says, 'even though they may display certain *formal* similarities' to the modern situation, 'they are incommensurable' with it (1999: 175).

In effect, Giegerich declares the Jungian method of mythological amplification to be invalid. Amplification is a comparative method. It compares images from the modern psyche to images from other sources – among them, ancient myths – in an effort to identify significant similarities, or parallels. Giegerich, however, maintains that the modern psychological situation is utterly without precedent, without parallel. It is so radically different – or, as he says, so logically different – from the ancient mythological situation that any similarity is merely formal and thus insignificant. Giegerich says that the modern situation has '*fundamentally broken with myth as such*, that is, with the entire level of consciousness on which truly mythic experience was feasible'. The modern situation has 'not broken with this or that myth, nor with all myths', he says, but with what 'made myths possible in the first place' (ibid.: 175).

In contrast to Giegerich, who posits a discontinuity between the ancient situation and the modern situation, Jung emphasizes what he calls 'the higher continuity of history' (1912/1952: 1). For example, Freud demonstrates that an ancient myth, the Oedipus myth, continues to exist in the modern psyche as the Oedipus complex. As a result, Jung says, 'the gulf that separates our age from antiquity is bridged over, and we realize that Oedipus is still alive for us' (ibid.). This realization, he says, establishes 'an identity of fundamental human conflicts' that are 'independent of time and place' and refutes the notion that modern people are '*different*' from (or 'better' than) ancient people. Jung says that 'an indissoluble link binds us to the men of antiquity' (ibid.). Oedipus is in ancient Thebes, and Oedipus is in modern New York. 'The latest incarnation of Oedipus', Joseph Campbell notes, is standing 'this afternoon on the corner of Forty-second Street and Fifth Avenue, waiting for the traffic light to change' (1968: 4). Of course, the modern Oedipus is simultaneously talking on a cellular phone and listening to a portable music player, but, to the extent that he is like the ancient Oedipus, he is still presumably motivated to commit patricide and incest: what Herman Melville calls 'the two most horrible crimes' (1971: 351).

Giegerich historicizes ancient mythology and, in the process, demythologizes modern psychology. Ancient mythological figures, he says, are inadequate to the modern situation precisely because they are ancient – that is, anachronistic. In the modern situation, they are obsolete and, as a result, irrelevant. What is the 'modern situation'? As Giegerich defines it, it is, in the history of consciousness, the stage of the computer, internet, cyberspace, and virtual reality. For Giegerich, the modern psychological situation is so technological that it is post-mythological. Jung believes that the more things change, the more they remain the same. In contrast, Giegerich is what I would call a 'situationist'. He believes that the situation –

something technological – has changed so much that nothing mythological remains the same or significantly similar.

Giegerich is a formidable, impressively erudite critic of Jungian psychology. If there is any 'post-Jungian', it is Giegerich. Does, however, the digital technology of the computer, internet, cyberspace, and virtual reality render mythological amplification – which as a comparative method is an analog technology – obsolete and irrelevant? I, too, have criticized amplification. I have advocated an expansive redefinition of amplification to include, in addition to the comparative method, what I call a 'contrastive method' (Adams 2004: 62–3). By this redefinition, amplification would not only compare images in order to identify significant similarities but would also contrast images in order to identify significant differences. I have not, however, proposed that Jungians discard mythological amplification as a method.

Mythological amplification is not, of course, the only Jungian method. Mythology is not absolutely indispensable to Jungian psychology. A Jungian might still be a Jungian and not practice mythological amplification. For example, Michael Fordham says that he 'never used amplification' as insistently as some Jungians do and 'largely eliminated it' as a method (1993: 74). Active imagination is also a Jungian method, and it does not entail any recourse to mythology. 'No myths', Sam Harris says, 'need to be embraced to commune with the profundity of our experience' (2004: 227). I agree with Harris that myths are not, in that sense, experientially necessary. They may, however, still be psychologically valuable, for certain dreams, fantasies, and experiences of modern people are conspicuously (and profoundly) similar to the myths of ancient people, as Jungians continue to demonstrate – and, contrary to what Giegerich says, those modern dreams, fantasies, and experiences are similar not only in form but also in content to ancient myths.

Sophia Heller, who acknowledges the influence of Giegerich, does not just assert, as Harris does, that myths are unnecessary. She contends that myth is 'absent' in the modern (or postmodern) situation. Heller says that 'myths today are studied rather than lived'. Myth still has a function, she affirms, but that function is now 'critical rather than existential' (2006: 2). In contrast to Heller, I would say that myth is not absent but present, although it is present in a way functionally different from the way it was previously present, and that Jungians study myth in order to demonstrate how contemporary people continue to live myth – or, more precisely, to demonstrate how myth continues to live in (the psyche of) contemporary people.

For Giegerich, mythological amplification is not only a nostalgic, sentimental exercise, but also an abusive method. In this respect, he criticizes Jungians who attempt, for example, 'to reclaim Aphrodite for modern life experience'. He says that this reclamation project is 'a terrible abuse of poor Aphrodite, who, being dead, has no way to defend herself against this abuse'. How, he wonders, can Jungians 'seriously want to recognize Aphrodite in, or find her relevant to', the sense of the beautiful, erotic, or sexual in modern fantasy and behavior, when the modern situation has so moralistically distorted and so commercially appropriated and exploited that sense (1999: 181)?

Giegerich does not mention Ginette Paris, but she, more eloquently than any other Jungian, reclaims Aphrodite for modern life experience. Paris is not naive. She, too, notes how the moralistic distortion and commercial appropriation and exploitation of the beautiful, erotic, or sexual in the modern situation abuse Aphrodite, but when Paris practices mythological amplification, she does not abuse Aphrodite. She describes how Aphrodite is alive and well in the modern psyche, and is still relevant to the modern situation (1986). For example, she recounts an anecdote in which Aphrodite manifested to a modern young woman. On a spring day, the young woman saw a pair of sexy sandals in a store window, and, although the sandals were extremely expensive, she impulsively bought them. The young woman called the impulse 'spring fever'. What impelled her, she remarked, was 'the season for love'. Paris says that if the young woman had been a Jungian, 'she would probably have said, "Here comes Aphrodite"' (1997: 88). The young woman, Paris notes, 'didn't know Greek mythology and didn't identify Aphrodite by her Greek name'. As Paris says, the young woman did not call her 'Aphrodite' but called her, equivalently, 'the season for love' (ibid.).

Aphrodite also manifests to modern young men. For example, a young man who entered analysis with me was in a marriage with a woman who he acknowledged was potentially – but only occasionally actually – an Aphrodite. What had attracted him to her was a 'love at first sight' moment, when had seen just how much an Aphrodite she might be. 'When I saw her, I thought here's this potentially beautiful girl with a pretty face and figure', he said. 'I thought she just needs to learn a few of the arts of beauty – then she'll be "perfect"'. Actually, to be an Aphrodite was, for his wife, an exertion. With effort, she could adopt the aesthetic style of an Aphrodite, but she did not often do so. On one occasion, she had surprised and pleased him immensely with an exhibition of initiative. 'She did the whole Aphrodite thing on her own', he said. 'I thought, "Oh, so *you* can do it too!"' His wife had returned from a weekend away, and after bathing herself and perfuming herself, she had made herself up and dressed herself up. They had gone out to a restaurant for dinner and then come back to the apartment for a movie. 'We watched Woody Allen's *Mighty Aphrodite*', the young man said with an ironic laugh, 'and then we had great sex'. Such experiences were, however, an exception to the rule. To the young man, his wife left something very much to be desired. 'The search for Aphrodite is part of my psyche', he said. 'That doesn't mean that my wife doesn't have those qualities that I'm looking for.' It was just that she did not often embody them. As a result, the young man was in a real quandary. 'I *really* like *feminine* women, and when I encounter other women, who are Aphrodites, something is really stirred up inside me', he said. 'The difficulty has been not to let the stirrings inside me happen, because I'm married – but I'm not getting what I need out of my marriage.' One day on the way to analysis, he had looked in a store window. 'I saw all these women's magazines – the photos on the covers of the magazines', he said. 'I thought, "Oh, there she *is*! There's Aphrodite. I'm being surrounded by her all the time".' The previous night, he had worked a job at a social event. 'Quite a few of the women there were Aphrodites', he said. 'It's not that my wife doesn't have *any* Aphrodite about her, but *they* – other women – have *more*, and it's something that I'm not getting enough of.'

In one aspect, Aphrodite is in love with Adonis. Like Aphrodite, Adonis is 'beautiful'. He dies, however, before Aphrodite can 'truly possess him'. At his death, Adonis metamorphoses into a flower, his blood transforms into 'red anemones' (Kerenyi 1951: 76). The young man who entered analysis with me said, 'I identify with Adonis'. Now, however, as he became older, he was ambivalent about the identification with Adonis, who, he noted, 'dies young'. He elaborated:

> Being identified with Adonis is a difficult thing for me to acknowledge about myself. When I was younger, I didn't feel it was difficult. The Adonis thing worked in the past but doesn't work so well now. Adonis doesn't have to try that hard. He gets petulant when his needs aren't met: 'Why aren't they being met? What's going on? Where are the Aphrodites?' I was really used to getting female attention. I took it for granted. I didn't have to try that hard to get attention. Now I'm getting older, but I still expect girls just to come to me. Of course, it can still happen once in a while. I still look young. If I see a girl on the subway and she's responding to how I look, I think to myself, 'I know what to do with *that* now'. If the Adonis thing continues much longer, however, it will come across as *strange* – and then, eventually, as *insane*. I don't think that will happen to me, because I don't identify solely with Adonis. The Adonis thing is only one of the parts of me, but it has to do with how I initially approach women. If you try to be Adonis past a certain point, women go, 'Huh?' That might have been enough when I was younger. Then all the other stuff is still 'potential', and girls can read that potential into you – they can project all that onto you. If you show a little 'intellectual' stuff, girls think, 'He'll *become* somebody'. But if you don't work at it, you get older, and it's no longer potential. Adonis turns into a flower. Women say, 'What are you going to do with *that*? It's just a *flower*. You were just a flower all along? What a shame!'

He realized, with chagrin, that Adonis is a 'pretty boy', who dies before Aphrodite can love him as a man – as if Adonis is always potential, never actual, as if Adonis has a time limit, an expiration date at which he prematurely perishes. From a Jungian perspective, Adonis is an image of the *puer aeternus* – who stays, Robert A. Segal notes, 'an adolescent for life' (1999: 108). As Segal succinctly says, 'He simply never grows up' (1999: 109). Such individuals are, Hillman says, 'only flower-people', who remain 'possibility and promise only' (1979b: 27).

Among mythologies, Greek mythology is exceptional, Paul Friedrich asserts, 'because of the number and stature of its female deities, so diverse in their personal, moral, and aesthetic characteristics, and for what it says about "the feminine"' (1978: 1). As the love goddess, Aphrodite is much more, he notes, than a mere 'fun girl' (ibid.: 2). What interests Friedrich are 'both the universal and the contemporary American meanings of Aphrodite, notably as these bear on our understanding of the psychology of women' (ibid.: 4). No other mythology, he contends, 'is richer in archetypes, implicit characterology, insight into the human psyche', than Greek mythology (ibid.: 7). In this respect, he says that Aphrodite is one of the 'emotional complexes', the 'one including sex and sensuousness' (ibid.: 8). I would merely add that, in spite of what Giegerich says, the Aphrodite complex continues to be a vitally decisive factor in the psychology of both modern women and modern men. As Jean Shinoda Bolen says, 'The Aphrodite archetype creates a personal charisma – a magnetism or electricity – that, combined with physical attributes, makes a woman "an Aphrodite"' (1984: 243). Paris says, 'The woman who has the qualities of Aphrodite knows how to move, breathe, and vibrate, and is capable of generating as well as receiving high-intensity sexual energy' (1986: 45).

There is no 'Aphroditic Personality Disorder' in the *Diagnostic and Statistical Manual of Mental Disorders*, but if, as Jung says, 'the gods have become diseases' (1929: 54), there well could be. For example, a psychiatric dictionary defines 'aphrodisia' as sexual excitation and 'aphrodisiomania' as excessive (by implication, pathological) sexual excitation (Hinsie and Shatzky 1940: 44–5). There is an intimate association between Aphrodite and the penis. After Ouranos is castrated by Kronos and the genitals are cast into the sea, Aphrodite is born from the white foam (*aphros*) and named after it. It is apt, Paris emphasizes, that 'intellectual Athena' is born from her father's head and 'sexy Aphrodite is born from her father's *genitals*' (1986: 15). Aphrodite is the mother not only of Eros but also of Priapos, who is 'excessively phallic' (Kerenyi 1951: 176) – most graphically (or pornographically) in the notorious mural from Pompeii, where Priapos weighs down the scales with the prodigiously disproportionate, heavy organ (Thorn 1990: 78). This enormity, which Aphrodite considers a deformity, is, indeed, a *membrum virile*, which implies, Hillman says, 'vulgar as it may seem to those who cling to prissy pretty sex, every hard-on is mothered by Aphrodite' (1995: 44). The condition of 'priapism' is a persistent erection of the penis (Hinsie and Shatzky 1940: 429).

Why not just say 'love' rather than 'Aphrodite'? Because, I would emphasize, 'love' is a concept, 'Aphrodite' an image. Concepts are abstract generalizations, in contrast to images, which are concrete particularizations. Images are preferable to concepts because they possess quite distinctive qualities that endow them with vitality. In this respect, Jung declares that, in contrast to concepts, 'images are life' (1955: 226). Aphrodite may be the 'goddess of love', but she is not the goddess of love in general. 'We cannot', Hillman says, 'place all love at Aphrodite's altar' (1972: 66). There are many varieties of love, not just one. Aphrodite is the goddess of a specific variety of love – in particular, sexual and sensual love, which is impulsive, even compulsive.

For example, the Aphrodite variety of love is not the 'moral' love of fidelity in marriage. That is the Hera variety of love. The numerous infidelities of Zeus offend the Hera variety of love. From that perspective, the Aphrodite variety of love is amoral, even 'immoral'. In one aspect, Aphrodite is the goddess of affairs. With Ares, Aphrodite is unfaithful in marriage to Hephaistos. Helios reports the adultery, and Hephaistos, god of the smithy, then forges a net of invisible chains that he secretly attaches to the bed. After sex, Ares and Aphrodite sleep, and when they awake, they are stark naked and snared. Hephaistos surprises them and then summons all the gods and goddesses to witness Ares and Aphrodite *in flagrante delicto*. The goddesses modestly demur, but the gods lewdly gather for a laugh. Apollo jokes that surely Hermes would not object if he, rather than Ares, were in that net with Aphrodite, and Hermes exclaims that he would not, even if the chains were 'three times as strong!' (Kerenyi 1951: 74). When, in 1910, the 34-year-old Jung says to the 53-year-old Freud, 'The prerequisite for a good marriage, it seems to me, is the license to be unfaithful' (Freud and Jung 1974: 289), he attempts, in effect, to reconcile the Hera variety of love with the Aphrodite variety of love.

Many modern people are not at all psychological. They remain strictly and exclusively mythological. That is, like ancient people, they still believe that gods exist, or at least that God with a capital 'G' exists, quite literally, in a supernatural dimension – in spite of the fact that, as Harris says, 'there is no more evidence to justify a belief in the literal existence of Yahweh' than, for example, 'Zeus' (2004: 16). Giegerich says that in the modern situation it is no longer feasible for people to have what he calls 'truly mythic experience'. On the contrary, many modern people have the same experience of myth as ancient people. These people are 'modern' only in the sense that they are in the modern situation. They do not have modern consciousness. They are 'ancient' people in the modern situation. Like ancient people, they have truly mythic experience. Of course, these ancient people in the modern situation are, as Harris notes, quite selective in what qualifies as truly mythic experience. For example, they arbitrarily believe in 'God', or Yahweh, but not in Zeus. 'Imagine', Harris says, 'President Bush addressing the National Prayer Breakfast in these terms: "Behind all of life and all history there is a dedication and a purpose set by the hand of a just and faithful Zeus"' (2004: 46–7). Or, I might say, imagine President Clinton interviewing an intern in the Oval Office of the White House and wearing a WWZD – 'What would Zeus do?' – bracelet. What, then, would Hera – I mean, Hillary – do? Is not this image hilarious?

It is the genius of Jung to argue that 'gods' exist, but only metaphorically and only in a natural dimension. That natural dimension is the psyche. 'All deities', William Blake says, 'reside in the human breast' (1976: 153) – or, as Jung says, in the psyche. From this perspective, the gods are dead, but the 'gods' are alive and well – or, I would say, the literal is dead, but the metaphorical is alive and well. As Hillman provocatively says, 'Nothing is literal; all is metaphor' (1975: 175). The 'gods' continue to 'exist', as they always have, in the psyche. In this respect, to be psychological is to be metaphorical. It is to realize, once and for all, that the 'gods' are metaphors – personifications (or deifications) in the psyche. There is still 'divine intervention', but now it is, as Jung says, psychic compensation.

Some people in the modern situation have modern consciousness. They do not have what Giegerich calls, 'truly mythic experience', but, like Jung, they have *psychic experience of myth.* As they experience myth, it is a projection of the psyche. Jungians psychologize the experience of myth. They deliteralize the gods, metaphorize them. They punctuate the 'gods' in quotation marks. Rhetorically, they regard ancient mythological figures figuratively. The decisive difference between people with modern consciousness – among them, Jungians – and people with ancient consciousness is a capacity for metaphor.

Harris says that, 'it does not seem out of place to wonder whether the myths that saturate our discourse will wind up killing many of us' (2004: 47). As Harris says, 'That it would be a horrible absurdity for so many of us to die for the sake of myth does not mean, however, that it could not happen' (2004: 129). What is dangerous, even deadly, I would argue, is not myths, as such, but an incapacity for metaphor in relation to myths. When people in the modern situation take myths literally rather than metaphorically, they have an all too convenient excuse to take lives in the name of the gods.

'Mythology is a psychology of antiquity', Hillman says. 'Psychology is a mythology of modernity' (1979a: 23). Jung says that the psyche is intrinsically mythopoeic. The psyche, he says, spontaneously projects myths – or produces modern dreams, fantasies, and experiences similar to ancient myths. Freud employs a special term for this process: 'Psycho-mythology' (1985: 286). In this respect, Jungians are neither exclusively mythological nor exclusively psychological, but are inclusively 'psycho-mythological'. Jungian psychology is not a 'psychology' in the conventional sense but a 'psycho-mythology'.

References

Adams, M.V. (2001) *The Mythological Unconscious*, New York and London: Karnac.

—— (2004) *The Fantasy Principle: Psychoanalysis of the Imagination*, Hove and New York: Brunner-Routledge.

Blake, W. (1976) 'The Marriage of Heaven and Hell', in G. Keynes (ed.) *Complete Writings*, London: Oxford University Press, pp. 148–60.

Bolen, J.S. (1984) *Goddesses in Everywoman: A New Psychology of Women*, San Francisco: Harper & Row.

Campbell, J. (1968) *The Hero with a Thousand Faces*, Princeton, NJ: Princeton University Press.

Fordham, M. (1993) *The Making of an Analyst: A Memoir*, London: Free Association Books.

Friedrich, P. (1978) *The Meaning of Aphrodite*, Chicago and London: University of Chicago Press.

Freud, S. (1985) *The Complete Letters of Sigmund Freud to Wilhelm Fliess, 1887–1904*, ed. and trans. J.M. Masson, Cambridge, MA, and London: Belknap Press of Harvard University Press.

Freud, S. and Jung, C.G. (1974) *The Freud/Jung Letters: The Correspondence between Sigmund Freud and C.G. Jung*, ed. W. McGuire, trans. R. Manheim and R.F.C. Hull, Princeton, NJ: Princeton University Press.

Giegerich, W. (1999) *The Soul's Logical Life: Towards a Rigorous Notion of Psychology*, Frankfurt am Main: Peter Lang.

Harris, S. (2004) *The End of Faith: Religion, Terror, and the Future of Reason*, New York and London: W.W. Norton.

Heller, S. (2006) *The Absence of Myth*, Albany, NY: State University of New York Press.

Hillman, J. (1972) *The Myth of Analysis: Three Essays in Archetypal Psychology*, Evanston, IL: Northwestern University Press.

—— (1975) *Re-Visioning Psychology*, New York: Harper & Row.

—— (1979a) *The Dream and the Underworld*, New York: Harper & Row.

—— (1979b) 'Senex and Puer: An Aspect of the Historical and Psychological Present', in C. Giles (ed.) *Puer Papers*, Irving, TX: Spring Publications, pp. 3–53.

—— (1995) 'Pink Madness, or Why Does Aphrodite Drive Men Crazy with Pornography?' *Spring: A Journal of Archetype and Culture*, 57, 39–71.

Hinsie, L.E. and Shatzky, J. (1940) *Psychiatric Dictionary: With Encyclopedic Treatment of Modern Terms*, London, New York, and Toronto: Oxford University Press.

Jung, C.G. (1912/1952) *Symbols of Transformation: An Analysis of the Prelude to a Case of Schizophrenia*, *CW* 5, 1956/1967.

—— (1929) 'Commentary on "The Secret of the Golden Flower"', *CW* 13, 1967, 1–55.

—— (1955) *Mysterium Coniunctionis: An Inquiry into the Separation and Synthesis of Psychic Opposites in Alchemy*, *CW* 14, 1963/1970.

Kerenyi, C. (1951) *The Gods of the Greeks*, London and New York: Thames & Hudson.

Kirk, G.S. (1970) *Myth: Its Meaning and Functions in Ancient and Other Cultures*,

Cambridge: Cambridge University Press and Berkeley, CA, and Los Angeles: University of California Press.

Melville, H. (1971) *Pierre; or The Ambiguities*, in H. Hayford, H. Parker and G.T. Tanselle (eds) *The Writings of Herman Melville*, vol. 7, Evanston, IL, and Chicago: Northwestern University Press.

Nabokov, V. (1973) *Strong Opinions*, New York: McGraw-Hill.

Paris, G. (1986) *Pagan Meditations: The Worlds of Aphrodite, Artemis, and Hestia*, trans. G. Moore, Dallas, TX: Spring Publications.

—— (1997) 'Everyday Epiphanies', in P. Clarkson (ed.) *On the Sublime in Psychoanalysis, Archetypal Psychology and Psychotherapy*, London: Whurr Publishers, pp. 85–95.

Segal, R.A. (1999) 'Adonis: A Greek Eternal Child', in *Theorizing about Myth*, Amherst, MA: University of Massachusetts Press, pp. 99–155.

Thorn, M. (1990) *Taboo No More: The Phallus in Fact, Fantasy, and Fiction*, New York: Shapolksy Publishers.

Chapter 8

Bringing myth back to the world: the future of myth in Jungian psychology

Robert A. Segal

Nineteenth-century theories of myth

There is a clear-cut divide between nineteenth- and twentieth-century theories of myth. In the nineteenth century myth was taken to be the 'primitive' counterpart to science, which was assumed to be entirely modern. Myth originated and functioned to do for primitive peoples what science now did for moderns: account for all events in the physical world. One could not consistently hold both kinds of explanations, and moderns, who were *defined* as scientific, were logically obliged to abandon myth. The rise of science thus spelled the death of myth.

The leading exponents of the nineteenth-century view of myth were the pioneering anthropologist E.B. Tylor, whose main work, *Primitive Culture*, was published in 1871, and the classicist and fellow pioneering anthropologist J.G. Frazer, whose key work, *The Golden Bough*, was first published in 1890. For Tylor, myth provides knowledge of the world as an end itself. For Frazer, the knowledge that myth provides is a means to control over the world, above all for securing food. For both Tylor and Frazer, the events explained or effected by myth are ones in the external world, such as rainfall and death, rather than ones in the social world, such as marriage and war. Myth is the primitive counterpart to natural, not social, science. It is the counterpart to biology, chemistry, and physics rather than to sociology, anthropology, politics, psychology, and economics. For Tylor, myth is the exact counterpart to scientific theory. For Frazer, myth is the exact counterpart to applied science.

Myth, which is part of religion, attributes rain to a decision by a god; science attributes it to impersonal, meteorological processes. For Tylor and Frazer, the explanations are incompatible because both are direct. In myth, gods operate not behind or through impersonal forces but in place of them. God does not set meteorological processes in motion but instead likely dumps accumulated buckets of water on a designated spot below. Therefore one cannot stack the mythic explanation atop the scientific explanation, crediting science with the direct explanation and crediting myth with the indirect explanation. Rather, one must choose between them. Because moderns by definition have science, the choice has been made for them. They must give up myth, which is not merely outdated but false. Moderns who still cling to myth have failed either to recognize or to concede the incompatibility of it with science.

Twentieth-century theories of myth

In the twentieth century myth was reconciled with science. Moderns, still defined as scientific, could now retain myth. Tylor's and Frazer's theories were spurned on many grounds: for precluding modern myths, for subsuming myth under religion and thereby precluding secular myths, for deeming the function of myth science-like, and for deeming myth false. Yet twentieth-century theorists did not try to reconcile myth with science by challenging science. They did not take any of the easy steps: 'relativizing' science, 'sociologizing' science, making science 'masculine', or making science 'mythic'.[1] No less than their nineteenth-century predecessors did they accept science as the reigning explanation of the physical world. Rather, they recharacterized *myth* as other than a *literal explanation* of the physical world.

Twentieth-century theories of myth can be divided into three groups. First are those theories which maintain that myth, while still about the world, is not an explanation of the world, in which case its function diverges from that of science. The true function of myth can range from acceptance of the world to escape from the world. The preeminent theorists here are the anthropologist Bronislaw Malinowski and the historian of religions Mircea Eliade. Second are those theories which maintain that myth is not to be read literally, in which case the subject matter of myth is not the physical world. The true subject matter of myth can range from the impact of the physical world on human beings to human beings themselves. The leading theorists here are the New Testament scholar Rudolf Bultmann and the philosopher Hans Jonas. Third and most radical are those theories which maintain both that myth is not an explanation and that myth is not to be read literally. Here fall, above all, Freud and Jung.[2] As much as these two differ from each other, both deem the subject matter of myth the human mind and deem the function of myth the experience of that mind.

For both Malinowski (1926) and Eliade (1968), myth is, to be sure, an explanation in part, but explanation is only a means to a non-scientific end rather than the end. For Malinowski, that end is to reconcile humans to disease, death, and other brute aspects of the physical world. For Eliade, the end is to carry humans back to the time of the myth, which is always the past, in order to encounter god. Myth is like a magic carpet.

For both Malinowski and Eliade, myth is as much about social phenomena – customs, laws, and institutions – as about physical ones. The subject matter of myth is thus more than the physical world. For Malinowski, myths about social phenomena serve to reconcile members to impositions that they might otherwise reject. The beneficiary is society, not the individual. For Eliade, myths about social phenomena serve the same magic carpet-like function as myths about physical ones.

Insofar as myth for Malinowski deals with the social world, it turns its back on the physical world. But even when myth deals with the physical world, its connection to that world is limited. Myth may explain how flooding arose – a god or a human brought it about – but science, not myth, explains why flooding occurs whenever it does. And even for those with myth, science says what to do about it. Indeed, myth assumes that nothing can be done about it. Myth and science are compatible because their functions are distinct.

So, too, for Eliade. But he goes beyond Malinowski and, even more, Tylor and Frazer in proclaiming myth universal and not merely primitive. Where for Malinowski primitive peoples have both myth and science and moderns have only science, for Eliade, as for Tylor and Frazer, primitive peoples have only myth. But for Eliade, in contrast to Malinowski, Tylor, and Frazer alike, moderns have myth as well as science, in which case myth must be universal.

Where neither Malinowski nor Eliade challenges Frazer's and especially Tylor's literal reading of myth, Bultmann and Jonas do. While they limit themselves to their specialties, Christianity and Gnosticism, they apply a theory of myth per se – a theory that comes from the early, existentialist philosophy of Martin Heidegger.

Bultmann (1953) acknowledges that, read literally, myth is about the physical world and is incompatible with science. It should therefore rightly be rejected as uncompromisingly as Tylor and Frazer reject it. But unlike both Malinowski and Eliade as well as both Tylor and Frazer, Bultmann proposes reading myth symbolically. In his celebrated, if excruciatingly confusing, phrase, myth should be 'demythologized', which means not that the mythology should be eliminated, or 'demythicized', but that the true, existential meaning of that mythology should be extricated. To seek evidence of an actual worldwide flood, while dismissing the miraculous notion of an ark containing all species, would be to *demythicize* the myth of Noah. To interpret the flood as a symbolic statement about the precariousness of human life would be to *demythologize* the myth.

Demythologized, myth ceases to be about the world itself and turns out to be about the human *experience* of the world. Demythologized, myth ceases to be an explanation at all and becomes an expression, an expression of what it 'feels' like to live in the world. The New Testament, when demythologized, contrasts the alienation from the world felt by those who have not yet found God to the at-homeness in the world felt by those who have found God. Myth ceases to be merely primitive and becomes universal. It ceases to be false and becomes true. It still speaks to humans because it depicts the eternal human condition.

Like Bultmann, Jonas (1963) seeks to show that ancient myths retain a message for moderns. For Jonas, as for Bultmann, myth read symbolically describes the alienation of humans from the world as well as from their true selves prior to their acceptance of God. Because ancient Gnosticism, unlike mainstream Christianity, sets the soul against the body and sets immateriality against matter, humans remain alienated from the material world and from their bodies even after they have found the true God. In fact, the true God can be found only by rejecting the false god of the material world. Gnostics overcome alienation from this world only by transcending the world. Gnostic mythology can still speak to moderns because, correctly understood, it addresses not the nature of the world but, like Christian mythology according to Bultmann, the nature of the experience of the world. Hence for Jonas, as for Bultmann, myth and science do not compete.

Freud and Jung offer the most extreme departure from Tylor and Frazer. For they transform both the literal meaning and the explanatory function of myth. The subject matter of myth – the human unconscious – is as far removed from the outer world as can be. In myth, the unconscious projects itself onto the world in the form of gods and heroes, so that the analysis of myth requires the disentangling of myth from the world. Myth functions as a means of encountering not the world but the unconscious.

Freud and Jung on myth and the external world

It is conventionally assumed that Jung, on myth as in general, is arguing against Freud. It is also commonly assumed that Freud or Freudians on myth are arguing against Jung and Jungians. But in fact both are arguing at least as much against nineteenth-century theorists like Tylor and Frazer. Freud and Jung are part of the same twentieth-century trend as Malinowski, Eliade, Bultmann, and Jonas. Before Freudians and Jungians can debate each other on the *psychology* of myth, they must show that myth is psychological in nature.[3]

In 'The Theme of the Three Caskets' Freud comments snippily on an interpretation made by one E. Stucken of the choice of the caskets in *The Merchant of Venice*:

> He [Stucken] writes: 'The identity of Portia's three suitors is clear from their choice: the Prince of Morocco chooses the gold casket – he is the sun; the Prince of Arragon chooses the silver casket – he is the moon; Bassanio chooses the leaden casket – he is the star youth'.
>
> Thus our little problem has led us to an astral myth! The only pity is that with this explanation we are not at the end of the matter. The

> question is not exhausted, for we do not share the belief of some investigators that myths were read in the heavens and brought down to earth; we are more inclined to judge with Otto Rank that they were projected on to the heavens after having arisen elsewhere under purely human conditions. It is in this human content that our interest lies.
> (Freud 1913: 291–2)

Rather than originating in the experience of the natural world, myth for Freud originates in the experience of the family and is then projected onto the world.

Along with Otto Rank's *The Myth of the Birth of the Hero* (1914/2003), to which Freud is referring, the other classically Freudian analysis of myth is Karl Abraham's *Dreams and Myths* (1913). Like Freud, both Abraham and Rank dismiss those theorists, called nature mythologists, who either take myth to be about the physical world rather than about the human mind or, worse, turn myths about humans into myths about the physical world. Rank is especially disdainful of those who, for example, turn the life of Oedipus into a symbol of the daily course of the sun:

> As given by a representative of the natural mythological mode of interpretation, Oedipus, who kills his father, marries his mother, and dies old and blind, is the solar hero who murders his procreator, the darkness; shares his couch with the mother, the gloaming, from whose lap, the dawn, he has been born; and dies blinded, as the setting sun.
> (Rank 1914: 9–10)

Here myth is not a literal explanation of the course of the sun, as it would be for Tylor, but a symbolic description of the course of the sun. Still, myth for Tylor, Frazer, and Rank's nature mythologists is about the sun, not the family.[4]

Toward nature mythologists, Jung is at least as dismissive as Freud, Abraham, and Rank. To begin with, he criticizes Tylor and Frazer for mischaracterizing primitive religion as animism, or the belief in individual souls, or spirits, in nature. Instead, primitive religion is the belief in an underlying universal spirituality. This criticism is not specifically psychological and was regularly made by anthropologists such as R.R. Marett, who contended that primitive peoples believe in a divine power, often called *mana*, that only subsequently is separated into distinct spirits.

Jung's psychological criticism of both Tylor and Frazer is that they misconstrue the source of *mana*, which comes not, as they assume, from conscious reflection but from the unconscious. Jung combines both criticisms as follows:

> [T]he idea of energy and its conservation must be a primordial image that was dormant in the collective unconscious. . . . [T]he most primitive religions in the most widely separated parts of the earth are founded upon this image. These are the so-called dynamistic religions whose sole and determining thought is that there exists a universal magical power [i.e. *mana*] about which everything revolves. Tylor, the well-known English investigator, and Frazer likewise, misunderstood this idea as animism. In reality primitive peoples do not mean, by their power-concept, souls or spirits at all, but something which the American investigator Lovejoy has appropriately termed 'primitive energetics'. . . . So this idea has been stamped on the human brain for aeons. That is why it lies ready to hand in the unconscious of every man. Only, certain conditions are needed to cause it to appear.
>
> (Jung 1917/1926/1943: 108–9)

The experience of the external world provides the 'condition' for the appearance of the unconscious. The awesome grandeur of the external world provides an ideal peg onto which to project the unconscious, which is always experienced as extraordinary rather than ordinary, as magical rather than natural, and as divine rather than human.[5]

Like many others, Jung turns to Frazer for examples of myths worldwide, but he then psychologizes whatever examples he uses. Above all, he enlists examples of Frazer's own chief myth, that of the death and rebirth of the god of vegetation. Unlike Tylor, who stalwartly reads myth literally, Frazer, like Rank's nature mythologists, alternatively reads the myth as symbolic of the course of vegetation itself. Thus:

> The story that Adonis spent half, or according to others a third, of the year in the lower world and the rest of it in the upper world, is explained most simply and naturally by supposing that he represented vegetation, especially the corn, which lies buried in the earth half the year and reappears above ground the other half.
>
> (Frazer 1922: 392)

True, Frazer, like Tylor, assumes that primitive peoples themselves take their myths literally and must do so in order for their myths to explain events in the world. But Frazer here breaks with Tylor in asserting that myths about either the decisions or the actions of gods are in fact, albeit unrecognized, symbolic descriptions of natural processes themselves.[6]

Against Frazer, Jung offers his own symbolic rendition of these myths: the myth of the death and rebirth of a god is a symbolic description of a process taking place not in the world but in the mind. That process is the return of the ego to the unconscious – a kind of temporary death of the ego – and its re-emergence, or rebirth, from the unconscious:

> I need only mention the whole mythological complex of the dying and resurgent god and its primitive precursors all the way down to the re-charging of fetishes and churingas with magical force. It expresses a transformation of attitude by means of which a new potential, a new manifestation of life, a new fruitfulness, is created.
>
> (Jung 1921a: 325)

Jung does not deny that the psychological process of the death and rebirth of the ego *parallels* the physical process of the death and rebirth of vegetation. Rather, he, like Freud, Rank, and Abraham, denies that the physical process *accounts for* the psychological one, let alone for the mythic one. For Frazer, as for Tylor, the leap from vegetation to god is the product of reasoning: primitive peoples observe the course of vegetation and hypothesize the existence of a god to account for it – even if, again, for Frazer himself the god can alternatively be a mere symbol of vegetation. For Jung, the leap from vegetation to god is too great for the human mind to make. Humans generally, not merely primitive peoples, lack the creativity required to concoct consciously the notion of the sacred out of the profane. They can only transform the profane into a sacred that already exists in their minds. Humans must already have the idea of god within them and can only be projecting that idea onto vegetation and other natural phenomena:

> This latter analogy [between god and natural phenomenon] explains the well-attested connection between the renewal of the god and seasonal and vegetational phenomena. One is naturally inclined to assume that seasonal, vegetational, lunar, and solar myths underlie these analogies. But that is to forget that a myth, like everything psychic, cannot be solely conditioned by external events. Anything psychic brings its own internal conditions with it, so that one might assert with equal right that the myth is purely psychological and uses meteorological or astronomical events merely as a means of expression. The whimsicality and absurdity of many primitive myths often makes the latter explanation seem far more appropriate than any other.
>
> (Jung 1921a: 325)

Jung's insistence on the divide between the sacred and the profane parallels Eliade's, though Jung, of course, translates the divide into that between the unconscious and consciousness.

Even early Jung, who was prepared to give more weight to experience than later Jung, distinguishes between the experience of the sun itself and the experience of the sun as a god. On the one hand early Jung seemingly derives the sun archetype from the experience of the sun:

> I have often been asked where the archetypes or primordial images come from. It seems to me that their origin can only be explained by assuming them to be deposits of the constantly repeated experiences of humanity. One of the commonest and at the same time most impressive experiences is the apparent movement of the sun every day. We certainly cannot discover anything of the kind in the unconscious, so far as the known physical process is concerned.
>
> (Jung 1917/1926/1943: 109)

On the other hand even early Jung proceeds to distinguish the sun archetype from the sun:

> What we do find, on the other hand, is the myth of the sun-hero in all its countless variations. It is this myth, and not the physical process, that forms the sun archetype. . . . The archetype is a kind of readiness to produce over and over again the same or similar mythical ideas.
>
> (Jung 1917/1926/1943: 109)

The experience of the sun thus provides the *occasion* for the manifestation of the sun archetype but does not *cause* that archetype.

It is not only allegories of physical processes that Jung rejects as the real subject matter of myth. It is also literal interpretations of myth like Tylor's, which still make the subject matter outer rather than inner. For Tylor, myths are explanations of natural phenomena and not merely, as sometimes for Frazer, colorful descriptions of them. As, indeed, Tylor writes against those who would interpret myths allegorically,

> When the Apache Indian pointed to the sky and asked the white man, 'Do you not believe that God, the Sun, . . . sees what we do and punishes us when it is evil?' it is impossible to say that this savage was talking in rhetorical simile.
>
> (Tylor 1871 (I): 262)

Jung conflates Tylor's theory with Frazer's in stating that 'People are very loath to give up the idea that the myth is some kind of explanatory allegory of astronomical, meteorological, or vegetative processes' (Jung 1928: 71). The phrase 'explanatory allegory' equates Tylor's theory – myth as explanation – with Frazer's – myth as allegory. Jung asks rhetorically 'why', if myth is really about the sun, 'the sun and its apparent motions do not appear direct and undisguised as a content of the myths' (Jung 1921b: 748). But the question is rhetorical only for Frazer's theory. For Tylor, a myth describes the sun god and not merely the sun because the myth is about the sun god and not merely about the sun. Yet even if Jung were to distinguish Tylor's view from Frazer's, he would still invoke his fundamental claim that human beings are incapable of consciously inventing gods and can only cast onto the world gods already in their minds.

For Jung, myth is no more about gods than about the physical world. It is about the human mind. Myth must be read symbolically, as for Frazer, and the symbolized subject is a process, as likewise for Frazer, but the process is an inner rather than outer one. If, on the one hand Jung would doubtless prefer Frazer's symbolic reading of myth to Tylor's literal reading, on the other hand he would surely prefer Tylor's appreciation of the divine referent of myth to Frazer's reduction of it to something natural, which psychologically means the reduction of the unconscious to consciousness.

Jung takes as projections not only nature myths but all other kinds of myths as well. He states that 'in fact, the whole of mythology could be taken as a sort of projection of the collective unconscious. . . . Just as the constellations were projected into the heavens, similar figures were projected into legends and fairytales or upon historical persons' (Jung 1927/1931: 325). Once Jung uncouples myth from the natural world, he is free to look for myths elsewhere. No longer confined, like Tylor and Frazer, to myths that at face value are about the external world – creation myths, flood myths, myths of the seasons, myths of paradise, and myths of the end of the world – he can now equally fix his psychological gaze on myths that at face value are about human beings – for example, myths about children, old persons, kings, and queens.[7]

Hero myths, to take one case, are projections onto mere human beings of a quasi-divine status: 'the hero myth is an unconscious drama seen only in projection, like the happenings in Plato's parable of the cave. The hero himself appears as a being of more than human stature' (Jung 1912/1952: 612).[8] Moderns, even while often professing atheism, still create myths by projecting onto their fellow human beings exaggerated qualities that turn those humans into superhuman figures – not only into heroes but also into saints and demons:

> [T]he archetypes usually appear in projection; and, because projections are unconscious, they appear on persons in the immediate environment, mostly in the form of abnormal over- or under-evaluations which provoke misunderstandings, quarrels, fanaticisms, and follies of every description. Thus we say, 'He makes a god of so-and-so', or, 'so-and-so is Mr. X's *bête noire*'. In this way, too, there grow up modern myth-formations, i.e., fantastic rumours, suspicions, prejudices.
>
> (Jung 1917/1926/1943: 152)

For Jung, traditional myths – the ones on which nature mythologists focused – have been religious myths. They have been either about gods acting in the world (Tylor) or about the world as symbolized by gods

(Frazer). The decline of religion in the wake of science has obliged moderns to seek secular myths, such as myths about heroes, who, if superhuman, are still not quite gods. The decline of religion has also spurred moderns to forge private myths. Jung had the creativity to forge or to find his own myth, and he announces at the outset of *Memories, Dreams, Reflections* that he will proceed to 'tell my personal myth' (Jung 1962: 3), which refers either to the course of his whole life or, less likely, to his speculations about life after death. But a personal myth is no more about the outer world than a group myth, and Jung's autobiography barely mentions the outer world.

Bringing myth back to the world

To me, the future of a Jungian approach to myth lies in trying to bring myth back to the outer world. Where theorists of the nineteenth century assumed that myth could not be dislodged from the world and therefore could not be saved from science, theorists of the twentieth century saved myth from science either by removing myth altogether from the world or by removing it as an explanation of the world. The question for the twenty-first century, if I may suggest, is whether myth can be returned to the world – but in a way still compatible with science. The postmodern dismissal of the authority of science, often evinced in labelling science itself mythic, cheapens both myth and science. My admiration for twentieth-century theorizing lies in its attempt to accommodate myth *to* science rather than to spurn science in the name of myth.

The burden of bringing myth back to the world scarcely falls on Jungians alone,[9] but the issue at hand is whether Jungian psychology offers any help. Jung himself, for all his relentless psychologizing of myth, waxes romantic about the existential function of myth – the function of myth for Bultmann and Jonas. To cite his favorite example:

> The Pueblo Indians believe that they are the sons of Father Sun, and this belief gives their life a perspective and a goal beyond their individual and limited existence. It leaves ample room for the unfolding of their personality, and is infinitely more satisfactory than the certainty that one is and will remain an underdog in a department store.
>
> (Jung 1964a: 567)

But Jung's appreciation is of the existential power of myth for primitive peoples only. The meaningfulness that myth offers Pueblo Indians works only by personifying the external world. This pre-scientific option is not available to moderns. And even existentialist theorists of myth, especially Bultmann, have difficulty offering moderns a comforting world without resurrecting God as an active agent in that world.

For Jung, modern myths are for the most part non-projective. They presuppose the withdrawal of projections from the outer world, which is now experienced as impersonal: 'We have stripped all things of their mystery and numinosity; nothing is holy any longer' (Jung 1964b: 582). Put another way, for Jung, modern myths are non-religious. They cannot do what religious myths used to do: 'giving [man] the security and inner strength not to be crushed by the monstrousness of the universe' (Jung 1912/1952: 343). Myths for moderns do not function to connect the inner world to the outer world, which remains impersonal. Instead, modern myths function to connect, or to reconnect, moderns to the inner world. Modern myths still provide meaningfulness, but that meaningfulness now lies entirely within humans rather than also within the world. In fact, Jung himself cannot resist asserting that the power of myth for even primitive peoples lies in the linkage between inner and outer rather than in the outer itself:

> Primitive man is not much interested in objective explanations of the obvious, but he has an imperative need – or, rather, his unconscious psyche has an irresistible urge – to assimiliate all outer sense experiences to inner, psychic events. It is not enough for the primitive to see the sun rise and set; this external observation must at the same time be a psychic happening: the sun in its course must represent the fate of a god or hero who, in the last analysis, dwells nowhere except in the soul of man.
>
> (Jung 1934/1954: 7)

Synchronicity

A more promising Jungian way of bringing myth back to the world – the outer world – doubtless lies in the concept of synchronicity (see Jung 1951: 969–97 and Jung 1952: 816–968).[10] The term refers, of course, to the coincidence between our thoughts and the behavior of the world, between what is inner and what is outer. As Jung writes of his favorite example of synchronicity, that of a resistant patient who was describing a dream about a golden scarab when a scarab beetle appeared, 'at the moment my patient was telling me her dream a real "scarab" tried to get into the room, as if it had understood that it must play its mythological role as a symbol of rebirth' (Jung 1973–74 (II): 541). Here the world apparently responds to the patient's dream; but understood synchronistically, the world merely, if most fortuitously, *matches* the patient's dream, not *causes* it or is caused by it. Synchronicity is not like astrology, in which the planets determine personality. The patient's conscious attitude, which dismisses the notion of an unconscious, is 'out of sync' with the world. The unconscious is using this coincidence to impress on the patient the kinship between humans and the world – exactly the kind of kinship that myth, as a person-like account of the world, provides the Pueblos.

With the concept of synchronicity, the world regains meaningfulness even without personalization. The world regains the meaningfulness that had been lost with the withdrawal of mythic projections. Furthermore, that meaningfulness is now inherent in the world rather than projected onto it: 'synchronistic experiences serve our turn here. They point to a latent meaning which is independent of [our] consciousness' (Jung 1973–74 (II): 495). Meaningfulness now stems not from the existence of god, or personality, in the world but from the symmetry between human beings and the world. Rather than alien and indifferent to humans, the world proves to be akin to them – not because gods respond to human wishes or because human wishes directly affect the world but because human thoughts correspond to the nature of the world.

But in the case of the patient, what exactly is the 'mythological role' of the beetle as 'a symbol of rebirth'? The patient's experience of synchronicity is not itself myth, which would be an account of that experience. But an account means a causal account. Can there be a causal account of non-causality? Can there be a myth of synchronicity – a myth accompanying a case of synchronicity?

In a forthcoming essay on 'Recaptured Time and the Re-Mythologisation of Modernity' Roderick Main takes this example of synchronicity and argues that synchronicity constitutes 'myth beyond projection'. He teases out the association for Jung, whether or not for the patient, of the scarab with ancient myths of rebirth, of creation, and of heroic rescue. He suggests that the incident with the scarab aroused in Jung his notion of himself as the heroic rescuer of not merely his psychologically imprisoned patient but, far more, the psychologically locked-up modern West.

The first question is whether the mythological associations really deal with the world. Even if synchronicity itself ties the inner world to the outer one, do the myths it stirs themselves deal with the outer world? If what is being rescued is the unconscious side of humanity, then surely the outer world is a mere steppingstone to the inner one. Undeniably, synchronicity, as a non-causal phenomenon, circumvents the issue that in the nineteenth century pitted myth against science: the cause of events in the outer world. But are myths that are tied to synchronicity really connected to the outer world? Main has explained to me that for Jung they are. Synchronicity *enhances* the meaningfulness of myths about the outer world but does not create it. The myth of the rebirth of the scarab is to be found in the outer world as well as in the world of the patient's dream. The outer myth is not a projection of the inner one and therefore does not need to be withdrawn.

With synchronicity, Jungian psychology offers an extraordinary vehicle for carrying myth back to the world – and without leaving science behind. Still, one question, not to be answered here, lingers: is the myth of the rebirth of the scarab *explaining* the appearance of the scarab or merely being invoked on the appearance of the scarab? Unless the myth explains the scarab, the myth may lie more in the background than in the foreground. Myth, then, may not yet be fully back in the world.

For exceedingly helpful comments on this essay, I thank Roderick Main, John Beebe, and Robert Ackerman.

Notes

1 Admittedly, Jung does 'mythicize' science to a degree, but never to the extent of turning science into myth. On the contrary, Jung seeks to use science – psychology – to fathom myth, which is the *subject* of science, not science itself.

2 The theory of the French anthropologist Claude Lévi-Strauss (1966) might seem to defy my characterization of twentieth-century theories. Myth for him is wholly primitive yet is not merely pre-scientific, let alone anti-scientific, but fully scientific. He deems the ordering of things the heart of science, and myths organize the world for primitive peoples as thoroughly as modern science does for moderns. The difference between primitive and modern science is only the level at which each works: primitive science works at the observable, sensory level; modern science, at the unobservable, nonsensory level, such as at the microscopic level. For Lévi-Strauss, ordering takes the form of not merely categorizing phenomena but also categorizing them into sets of logical oppositions – for example, into the opposition between food eaten raw and food first cooked. Lévi-Strauss credits myth with not merely presenting these oppositions, which are actually experienced, but also resolving or at least tempering them. Still, the oppositions experienced in the world stem from the projection onto the world of the human mind, which thinks oppositionally. Thus myth is really about the human mind, not about the world, and so Lévi-Strauss' theory fits my depiction of twentieth-century theories of myth.

3 The following presentation of Freud's and Jung's rejection of the views of Tylor and Frazer comes from Segal 2003: 607–12.

4 On nature mythologists, see Abraham 1913: 41; Rank 1914: 8–10; 1992: 224–25; Rank and Sachs 1916: 37–42.

5 For the nineteenth-century theorist Friedrich Max Müller, the grandeur of the sky provides the ideal 'condition' for the experience of the non-physical god, or the 'Infinite'. Even if myth for Müller is not about the physical world, which merely symbolizes the Infinite, myth is still about the cosmos and not about human beings: see Müller 1878, lecture I.

6 Where for Frazer gods symbolize nature, for Müller nature symbolizes gods.

7 It is true that Tylor allows for hero myths (see *Primitive Culture*, I, 281–2), but his allowance for them is inconsistent with his overall characterization of myths as nature myths. Conversely, Frazer turns myths of mere human beings, such as Adonis and Attis, into myths of gods in order to advance his claim that the chief myth of every culture is that about the death and life of the god of vegetation.

8 For Jung, heroes are mythical because they are more than human. For Lord Raglan, who extends Frazer's theory of myth to heroes, heroes are mythical because they are not historical. That is, Raglan concentrates on disproving the historicity of hero stories in order to make them mythical, whereas Jung takes for granted that heroes cannot be historical because they are quasi-divine. See

Raglan 1936, pt. 2. John Beebe has kindly corrected my undue elevation of the place of hero myths in the Jungian pantheon.

9 I myself have enlisted the theory of play of D.W. Winnicott to suggest one way of bringing myth back to the world: see Segal 2004: 137–42.

10 On synchonicity, see Aziz 1990; Main 1997, 2004.

References and further reading

Abraham, K. (1913) 'Dreams and Myths', trans. W.A. White, New York: *Journal of Nervous and Mental Disease* Publishing.

Aziz, R. (1990) *C. G. Jung's Psychology of Religion and Synchronicity*, Albany, NY: State University of New York Press.

Bultmann, R. (1953) 'New Testament and Mythology' [1944], in H.-W. Bartsch (ed.) *Kerygma and Myth*, vol. I, trans. R.H. Fuller, London: SPCK, pp. 1–44.

Eliade, M. (1968) *The Sacred and the Profane*, trans. W.R. Trask, New York: Harvest Books.

Frazer, J.G. (1890) *The Golden Bough*, 1st edn, 2 vols, London: Macmillan.

—— (1922) *The Golden Bough*, abridged, 1-vol. edn, London: Macmillan.

Freud, S. (1913) 'The Theme of the Three Caskets', Standard Edition of the Complete Psychological Works of Sigmund Freud, ed. and trans. J. Strachey (in cooperation with Anna Freud, Alix Strachey and Alan Tyson), 12: 289–301, London: Hogarth Press and Institute of Psycho-Analysis, 1958.

Jonas, H. (1963) 'Gnosticism, Existentialism, and Nihilism', *The Gnostic Religion*, 2nd edn, Boston: Beacon Press, pp. 320–40.

Jung, C.G. (1912/1952) *Symbols of Transformation*, *CW* 5, 1956/1967.

—— (1917/1926/1943) 'On the Psychology of the Unconscious', *CW* 7, 1953/1966: 1–200.

—— (1921a) 'The Type Problem in Poetry', *CW* 6, 1921/1971: 275–460.

—— (1921b) 'Definitions', *CW* 6, 1921/1971: 672–844.

—— (1927/1931) 'The Structure of the Psyche', *CW* 8, 1960/1969: 283–342.

—— (1928) 'On Psychic Energy', *CW* 8, 1960/1969: 1–130.

—— (1934/1954) 'Archetypes of the Collective Unconscious', *CW* 9i, 1959/1968: 1–110.

—— (1951) 'An Appendix: On Synchronicity', *CW* 8, 1960/1969: 969–97.

—— (1952) 'Synchronicity: An Acausal Connecting Principle', *CW* 8, 1960/1969: 816–968.

—— (1962) *Memories, Dreams, Reflections*, ed. A. Jaffé, trans. R. and C. Winston, New York: Vintage Books.

—— (1973–74) *C.G. Jung: Letters*, eds G. Adler and A. Jaffé, 2 vols, Princeton, NJ: Princeton University Press.

—— (1964a) 'The Function of the Religious Symbols', *CW* 18, 1976: 560–77.

—— (1964b) 'Healing the Split', *CW* 18, 1976: 578–607.

Lévi-Strauss, C. (1966) *The Savage Mind*, trans. not given, Chicago: University of Chicago Press.

Main, R. (ed.) (1997) *Jung on Synchronicity and the Paranormal*, Princeton, NJ: Princeton University Press; London: Routledge.

—— (2004) *The Rupture of Time*, Hove and New York: Brunner-Routledge.

—— (forthcoming) 'Recaptured Time and the Re-Mythologisation of Modernity', *Who Owns Jung?*, ed. Ann Casement, London: Karnac.

Malinowski, B. (1926) *Myth in Primitive Psychology*, London: Kegan Paul; New York: W.W. Norton.

Müller, F.M. (1878) *Lectures on the Origin and Growth of Religion*, 1st edn, London: Longmans, Green.

Lord Raglan (1936) *The Hero*, London: Methuen.

Rank, O. (1914) *The Myth of the Birth of the Hero*, 1st edn, trans. F. Robbins and S.E. Jelliffe, New York: *Journal of Nervous and Mental Disease Publishing*.

—— (1992) *The Incest Theme in Literature and Legend*, 1st edn, trans. G.C. Richter, Baltimore, MD: Johns Hopkins University Press.

—— (2003) *The Myth of the Birth of the Hero*, 2nd edn, trans. E.J. Lieberman and G.C. Richter, Baltimore, MD: Johns Hopkins University Press.

Rank, O. and Sachs, H. (1916) *The Significance of Psychoanalysis for the Mental Sciences*, trans. C.R. Payne, New York: *Journal of Nervous and Mental Disease Publishing*.

Segal, R.A. (ed.) (1992) *The Gnostic Jung*, Princeton, NJ: Princeton University Press; London: Routledge.

—— (ed.) (1998) *Jung on Mythology*, Princeton, NJ: Princeton University Press; London: Routledge.

—— (1999) *Theorizing about Myth*, MA, Amherst: University of Massachusetts Press.

—— (2003) 'Jung's Very Twentieth-Century View of Myth', *Journal of Analytical Psychology*, 48, 593–617.

—— (2004) *Myth: A Very Short Introduction*, Oxford: Oxford University Press.

Tylor, E.B. (1871) *Primitive Culture*, 2 vols, 1st edn, London: Murray.

Part 3

Myths at play

Chapter 9

Active imagination in *Answer to Job*

Leon Schlamm

Introduction

In this chapter I will address one significant theme in *Answer to Job* given insufficient attention by Jung scholars to date: the role of active imagination in the creation of the narrative of this much criticized and misunderstood monograph. More specifically, I will not only argue that Jung's reading of the biblical figures of Yahweh and Job was the product of active imagination, which led him to the 'difficult and unpopular task of talking *with* God, rather than *about* him' (Adler 1976: 34),[1] but also that the relationship between Job and Yahweh is, for Jung, a paradigmatic *expression* of this Jungian meditative practice of 'dreaming with open eyes' (Jung 1921: 723n; 1955–6: 706).

Jung's active imagination on the Job/Yahweh relationship (as well as his alchemical and kabbalistic observation that 'whoever knows God has an effect on him', 1952/1954: 617) triggered his perception of the 'immensity of God' (1952/1954: 732). And this perception, I will argue, provides the point of departure for Jung's conscious, speculative, and hermeneutical engagement with other biblical figures addressed in the text (including Satan, Sophia, Christ, the Paraclete, the Virgin Mary), informed by his earlier writings, particularly *Aion* (Bishop 2002: 38–41; Heisig 1979: 70–9; Lammers 1994: 154–92; Stein 1985: 147–62).

Active imagination

I begin with a brief account of Jung's active imagination, instrumental in the creation of *Answer to Job*. This meditative practice initiates a dynamic, confrontational exchange between consciousness and the unconscious, in which each is totally engaged with the other, which, in turn, activates a stream of powerful, unconscious emotions and impulses (cf. Chodorow 1997: 6, 10; Jung 1916/1958: 167, 183, 185–6; 1955–6: 706, 753). For Jung, the function of this meditative practice is to access numinous unconscious images concealed by these emotions and impulses (1963: 201–2).

By consciously dialoguing with the flow of images produced by active imagination (1955–6: 706, 749, 753), one can transform and control these powerful emotions and impulses (1963: 201–2). This subsequently leads to the discovery of the transcendent function (1916/1958: 145, 167, 181, 189), the union of the opposites of consciousness and the unconscious – 'embodying the striving of the unconscious for the light and the striving of the conscious for substance' (1916/1958: 168) – and the healing of oneself. However, it is important to remember that, for Jung, 'It is through the "affect" that the subject [of active imagination] becomes involved and so comes to feel the whole weight of reality' (1951: 61). Numinous images encountered during active imagination are based 'on an emotional foundation which is unassailable by reason' (1952/1954: 556). Indeed, 'The whole procedure is a kind of enrichment and clarification of the affect, whereby the affect and its contents are brought nearer to consciousness, becoming at the same time more impressive and more understandable' (1916/1958: 167).

Jung was well aware that the practitioner of active imagination who was unable to maintain a differentiated, self-reflective conscious point of view in the face of unconscious visionary material would be vulnerable to mental illness: either in the form of psychosis where consciousness is overwhelmed by unconscious visionary materials; or in the form of conscious identification with numinous unconscious contents leading to possession by them (Chodorow 1997: 12; Jung 1916/1958: 183). However, Jung insisted that his visionary practice, if approached responsibly by an individual endowed with a well-developed consciousness, could bring considerable rewards. In addition to the strengthening and widening of consciousness itself, dreaming with open eyes could enable the practitioner to realize that unconscious contents that appear to be dead are really alive (1963: 196), and, furthermore, this content desires to be known by, and enter into dialogue with, consciousness (1963: 211–12). If one rests one's conscious attention on unconscious contents without interfering with them (Chodorow 1997: 10; Jung 1916/1958: 155; 1955–6: 749; 1931/1962: 20): 'It is as if something were emanating from one's spiritual eye that . . . activates the object of one's vision' (1930–4: 661). Unconscious contents begin to spontaneously change or move, begin to become dynamic or energetic, to 'come alive'. Jung characterizes this process by the German term *betrachten*: to make pregnant by giving an object your undivided attention (1930–4: 661; 1935/1968: 397–8, 406; 1955–6: 706). The characterization of this psychological process was anticipated by his 1912 dream of a lane of sarcophagi, which sprang to life as he examined them (1963: 196–7). These numinous experiences, however, require a vigorous, active, self-reflective conscious response endowing them with meaning, and thereby changing them (1955–6: 706, 753; 1916/1958: 185–6; 1963: 207–12, 218). This process of continuous dynamic interaction and collaboration between consciousness and the unconscious is expressed by the German term *Auseinandersetzung* – 'coming to terms with', or 'having it out with', or 'confronting' unconscious psychic contents (Chodorow 1997: 10–11; Jung 1916/1958: 183, 185, 189) – and it is a process that is actually mirrored in Jung's plea for divine–human collaboration in *Answer to Job*: which is most notably expressed in the observation that 'Whoever knows God has an effect on Him' (1952/1954: 617; for Jung's plea, see 675, 677, 686, 756).

The dream foreshadowing *Answer to Job*

The writing of *Answer to Job* in 1951 was foreshadowed by a dream in 1948, which anticipates the biblical image of God's tragic contradictoriness (the main theme of *Answer to Job*) (1963: 243–4) as well as the role of active imagination in the creation of the narrative. This much commented on dream concludes with Jung's father saying to Carl:

> 'Now I will lead you into the highest presence' [Uriah]. Then he knelt down and touched his forehead to the floor. I imitated him, likewise kneeling, with great emotion. For some reason I could not bring my forehead quite down to the floor – there was perhaps a millimetre to spare. But at least I had made the gesture with him.
>
> (1963: 245–6)

Jung informs his readers that Uriah, the guiltless victim of David's adulterous love for Bathsheba (2 Samuel 11: 1–27) 'is a prefiguration of Christ, the god-man . . . abandoned by God' (Battye 1994: 169, 172; Bishop 2002: 38). The manifestation of Uriah in his dream signified that Jung would be 'forced to speak publicly, and very much to [his] detriment, about the ambivalence of the God-image in the Old Testament' (1963: 246).[2] Jung's judgement on the meaning of the dream follows:

> These were the things that awaited me, hidden in the unconscious. I had to submit to this fate, and ought really to have touched my forehead to the floor, so that my submission would be complete. But something prevented me from doing so entirely, and kept me just a millimetre away. Something in me was saying 'All very well, but not entirely'. Something in me was defiant and determined not to be a dumb fish; and if there was not something of the sort in free men, no Book of Job would have been written several hundred years before the birth of Christ. Man always has some mental reservation, even in the face of divine decrees. Otherwise, where would be his freedom? And what would be the use of that freedom if it could not threaten Him who threatens it . . . The dream discloses a thought and a premonition that

> have long been present in humanity: the idea of the creature that surpasses its creator by a small but decisive factor [consciousness].
> (1963: 246–7)

Clearly Jung's reading of this dream, celebrating the 'millimetre to spare' of consciousness (equated with Job), provides, at least in Jung's view, the key for interpreting the narrative of *Answer to Job*, and particularly the relationship between Job and Yahweh in the first nine chapters of the book. Indeed, Jung's active imagination in the text re-enacts his refusal in the dream to relinquish the millimetre to spare of consciousness in the face of the 'highest presence'. Equally clearly, the dream signals the role of active imagination in the creation of the text.[3] Jung's emotional experience (in the dream) of kneeling before the highest presence is mirrored in both his confession in *Memories* that the confrontation with the darkness of the biblical image of God was 'an experience charged with emotion' (1963: 243) and the emotional nature of active imagination itself. Moreover, we must not forget the critical role of consciousness in the successful practice of active imagination.

Active imagination in *Answer to Job*

In spite of the considerable body of secondary literature on *Answer to Job*,[4] I know of only one systematic study of the role of active imagination in the creation of the narrative in the text, and this significant article published in 1997 appears to have been ignored by subsequent Jung scholarship. While Michael Fordham long ago referred to the source of *Answer to Job* as 'an active imagination by proxy' (Fordham 1955: 273), presumably meaning that for Jung the book of Job functioned as a vehicle through which to enter the meditative process, only Malcolm Welland has identified the references to active imagination in the text, signalling that Jung's reading of the biblical figures of Yahweh and Job as well as their relationship (in the first nine chapters of the book), is the *product* of active imagination (Welland 1997: 297–308). However, even he does not go beyond a cursory examination of the relationship between Job (equated with consciousness) and Yahweh (equated with the unconscious) in *Answer to Job*. In what follows, I will argue that, for Jung, this relationship provides, on the one hand, a paradigmatic *illustration* of the meditative practice of 'dreaming with open eyes', and on the other, independent confirmation of the efficacy and value of this practice. There is a reciprocal relationship between Jung's reading of the images of Job and Yahweh (and indeed the incarnation of God in man in Christ and the Paraclete, followed by the Christification of many) and the dynamic interaction between consciousness and the unconscious in active imagination. Each can be read through, or from, the other.

There are two passages, ignored by Jung's theological critics, preceding the first chapter of the text, which warn the reader of the role of active imagination in the subsequent narrative. In the *Lectori Benevolo*, Jung observes:

> In what follows I shall attempt just such a discussion, such a *'coming to terms'* with certain religious traditions and ideas. Since I shall be dealing with numinous factors, my feeling is challenged quite as much as my intellect. I cannot, therefore, write in a coolly objective manner, but must allow my emotional subjectivity to speak if I want to describe what I feel when I read certain books of the Bible . . .
>
> (1952/1954: 559)

In the second, much longer passage there is a far more detailed account of the practice of active imagination driving the argument of the text.

> How the people of the Old Testament felt about their God we know from the testimony of the Bible. That is not what I am concerned with here, but rather with the way in which a modern man with a Christian education and background *comes to terms with* the divine darkness that is unveiled in the Book of Job, and what effect it has on him. I shall not give a cool and carefully considered exegesis that tries to be fair to every detail, but a purely subjective reaction. In this way I hope to act as a voice for many who feel the same way as I do, and to give expression to the shattering emotion that the unvarnished spectacle of divine savagery and ruthlessness produces in us . . .
>
> The Book of Job serves as a paradigm for a certain experience of God, which has a special significance for us today.[5] These experiences come on man from inside as well as from outside, and it is useless to interpret them rationalistically and thus weaken them by apotropaic means. It is far better to admit the affect and submit to its violence than to try to escape it by all sorts of intellectual tricks and emotional value judgements. Although, by giving way to the affect, one imitates all the bad qualities of the outrageous act that provoked it and thus makes oneself guilty of the same fault, that is precisely the point of the whole proceeding: the violence is meant to penetrate to a man's vitals, and he to succumb to its action. He must be affected by it; otherwise its full effect will not reach him.[6] But he should know, or learn to know, what has affected him, for in this way he transforms the blindness of the violence on the one hand and of the affect, on the other into knowledge.

Thus, Jung concludes:

> For this reason I shall express my affect fearlessly and ruthlessly in what follows, and I shall answer injustice with injustice, that I may

> learn to know why and to what purpose Job was wounded, and what consequences have grown out of this for Yahweh as well as for man.
> (1952/1954: 561–3)

Here Jung sets out what he means by the intensely emotional practices of becoming receptive to, and then *coming to terms with* (*Auseinandersetzung*), the divine darkness unveiled in the Book of Job, which he equates with the 'difficult and unpopular task of talking *with* God, rather than, as philosophers do, *about* him' (Adler 1976: 34). By identifying Yahweh's injustice in his dealings with Job – in having 'no compunction, remorse, or compassion, but only ruthlessness and brutality' (1952/1954: 581) – and by arguing that He is less conscious and moral than Job, Jung invites his readers to abandon Patristic and later Christian readings of Job as either patient or impatient, persistently attempting to justify the ways of God to man.[7] As daring as Job's questioning of God is in the Book of Job,[8] it is only through challenging the theodicy supporting the cultural repression of the experience of Yahweh's *antinomy* (a totality of inner opposites) (1952/1954: 567) during the last 2000 years, that contemporary Europeans can then begin to become fully conscious of their defensive distancing from the 'immensity of God'. By identifying himself with Job, Jung insists that active imagination necessitates a full confrontation by consciousness with the divine violence of Yahweh and the pain inflicted on it by Him. If the divine wound is not fully experienced in consciousness, it, and the divine numinous weapon in the unconscious that caused it (1952/1954: 561), will not be fully understood. Only through a full confrontation with the archaic brutality of Yahweh can one learn to know what has affected consciousness, and thus transform the blindness of the violence and the affect into knowledge.

However, what we have discussed so far is only the first, receptive stage of active imagination. This is followed by the dynamic, interrogatory response of consciousness. Jung's conscious responses to Yahweh's immorality take many forms. For example, Yahweh is identified as a monster (1952/1954: 621), a senseless savage (1952/1954: 572), an unconscious being, a *phenomenon* and not a human being (1952/1954: 600). At this stage, through questioning and interacting with the dark side of God, consciousness (standing on its own authority) brings about not only a change in itself but also exerts a transformative effect on the God-image (Welland 1997: 304–5). Thus, Jung makes the claim: 'Whoever knows God has an effect on him' (1952/1954: 617). More specifically, there are two transformative effects on the God-image. The first is to make the God-image fully conscious, as numinous God-images of the unconscious long to be known by the light of consciousness as much as consciousness longs to be acquainted with these God-images. In this effect can be found the first transcendent function. The second transcendent function emerges in the new image of

God created by the unification of the dark and light aspects of God brought about by consciousness (Welland 1997: 305).

There is another significant conclusion, which can be drawn from the passages on active imagination in *Answer to Job* cited earlier. It is that the dynamic, reciprocal relationship between consciousness and the unconscious, or Job and Yahweh, can be seen as a healing one for both. Murray Stein, commenting on the second longer passage, while not identifying it as a description of the process of active imagination, acknowledged that it could be understood as an expression of, what he calls, 'shamanic countertransference':

> This is the approach of the shamanic healer who allows himself to become infected with the illness of the patient. This type of healer takes the disease in, creates a medicine to cure it, and then returns the medicine to the patient by means of influence. In this instance, Jung was prepared to allow himself to be emotionally affected by the contradictoriness of the God-image at the heart of Biblical tradition, even to the point of imitating Yahweh's irrational behaviour and rageful outbursts, for the purpose of transforming this inner violence into conscious knowledge . . . This is the transformational feedback loop of the transference/countertransference process as Jung described it in several of his writings.
>
> (Stein 1985: 164–5)

Clearly, Yahweh or the unconscious is in need of as much healing as Job or consciousness, and one of the functions of active imagination is to trigger it. Jung declared to Erich Neumann in January 1952, after completing *Answer to Job*, that 'God is an ailment man has to cure. For this purpose God penetrates into man' (Adler 1976: 33). For Jung, it is man (or consciousness) who has the responsibility to provide this cure. Indeed, for Jung, the healing of God or the unconscious by man is as much an ethical as a psychological obligation (von Franz 1980: 91; Welland 1997: 306–7); and this is mirrored in Jung's plea in *Answer to Job*, for divine–human collaboration – a preoccupation not only of alchemy but also Kabbalah (Drob 2000a, 2000b, 2002, 2003; Schlamm 2004).

What I have established so far, through an examination of the materials of this paper, is that the relationship between Job (equated with consciousness) and Yahweh (equated with the unconscious) in *Answer to Job*, provides a paradigmatic *illustration* of the meditative practice of 'dreaming with open eyes'. I will conclude this chapter by citing a sample of passages in *Answer to Job* in support of my more radical claim that there is a reciprocal relationship between Jung's reading of the images of Job and Yahweh (and indeed, the incarnation of God in man in Christ and the Paraclete) and the dynamic interaction between consciousness and the unconscious in active imagination. Each can be read through, or from, the other:

[F]or, if Job gains knowledge of God, then God must also learn to know himself. Whoever knows God has an effect on him. The failure of the attempt to corrupt Job has changed Yahweh's nature.

(1952/1954: 617)

One should make clear to oneself what it means when God becomes man. It means nothing less than a world-shaking transformation of God. It means more or less what creation meant in the beginning, namely an objectivation of God. At the time of the Creation he revealed himself in Nature; now he wants to be more specific and become man.

(1952/1954: 631)

But the pleromatic split is in its turn a symptom of a much deeper split in the divine will: the father wants to become the son, God wants to become man, the amoral wants to become exclusively good, the unconscious wants to become consciously responsible . . . in the same measure as God sets out to become man, man is immersed in the pleromatic process.

(1952/1954: 675, 677)

The inner instability of Yahweh is the prime cause not only of the creation of the world, but also of the pleromatic drama for which mankind serves as a tragic chorus. The encounter with the creature changes the creator.

(1952/1954: 686)

Since he [the Paraclete] is the Third Person of the Deity, this is as much as to say that *God will be begotten in creaturely man*. This implies a tremendous change in man's status, for he is now raised to sonship and almost to the position of a man-god . . . But that puts man, despite his continuing sinfulness, in the position of the mediator, the unifier of God and creature . . . The future indwelling of the Holy Ghost in man amounts to a continuing incarnation of God.

(1952/1954: 692–3)

The unconscious wants to flow into consciousness in order to reach the light, but at the same time it continually thwarts itself, because it would rather remain unconscious. That is to say, God wants to become man, but not quite . . . We . . . need more light, more goodness and moral strength, and must wash off as much of the obnoxious blackness as possible, otherwise we shall not be able to assimilate the dark God who also wants to become man, and at the same time endure him without perishing.

(1952/1954: 740, 742)

What is clear from these passages, and many more in the text, is that Jung's 'poisonous' (Bishop 2002: 45; Brome 1978: 252) theological narrative (triggered by active imagination), the thrust of his psychological argument celebrating the transcendent function (itself the goal of active imagination), and the millimetre to spare of consciousness (necessary for the practice of active imagination) all mirror or illuminate one another, because of Jung's identification of Job or man with consciousness and Yahweh with the unconscious.

On the one hand, Jung's account of the evolution of the Western God image and Job's pivotal role in his theologically 'incomprehensible' (Bishop 2002: 44–6; Heisig 1979: 78–9) revisioning of Christian salvation history both serve to deepen our understanding of the dialectical process as well as the goal of active imagination. For example, just as Jung's preoccupation with the darkness of the Western God-image is mirrored in his understanding of the unconscious, which must be feared as well as loved (1952/1954: 732), so the biblical figure of Job is identified by Jung with the beginning – but only the beginning – of a *consciously* realized individuation process (expressed theologically by the image of the Christification of many – 1952/1954: 758) rather than a *natural* one that runs its course unconsciously (1952/1954: 756).

On the other hand, however, since Jung's theological narrative – which had been triggered by active imagination, and which describes the godhead as having created the world and humankind so that it might fully realize itself (1952/1954: 631, 686) – parallels alchemical and kabbalistic accounts of the reciprocal relationship between God and man,[9] these Western esoteric traditions provide independent confirmation for his conclusions. In other words, these traditions support Jung's conclusion that the unconscious mind manifests itself in a conscious, reflective ego in order to complete and know itself as a 'self'.[10] Consequently, they also lend support to the practice of active imagination, and indeed, to Jung's own relationship to the biblical figure of Yahweh.

Notes

1 Jung informed Erich Neumann that he needed an energetic illness to break down his resistance to talking *with* God rather than, as philosophers with a false sense of security are predisposed to do, *about* him. 'How', he asked, 'would Job have looked had he been able to keep his distance?' (Adler 1976: 34). To Aniela Jaffe he reported that 'If there is anything like the spirit seizing one by the scruff of the neck it was the way [*Answer to Job*] came into being' (Adler 1976: 20). And to Jakob Amstutz he confided that he regarded its contents as the 'unfolding of divine consciousness in which I participate, like it or not', 'a drama that was not mine to control' (Adler 1976: 112). For further comments by Jung on *Answer to Job* in his correspondence, see Bishop 2002: 41–4; Schlamm 2004: 181–95.

2 The dream, for Jung, through the biblical reference to Uriah (whose wife, Bathsheba, was taken from him by David), links his 'great whale' (referring to

Answer to Job) (Adler 1976: 17–18) with the subsequent death of Emma Jung in 1955 (Battye 1994: 169, 172, 190).

3 An earlier scene in the 1948 dream, where Paul Jung informs his son that a shed is haunted (indicating poltergeist activity) (1963: 245), may provide a textual link between *Answer to Job* and *Septem Sermones ad Mortuos*, the writing of which exorcised the ghosts in Jung's house in 1916 (1963: 215–17). Deirdre Bair, drawing on material in the *Protocols*, identifies *Septem Sermones* as a product of active imagination. Jung described the work as akin to 'phenomena that taught me there are things that I don't make, but make themselves' (Bair 2004: 290). Nevertheless, Jung was not entirely satisfied with the text because it was the product of an incomplete active imagination. He regarded it as 'raw material that flows forth, but that just does not contain the entire person. One must not overestimate the unconscious' (Bair 2004: 295).

4 Bishop 2002; Corbett 1996; Edinger 1984, 1992; Goldenberg 1990; Heisig 1979; Hoeller 1989; Kaufmann 1980; Lammers 1994; Raine 1981; Ryce-Menuhin 1994; Schlamm 1991; Slochower 1981; Smith 1996; Stein 1985; von Franz 1975; Wehr 1987; White 1959, 1960.

5 Jung is referring to 'the truly diabolical deeds of our time: the six million murdered Jews, the uncounted victims of the slave labour camps in Russia, as well as the invention of the atom bomb' (1952/1973: 1505). See also Jung's letter to Erastus Evans (Adler 1976: 155–7).

6 To Neumann he declares: 'In order to reach man, God has to show himself in his true form, or man would be everlastingly praising his goodness and justice and so deny him admission' (Adler 1976: 34).

7 In a survey of Patristic and Rabbinic readings of the Book of Job, Nahum Glatzer observes that Christian and Jewish interpreters in the premodern period:

> [W]ith exceptions, avoided a direct confrontation with the text of the book, in order not to be exposed (or not to expose the pious reader) to the bluntness of the hero's speeches and the shattering self-revelation of God in His answer to Job. The heritage of faith and the belief in a benevolent, providential deity were too strong to admit a position so greatly at variance with the accepted basic religious attitudes . . . By concentrating on the story of the patient, *saintly* Job, the reader could absorb the shock of the drama of the impatient, *rebellious* hero; he could 'interpret' the latter in the light of the former.
>
> (Glatzer 1969: 11)

8 Gershom Scholem, the historian of Jewish mysticism associated with Jung through the Eranos conferences in Ascona, echoing Jung's reading of the Book of Job as a primordial scandal in heaven (1952/1954: 607), observed that 'a tremendous agitation came into the world with the Book of Job and its daring questioning' (Wasserstrom 1999: 233).

9 For further discussion of the striking similarities between the Kabbalistic perspective and the thrust of Jung's argument in *Answer to Job*, as well as his growing appreciation of Jewish mysticism after 1945, see Schlamm 2004. Jung's theological critics have persistently failed to acknowledge the Kabbalistic (and indeed Rabbinic) provenance of Jung's ideas on the darkness of God celebrated in *Answer to Job* and *Aion* (Hurwitz 1994: 45–55; Jung 1951: 105–10; Schlamm 2004: 191).

10 Similarly, he observed in a 1953 letter to Jakob Amstutz: 'Man is the mirror which God holds up to himself, or the sense organ with which he apprehends his being' (Adler 1976: 112). There is a striking parallel between Jung's language

here and Henry Corbin's seminal study (first published in 1955/1956 in *Eranos-Jahrbücher*) of the relationship between God and man in Ibn 'Arabi's Sufism (Corbin 1997: 179–200, 216–36, 246–57), where his appropriation of many of Jung's technical psychological terms is transparent. Indeed, Corbin's enthusiastic review of *Answer to Job* (1953/1985) was acknowledged by Jung as 'not only the rarest of experiences, but even a unique experience, to be fully understood . . . I have received hundreds of critical reviews, but not a single one that comes anywhere near yours in its lucid and penetrating understanding' (Adler 1976: 115). For further discussion of Corbin's collaboration with Jung especially during the 1950s, see Wasserstrom 1999: 186–7, 232–3, 330, 348.

References

Adler, G. (ed.) (1976) *C. G. Jung Letters* (1951–1961), vol. 2, London: Routledge & Kegan Paul.

Bair, D. (2004) *Jung: A Biography*, London: Little Brown.

Battye, N. (1994) 'Khidr in the Opus of Jung: The Teaching of Surrender', in J. Ryce-Menuhin (ed.) *Jung and the Monotheisms: Judaism, Christianity and Islam*, London: Routledge.

Bishop, P. (2002) *Jung's Answer to Job: A Commentary*, Hove and New York: Brunner-Routledge.

Brome, V. (1978) *Jung: Man and Myth*, London: Macmillan.

Chodorow, J. (ed.) (1997) *Jung on Active Imagination*, London: Routledge.

Corbett, L. (1996) *The Religious Function of the Psyche*, London and New York: Routledge.

Corbin, H. (1953/1985) 'A retrospective paper: the eternal Sophia', trans. and ed. M. Tuby, *Harvest: Journal for Jungian Studies*, 31, 7–23.

—— (1997) *Alone with the Alone: Creative Imagination in the Sufism of Ibn 'Arabi*, Princeton, NJ: Princeton University Press.

Drob, S.L. (2000a) *Kabbalistic Metaphors: Jewish Mystical Themes in Ancient and Modern Thought*, Northvale, NJ: Jason Aronson.

—— (2000b) *Symbols of the Kabbalah: Philosophical and Psychological Perspectives*, Northvale, NJ: Jason Aronson.

—— (2002) 'Jung, Kabbalah, and Judaism', in A. Maidenbaum (ed.) *Jung and the Shadow of Antisemitism*, Berwick, ME: Nicolas-Hays, pp. 175–92.

—— (2003) 'Towards a Kabbalistic Psychology: C.G. Jung and the Jewish Foundations of Alchemy', *Journal of Jungian Theory and Practice* 5, 2, 77–100.

Edinger, E.F. (1984) *The Creation of Consciousness: Jung's Myth for Modern Man*, Toronto: Inner City Books.

—— (1992) *Transformation of the God-Image: An Elucidation of Jung's* Answer to Job, (ed.) L.W. Jaffe, Toronto: Inner City Books.

Fordham, M. (1955) 'An appreciation of *Answer to Job*', *British Journal of Medical Psychology* 28, 4, 271–3.

Glatzer, N.N. (ed.) (1969) *The Dimensions of Job: A Study and Selected Readings*, New York: Schocken Books, pp. 1–48.

Goldenberg, N.R. (1990) *Returning Words to Flesh: Feminism, Psychoanalysis, and the Resurrection of the Body*, Boston, MA: Beacon Press.

Heisig, J.W. (1979) *Imago Dei: A Study of C. G. Jung's Psychology of Religion*,

Lewisburg, WV: Bucknell University Press, London: Associated University Presses.

Hoeller, S. (1989) *Jung and the Lost Gospels: Insights into the Dead Sea Scrolls and the Nag Hammadi Library*, Wheaton, IL: Theosophical Publishing House.

Hurwitz, S. (1994) 'The Dark Face of God in Judaism', in J. Ryce-Menuhin (ed.) *Jung and the Monotheisms: Judaism, Christianity and Islam*, London: Routledge.

Jung, C.G. (1916/1958) 'The transcendent function', *CW* 8, 1969, 67–91.

—— (1921) *Psychological Types*, *CW* 6, 1971.

—— (1930–4) *Visions: Notes of the Seminar Given in 1930–1934*, C. Douglas (ed.), 2 vols, London: Routledge, 1998.

—— (1931/1962) 'Commentary on *The Secret of the Golden Flower*', *CW* 13, 1968, 1–56.

—— (1935/1968) 'The Tavistock lectures', *CW* 18, 1976, 3–182.

—— (1951) *Aion: Researches into the Phenomenology of the Self*, *CW* 9ii,1968..

—— (1952/1954) 'Answer to Job', *CW* 11, 1958, 355–470.

—— (1952/1973) 'Religion and Psychology: A Reply to Martin Buber', *CW* 18, 1976, 663–70.

—— (1955–6) *Mysterium Coniunctionis: An Enquiry into the Separation and Synthesis of Psychic Opposites in Alchemy*, *CW* 14, 1970.

—— (1963) *Memories, Dreams, Reflections*, ed. A. Jaffe, trans. R. and C. Winston, London: Fontana Press/Harper Collins, 1995.

Kaufmann, W. (1980) *Freud, Adler and Jung* (*Discovering the Mind*, vol. 3), New York: McGraw-Hill.

Lammers, A.C. (1994) *In God's Shadow: The Collaboration of Victor White and C.G. Jung*, New York and Mahwah, NJ: Paulist Press.

Raine, K. (1981) 'Blake's Job and Jung's Job', *Harvest: Journal for Jungian Studies*, 27, 14–37.

Ryce-Menuhin, J. (1994) 'Jung's *Answer to Job* in the light of the Monotheisms', in J. Ryce-Menuhin (ed.) *Jung and the Monotheisms: Judaism, Christianity and Islam*, London: Routledge, pp. 111–24.

Schlamm, L. (1991) 'The Bible and Jungian Depth Psychology', in D. Cohn-Sherbok (ed.) *Using the Bible Today: Contemporary Interpretations of Scripture*, London: Bellew Publishing, pp. 76–86.

—— (2004) 'Review of P. Bishop, *Jung's Answer to Job: A Commentary*', *Harvest: International Journal for Jungian Studies* 50, 2, 181–95.

Slochower, H. (1981) 'Freud as Yahweh in Jung's *Answer to Job*', *American Imago*, 38, 3–60.

Smith, R.C. (1996) *The Wounded Jung: Effects of Jung's Relationships on His Life and Work*, Evanston, IL: Northwestern University Press.

Stein, M. (1985) *Jung's Treatment of Christianity: The Psychotherapy of a Religious Tradition*, Wilmette, IL: Chiron Publications.

von Franz, M.L. (1975) *C.G. Jung: His Myth in Our Time*, New York: G.P. Putnam's Sons.

—— (1980) 'On Active Imagination', in *Methods and Treatment in Analytical Psychology*, Fellbach: Bent.

Wasserstrom, S.M. (1999) *Religion after Religion: Gershom Scholem, Mircea Eliade, and Henry Corbin at Eranos*, Princeton, NJ: Princeton University Press.

Wehr, G. (1987) *Jung: A Biography*, trans. D. M. Weeks, Boston, MA and London: Shambhala.

Welland, M. (1997) 'Active Imagination in *Answer to Job*', *Studies in Religion* 26, 3, 297–308.

White, V. (1959) 'Review of C.G. Jung's *Psychology and Religion: West and East*', *Journal of Analytical Psychology* IV, 1, 73–8.

—— (1960) *Soul and Psyche: An Enquiry into the Relationship of Psychotherapy and Religion*, London: Collins/Harvill Press.

Chapter 10

Active imagination and countertransference enchantment: space and time within the analytic frame

Joy Schaverien

I am in my consulting room with Ms X. It is 20 minutes into a 50-minute session, and Ms X has been describing various incidents in her week and relating them to her past life and she is now recounting a dream. There is a sudden loud rap on the door. We both jump; shocked out of our shared reverie. I do not answer the door, but, nonetheless, the spell is broken. Without realizing it, we had both become immersed in a depth experience – we were together in a room but, in our imaginations we had travelled to a realm where past combines with present, then with now. It is often thus in analysis; for 50 minutes we occupy a different sense of time and space. Our bodies are present in a room but our imagination has taken us to another location.

The man who had come to read the electric meter – for it was he who had rapped on the door – had intruded into this shared reverie and, as a result of this interruption, it became apparent that we had been in a kind of shared dreaming together. We had journeyed to a world inhabited by Ms X and something of her past had become live in the present.

As her analyst, I had accompanied Ms X in her reverie, peopled by her memories and imaginings, but, until this interruption, I was unaware that I had become immersed in her story. Her story and her presence had evoked my imagination. Is it too technical to call this shared reverie transference, countertransference or active imagination; and too esoteric to call it enchantment? I think not – because to do so, combines technical terms with the magic of storytelling. It places the analyst in the position of the imaginer or of the audience – a witness, who, through a leap of imagination, sees Ms X in the drama described.

The analyst could be viewed as a time traveller, who witnesses and journeys with the analysand into the realms of the past, present and future. This time traveller, in the course of a day, sees a series of analysands and so makes several such journeys. Of course not all sessions have this impact; some fail to engage the analyst with this intensity. So why is this the case?

Transference and imagination

Analysis starts, as do most creative enterprises, with a framed space. The analyst creates a particular form of time and space in which imagination can range freely. The atmosphere of the room, sense impressions of the person of the analyst, and the analytic setting as a whole set the scene. Together analyst and patient embark on a shared venture, which begins for the patient with a real and transparent need and which may develop into a journey, bringing the past into the present, in surprisingly vivid ways. In psychoanalysis this re-presentation of the past, as we know, is called transference (Freud 1915, 1917). As Bachelard puts it, 'psychoanalysis sets the person in motion rather than at rest' (1964: 10). Transference mobilizes the psyche and sometimes this deepens into a form of active imagination.

Jung's concept of active imagination is sometimes applied rather uncritically to any form of imaginal activity or art within analysis and so, in this chapter, I will explore facets of imagination and what is active about it. Jung writes, 'I therefore took up a dream-image or an association of the patient's, and, with this as a point of departure, set him the task of elaborating or developing his theme by giving free rein to his fantasy' (1947: 400). This describes the experience of the analysand. Active imagination is an imaginal journey, taken by the analysand and not the analyst; the analyst does not give free rein to his or her own fantasy within the analytic work. However, here I am extending active imagination to include facets of the analyst's *reciprocal* imaginative experience. When imagination is active in the analysand, it might evoke a countertransference or a *counter-imaginal* experience in the analyst.

In active imagination the patient, while awake, is encouraged to journey with the images and personifications that emerge from the unconscious (Watkins 1984). Active imagination might imaginatively be configured as an inward journey, peopled by dream-like figures and actions. It is a 'waking dream' (ibid.) that may begin with a dream or a memory or may emerge spontaneously of its own accord. The images are described to the analyst or they are written, painted or danced, either within the analytic frame or between sessions. Jung makes it clear that active imagination is not merely imaginative activity, but a vibrant and living movement into psyche, 'active imagination, as the term denotes, means that the images have a life of their own and that symbolic events develop according to their own logic' (Jung 1935: 397). For those who are able to lower consciousness and so tap into this source, it opens a channel to an extra dimension in the analytic process. Like the transference, active imagination mobilizes the psyche.

As transference develops, some event or affect from the past may become re-activated emotionally in the present. Thus the past is transposed from story into drama and, temporarily, lived in the analytic present. The affective memory or sense impression is transformed from reminiscence to re-enactment or, when pictures are involved, from mental image to pictorial one. A person may have been arrested by a trauma or event from the past, which may remain as an image or series of half-formed images that hover on the edge of consciousness or repeat in unconscious re-enactment. Through transference the original memory may return, becoming live in the present. In this way it begins to become conscious and to differentiate, evoking imaginal connections and gradually becoming amenable to transformation. Significantly, in its return, it can be witnessed by the analyst and so validated.

Wollheim, in his depth discussion of imagination (1984), describes the different roles and positions we take when imagining an event. Sometimes we imagine from the inside; that is, the imaginer is central in the action – Wollheim calls this 'centrally imagining' (1984: 74). In 'centrally' imagining, the protagonist is at the centre of the imagined event. At other times we imagine as if from outside the event, as observer: present but removed from the action, and this he calls 'acentrally imagining' (ibid.). In 'acentrally' imagining he or she observes the event but not as a participant in it. Wollheim distinguishes between iconic mental states, in which visualizing is central, and its counterparts in other sense modalities, such as 'event memory: dreams: and phantasy' (ibid.: 62). He considers that:

> Iconic mental states . . . are crucial to the way in which the past exercises an influence over the present, and we draw upon them when we try to predict, or anticipate, or control, the future . . . iconic mental states are a certain kind of imagination.
>
> (Wollheim 1984: 62)

I would add that when art is involved in analysis, a distance might be created. This is because, in this instance previously unconscious imagery is literally brought out into the light of day and in viewing the image we create a distance from the imagined or depicted affect.

Thus a move is made from a form of imagining from the *inside* to imagining from the *outside* (ibid.: 74). We might consider that a picture contributes to transforming the state of the artist from 'centrally imagining' to 'acentrally imagining' in a rather concrete sense. It may be similar when the analyst, through interpretation, facilitates separation from a state of unconscious identification with some affect. A distance is created between the mental image and the act.

Imagination: active and passive

Imagination, or its lack, is central in the work of the Jungian analyst. The analyst offers the potential for acentrally imagining and, so, for psychological separation and differentiation. The connection between conscious and unconscious and the transformation from thinking in a literal or concrete manner, to symbolization is revealed in the work of the imagination (Jung 1916). For some people, who enter analysis, the imaginative faculty and so the symbolic function, is lacking; for others, imagination is out of control and is overwhelming (for example, in psychosis). My point is that the work of the imagination in analysis takes place within the context of a therapeutic relationship and so the transference and countertransference dynamic is essential as a base or grounding element. Attention to the transference/countertransference dynamic is by no means always reductive, as is sometimes suggested. However, if the transference is left unexplored, even though rich imaginative material may be explored, the suffering and loneliness that brought the client to analysis is likely to continue. When attention to active imagination is tempered by attention to the transference, relational aspects of the psyche are included in amplification. A delicate balance can be achieved between the archetypal and the developmental approaches (Samuels 1985a) and this helps the client to find a balance in his or her own psyche.

In 1966 both Fred Plaut and Dorothy Davidson published papers relevant to this discussion. Plaut's paper, 'On Not Being Able to Imagine', links the inability to imagine to the inability to trust. I suggest that, in such a case, imagination could be considered to be *passive* rather than *active*. In her paper, 'Transference as Active Imagination', Davidson claims that the analyst is the one who temporarily holds the symbolic function for the patient who cannot do so for him or herself. In such cases the analyst's imagination – which is sometimes *active* – becomes significant. Davidson's article has led me to develop her ideas and to consider *countertransference* as a form of active imagination (Schaverien 2004, 2007a). And it is this theme that I am developing here.

When the analyst – working from either a developmental or an archetypal stance – sees the child in the adult analysand, he or she is applying their imaginative capacity. Hillman evokes this beautifully in his paper 'Abandoning the Child' (1975: 22). Similarly, imagination is required when the analyst accompanies the analysand in dreaming the present and the future. When the analysand is unable to imagine, the analyst holds the transcendent function (Jung 1916), imaginatively placing him or herself in relation to the client's situation. We could say that he or she is 'acentrally imagining' in this instance. The imaginative capacity in the analyst, particularly with regard to countertransference imagery and somatic experiences, was researched and, I think, validated by Andrew Samuels (1985b). And it has been developed by a number of analysts, who have explored the analyst's somatic experiences (see, for example, Field 1989; Orbach 2006; Stone 2006; Wiener 1994). The link between psyche and soma brings the analyst's imaginal experience to the fore; the analyst as an embodied person is imaginally engaged in the process.

Reverie and countertransference enchantment

The analyst is active in her or his imagination and is sometimes enchanted too. For 50 minutes the analyst is woven into the patient's story, becoming a temporary participant or a witness as the drama unfolds; sharing the horror of remembered abuse, the gentle recall of a beloved grandparent, the construction of a half-remembered story. The analyst may 'centrally' imagine him or herself in the client's drama, identifying with it, and sometimes 'acentrally' observing it, as if from a distance. Hillman maintains that the analysand who has 'story awareness' is more likely to do well in analysis than the one who does not (1975: 1). Furthermore, the one who is able to convey his or her story is more likely to evoke a vividly imagined or experienced countertransference. Bachelard, who has the gift of expressing the depth of story, writes vividly:

> There are reveries so deep, reveries which help us to descend so deeply within ourselves that they rid us of our history. They liberate us from our name. These solitudes of today return us to the original solitudes. Those original solitudes, the childhood solitudes leave indelible marks on certain souls.
>
> (Bachelard 1960: 99)

Sometimes, as the analysand develops such reverie, the analyst's own imagination is evoked. The analyst may drift into a reverie of his or her own, temporarily becoming both witness and participant. This is the ancient enchantment of the story: the archetypal appeal of the fairy tale (Bettelheim 1976). Although he does not use the term, Wilfred Bion (1970) evokes 'enchantment' when he writes of the reverie near sleep, to which the analyst lends him or herself in a state of openness to the patient. This, too, is a form of time travel, as the analyst becomes absorbed by, and imaginatively engaged in, the analytic present. Bion's is a Kleinian viewpoint but it is by no means reductive; it merely approaches the imaginal world through another lens.

This *act* of imagination, in the analyst, is not necessarily *active* imagination, as the analyst stays close to the analysand's story. However it might sometimes lead to active imagination, such as when the analyst, starting from the patient's material, sees imagery of his or her own that at first appears to have no obvious connection to the patient's material (Schaverien 2007a). It is only with reflection that it begins to become evident that this, apparently random imagining of the analyst, is actually evoked by something in the unconscious dynamic constellated in the analytic dyad. Bachelard's discourse shows how when we read about a place, our own imaginative memories are evoked (Bachelard 1964: 14). It is thus the case with the patient's story: it evokes memories and stories in the analyst too and so becomes a form of countertransference. These are forms of what I am calling countertransference enchantment. 'Countertransference enchantment' is like a spell, temporarily created though association with the inner world of the other (Schaverien 2007b).

This is enchantment in its widest sense, not a romantic state but one that carries all the elements of a good fairytale and so it is sometimes quite fearsome. The appeal of enchantment is what Bachelard calls the attraction of the domains of intimacy: 'There does not exist a real intimacy that is repellent. All the spaces of intimacy are designated by attraction' (Bachelard 1964: 12). However, this is complex because, in analysis, it may have the force of dynamic progression and regression of the libido discussed by Jung in terms of 'psychic energy' (Jung 1928: 61) and in terms of the transference/countertransference dynamic (Jung 1946: 364). This attraction is accompanied by its opposite – its *counter*part – repulsion. So while it might evoke temporary seduction – a moment of delight, sexual arousal or humour – it will also evoke a shudder of fear, a flash of disgust or horror. The atmosphere suffused with nostalgia may turn to terror, as memories become a lived narrative in the present of analysis. The analyst may become temporarily 'spellbound'. It is then that the witnessing function of another (a supervisor) is needed to extract her or him from this state (Schaverien 2007).

These are elements to which the analyst lends her or himself in a day's work. The analysand who is unable to imagine is also unable to evoke true intimacy in the other; consequently, there is little apparent psychological movement. In this case, the enchantment of the analyst may be an uncomfortable, unconscious and rigid identification, with some unconscious element located in the psyche of the analysand. The lack of the symbolic function creates a static feel in the session. The manifestation of this in the analyst may be intense boredom, an overwhelming impulse to sleep or an inability to find words or images with which to meet the patient's experience. It is as if both are arrested in a kind of becalmed state. In contrast the analysand, who is able to imagine, takes the analyst on a journey and I will now give a brief example of such an imaginal countertransference.

The narrator

Mr Y was referred to me for analysis because he had suffered from a severe clinical depression for much of his life. Indeed, my first impression was of a rather grey man; he wore a dull brown jacket as he sat hunched in the chair in my room. He was burdened with guilt due to the death of a sibling from a childhood illness when Mr Y was 5. As a child he was sure that his sibling rivalry had brought about this event. The sense of guilt, which accompanied this conviction, had unconsciously haunted Mr Y throughout his life. He had suffered years of misery, and the weight of his self-blame was such that he did not really engage with life. Through analysis he came to realize that, as a child, he could not have been responsible for this event. The depression began to lift and very gradually he came to feel that he could live his own life. He became more colourful.

Mr Y was a great storyteller. He would lie on the couch recounting his memories and dreams. Stories of his childhood experiences filled the sessions and, with him, I saw his young mother in her summer dress when he was a very small boy. I witnessed the pair of little boys that he and his brother had been. I accompanied him as he described the traumatic memory and incomprehension at the loss of his childhood companion. I saw it all from the viewpoint of the child he had been. As he talked he too understood the child he had been and realized that a part of him had been unable to develop beyond that time in his life. The sessions felt emotionally very live and, consequently, I was present with him and, as he recounted his tales, I could see vividly the characters and witness the events he described.

His was an unusually vivid form of narration. The origins of this became evident when he explained that his grandmother had lived with his family when he was a child and he would often sleep in her bed. He would delight in the stories she would tell him. Now, as he lay on the couch, I realized that he was recreating this in analysis; he was evoking the sense of his grandmother's storytelling. He was recreating the atmosphere for himself of listening; it was as if he was again that little boy in the analytic present. This was not all, because he was now the storyteller; and, as his grandmother had enchanted him, he now enchanted himself and me as well. I listened to his memories, his present fantasies and his dreams and, in my imagination, I visualized the pictures his words created, in between us.

The internal drama

With this vignette as a background, I turn again to Wollheim, who suggests that imagined events are dramas peopled by an *internal dramatist, an internal actor and an internal audience* (1984: 69). The *internal dramatist* makes up actions and lines for the invented characters. The actions and characters can be modelled on people in the real world or invented, but as imaginal figures, they are roles and not persons (ibid.: 65). *The internal actor* is assigned a character or characters that are represented for the benefit of the *internal audience* (ibid.: 66). Wollheim is describing a person's private imaginings and so the internal audience is part of a person's inner experience. I am departing from the specific meaning of Wollheim's project and borrowing from it to consider the imaginative elements of the inner world of analysis and the symbolic enchantment of transference and countertransference.

In analysis, we might see the internal audience as both the imaginal experience of the analysand and that of the analyst. Both imagine the actions and events described in the analysand's free association or active imagination. The analytic narrative is drama based, in part on memory, fantasy or unconscious phantasy, imagination and, in part, in unconscious repetition. However, in analysis – unlike in the internal imaginative drama – there is an actual, external, audience.

Without intending to concretize Wollheim's explication of a set of non-material, imaginal circumstances, I suggest that, in the case of analysis, the internal audience of the analysand's imagination will have a semi-conscious awareness of the culture in which it is created. Therefore, as well as the internal audience, an external audience will play a background role in the drama. The analyst is both witness and mirror.

In Wollheim's account, *the internal audience of imagination* is composed of three different types of internal state: the *sympathetic audience*, the *detached audience* and the *empathic audience* (ibid.: 67). The *detached audience* may note the state of each character and 'may try to comprehend that mental state, but holds back from any further involvement. It permits itself no affective response' (ibid.). This audience may *favour* one character over another, but there is no further involvement. Often the external role of the analyst is rather like this, as she or he listens dispassionately to the analysand's account. The mental states of the *sympathetic audience* are influenced by the 'favour' in which it holds the character, whose states they are. The sympathetic audience models the normal participant in human intercourse (ibid.). The mental state of the *empathic audience* is in unison with the protagonist. Wollheim distinguishes *empathy* from *favour*: favour starts in the intellect and it may or may not spread to the feelings, while *empathy* is based in the feelings.

While Wollheim's audience is an internal one, which belongs solely to the protagonist, it lends itself to consideration of the analyst's role. When engaged in analysis, all of these roles are drawn on intuitively. The analyst is external to the events described, however the role may sometimes be that of the detached audience, sometimes the sympathetic or the empathic one and frequently the analyst's position is a combination of all three. The analyst uses her or his imaginative capacity to venture imaginatively into the inner world, as expressed by the analysand, however it emerges. It may be spoken, painted or enacted; it may emerge through repetition in the transference of an atmosphere of the past.

We saw this with Mr Y. He evoked his own imagination and enjoyed it and having an interested witness generated this. He was participant and observer of his stories, which were sometimes, but not always, active imagination in the classic sense. As he recounted his stories, he imagined himself 'centrally' in the drama; in his mind's eye he visualized his past. He took all the positions: *internal* narrator, (dramatist), *internal actor* and *internal audience*. However, and here we move from imagining to communicating (and this is where the analyst comes in), it was important that there was also an *external* audience.

My own imagination was evoked and as I listened, I travelled with him and visualized the situations he described. I saw his mother and his little brother. (Of course I did not see what he saw exactly; we can never actually see the picture in the imagination of another however vividly it is described.) But the point is that I was, in part, the *detached* audience, observing all the characters objectively, but *favouring* his viewpoint. I was also, in part, the *sympathetic* audience, but mostly the *empathic* audience (this is the one that feels with the protagonist). This is the role of the analyst – she draws on her or his own imagination, feels with the analysand and yet remains detached as well. As analyst I was applying my own internal dramatist, actor and audience. Staying close to the material of Mr Y was an act of imagination, but was it active imagination? I was not, as Jung suggests, 'giving free rein to my fantasy', rather, I was following the lead of the analysand, so, perhaps, it was not active imagination in the true sense. However, imagination was certainly active; it was a waking dream and so I would suggest that it was a form of active imagination.

Imagination and countertransference enchantment

I have suggested that analysis is enchantment to which the analyst lends her or himself. It is a spell cast by the analysand's narrative and way of being. It weaves a complex web of feelings, which draws in both participants. Countertransference is an imaginal act: an act of generosity of spirit, in the sense of the analyst lending her or himself, for the 50-minute hour, to the inner world of this particular person. The analyst travels in time and space and opens to enchantment.

In conclusion, I return to my consulting room and Ms X conjuring up a picture of her dream and her past. As I listened to her I was imagining – seeing pictures in my mind: of course, neither of us could know if the pictures in my mind were the same as those in hers. However, what became clear from the interruption, was that we had shared a reverie, a kind of enchantment, where time and space were of a different order from the usual. We were both awake, but not in the usual sense; this was a waking dream. Our imaginations were active while our bodies were relaxed. We had travelled out of the time, space and pace of everyday life and, for the moment, we were together in a space set apart. This rendered us as time travellers, partly residing in the present reality of the place where we were and partly journeying into the realm of memory and imagination. The mundane nature of the electricity meter did not feature in such a space and this is why it was such a shock when the man rapped on the door. As with Mr Y, there was an element of enchantment that had enveloped us both – we were encapsulated in a room in a shared dreaming: separated from the rest of the world for that particular 50 minutes.

References

Bachelard, G. (1964) *The Poetics of Space*, trans. M. Jolas, Boston, MA: Beacon Press.

—— (1960) *The Poetics of Reverie: Childhood Language and the Cosmos*, trans. D. Russell, Boston, MA: Beacon Press, 1969.

Bettelheim, B. (1976) *The Uses of Enchantment: The Meaning and Importance of Fairy Tales*, Harmondsworth: Penguin Books.

Bion, W.R. (1970) *Attention and Interpretation*, London: Maresfield Reprints, 1984.

Davidson, D. (1966) 'Transference as Active Imagination', *Journal of Analytical Psychology*, 11, 135–45.

Field, N. (1989) 'Listening with the Body', *British Journal of Psychotherapy*, 5, 4, 512–22.

Freud, S. (1915) 'Observations on Transference Love', *SE* 12, London: Hogarth.

—— (1917) 'Transference', *SE* 16, London: Hogarth.

Hillman, J. (1975) 'Abandoning the Child', *Loose Ends*, Dallas, TX: Spring.

Jung, C.G. (1916) 'The Transcendent Function', *CW* 8, 1960: 131–93.

——(1928) 'On Psychic Energy', *CW* 8, 1960: 1–130.

—— (1935) 'Lecture 5', Tavistock Lectures, *The Symbolic Life*, *CW* 18, 1977: 304–415.

—— (1946) 'The Psychology of the Transference', *CW* 16, 1954: 353–539.

—— (1947) 'On the Nature of the Psyche', *CW* 8, 1960: 343–442.

Orbach, S. (2006) 'What Can we Learn from the Therapist's Body?', in J. Schaverien (ed.) *Gender, Countertransference and the Erotic Transference: Perspectives from Analytical Psychology and Psychoanalysis*, London and New York: Routledge.

Plaut, F. (1966) 'On Not Being Able to Imagine', *Journal of Analytical Psychology*, 11, 113–31.

Samuels, A. (1985a) *Jung and the Post Jungians*, London and New York: Routledge.

—— (1985b) 'Countertransference, the "Mundus Imaginalis" and a Research Project', *Journal of Analytical Psychology*, 30, 47–71.

Schaverien, J. (1992) *The Revealing Image: Analytical Art Psychotherapy in Theory and Practice*, London and New York: Routledge.

—— (2004) 'Art, Dreams and Active Imagination', *Journal of Analytical Psychology*, 50, 127–54.

—— (2007a) 'Countertransference as Active imagination: Or Whose Active Imagination?', *Journal of Analytical Psychology*, 52, 4.

—— (2007b) 'Framing Enchantment: Countertransference in Analytical Art Psychotherapy Supervision', in J. Schaverien and C. Case (eds) *Supervision in Art Psychotherapy*, New York: Routledge.

Stone, M. (2006) 'The Analyst's Body as Tuning Fork: Embodied Resonance in Countertransference', *Journal of Analytical Psychology*, 51, 1, 109–124.

Watkins, M. (1984) *Waking Dreams*, Dallas, TX: Spring.

Wiener, J. (1994) 'Looking Out and Looking In: Some Reflections on "Body Talk" in the Consulting Room', *Journal of Analytical Psychology*, 39, 331–50.

Wollheim, R.A. (1984) *The Thread of Life*, Cambridge: Cambridge University Press.

Chapter 11

The image emerging: the therapist's vision at a crucial point of therapy

Konoyu Nakamura

Jungian psychotherapy progresses by interaction between a therapist and a patient, and Jung realized the enormous importance of transference phenomenon. Jung says:

> It is probably no exaggeration to say that almost all cases requiring lengthy treatment gravitate round the phenomenon of transference, and that the success or failure of the treatment appears to be bound up with it in a very fundamental way.
>
> (1946a)

He also says:

> The patient, by bringing an activated unconscious content to bear upon the doctor, constellates the corresponding unconscious material in him, owning to the inductive effect which emanates from projections in greater or lesser degree. Doctor and patient thus find themselves in a relationship founded on mutual unconsciousness.
>
> (1946b: 364)

The therapist and the patient are involved with each other, in a 'mystical *coniunctio*', of conscious and unconscious relations. Moreover, Jung claims that:

> The doctor knows – or at least he should know – that he did not choose this career by chance; and the psychotherapist in particular should clearly understand that the psychic infections, however superfluous they seem to him, are in fact the predestined concomitants of his work, and thus fully in accord with the instinctive disposition of his own life.
>
> (ibid.: 365)

So, Jung insisted that therapeutic transformation resulted from the conscious and unconscious bond of patient and therapist, and that this bond reflects the instinctive lives of these two persons.

In this chapter, I will consider an image emerging from the therapist at a crucial point of therapy: the *Mahavairocana-tatha-gata* – the universal or primordial Buddah. In particular, I will examine the meaning of this image in the context of transference and countertransference, from the perspective of the therapist's personal background, and in terms of how this image induces transformation in both patient and therapist.

Although the background of the therapist is rarely considered in public or professional debates (Papadopoulos 1998), I would like to start this paper with discussion of my background, family, religion, and training. This is because it plays a very important part in the understanding of the clinical experience that I will come to describe.

My background in Jungian psychology and Buddhism

Since birth, I have been a Buddhist of the True Pure Land Sect, founded by Shinran. The majority of Japanese families belong to a temple of an institutional Buddhist sect. The system of family temples started in the seventeenth century by the governor, Iemitsu Tokugawa. The main purpose of the family temple system was political: to exclude Christianity and to control people. Japanese Buddhism is characterized by ancestor worship, which is not found in original Buddhism. The ancestor worship is the spiritual core of the family system, which bonds family members to one another, and keeps the family in order. While dogma and practice of the True Pure Land Sect intends salvation for all individuals (no matter their class, race, or gender), its institutional system is marked by a patriarchal hierarchy (Takasaki 1988). My parents were liberal for their generation, and were not interested in any religious activity, which meant that I grew up without receiving any religious education within my family. I had never approached spiritual problems through Buddhism, and I would not submit to Buddhist doctrine because of its authoritarian and patriarchal character.

While I am now teaching clinical psychology and analytical psychology at a university, I have been working as a psychotherapist for more than 20 years at various clinical facilities around Kyoto in Japan. Regarding my psychotherapeutic background, I identify myself as a Jungian-oriented psychotherapist, having trained as a Jungian therapist in my 30s.

It is well known that Jung was greatly interested in religious problems throughout his life. He was not only interested in Christianity but other past and present religions, including Eastern faiths. He integrated the ideas of these religions into his theories and practices. (For example, Jung famously respected the *mandala* as a symbol of the Self or totality.) Of the many schools of psychology, Jungian psychology most directly deals with spirituality and the soul of the human being. Therefore, Jungian psychotherapy demands both therapists and clients confront their own religious or spiritual problems. Through my own experiences in my training analysis, I gradually started to develop an interest in spiritual and religious problems. I realized that religious symbols or images appearing in my dreams actually provided me with meaningful insight, comfort, and salvation.

I was fortunate to find an encouraging personal analyst. She is American, and not only a Jungian analyst but also both a feminist and a Buddhist with a deep knowledge of Japanese Buddhism. While she accepted and understood my frustration, negative thoughts and feelings towards institutional Buddhism in Japan, she introduced me to the essence of Buddhism. Learning about Buddhism through English texts written by women led me to a more profound personal understanding of my religion than my earlier experience – of learning through texts by Japanese male authority figures – had allowed.

When I attended the international conference for Buddhism and Depth Psychology at the Hanazono University in Kyoto in 1999, I was surprised to discover that many psychotherapists outside Japan were interested in Buddhism. This fact made me pay closer attention to Buddhism, and to respect the values of Eastern religions and philosophies in the foundation of psychotherapy. At that time I also experienced meditation with foreign colleagues for the first time. After the conference, I visited Toji temple (which is the head temple of Shingon, a Japanese esoteric Buddhism sect) where I was able to look at a variety of *mandalas* with fresh impressions, and engage with them with an intensity that I could not have achieved in my previous visits. Whenever I experienced personal difficulty, I used to visit various temples of the Shingon sect near to my home. I found some comfort and peace in the sacred and mysterious atmosphere of these temples. However, honestly speaking, I am neither a pious Buddhist nor a scholar of Buddhism, and I have never been involved in any specific practice or training as a Buddhist.

Now that I have considered myself, the therapist, I will now consider the other half of the therapeutic interaction: my patient.

My patient

My patient was a young man when I first met him. For the purpose of this chapter, I will call him Tomita-san (Tomita is a family name and 'san' means 'light respect'). Tomita-san had grown up in the Kansai area of Japan. He was a good student and entered a major corporation after his university graduation. He married a woman from his home town, and they moved to Tokyo for his job. Tomita-san was on a fast-track scheme to a higher, managerial position within his company, which would enable him to take up employment abroad. His future appeared bright. His company sponsored his training in New York following his training in Tokyo. Tomita-san moved to New York by himself, leaving his wife behind, and, shortly after he had a breakdown with psychosomatic symptoms, caused by intense home sickness. After a 6-month break from work, he was ordered to go back to work in Kansai, his childhood home. The next year, he was involved in a great project, which went well until his supervisors decided to leave him to complete it on his own, causing him to feel stifled. He voluntarily visited a therapist, one who worked in the counseling room of his company. This therapist was me. I worked with him through several interruptions, from 1992 to 2000.

When I first met Tomita-san he did not seem to care about his physical appearance. His speech was highly logical and rational but he could not emotionally communicate with me; for example, he couldn't sustain eye contact with me. He reluctantly saw a psychiatrist, who diagnosed him as having a compulsive personality, a panic disorder and depression. Tomita-san also had difficulties managing relationships with others, due to his aggression and lack of sympathy. He was also overly concerned with other people's opinions and estimations of him. He would not directly express emotions in my presence, and it became obvious to me that the more distant our conscious relationship became, the more dependent he became on the psychiatrist (furthermore, his unconscious transferential relationships with both of us, with his psychiatrist and with me, his therapist, would deepen and intensify). This was demonstrated in the following episode.

In 1998 I left Japan to train in America for 6 months. Tomita-san appeared calm and accepting of my impending absence and of the long break in our therapeutic sessions together. He showed no complaint or negative feeling, and even agreed to see another, younger, female therapist in the meantime. However, he stopped seeing his new therapist shortly after his sessions began, and he subsequently suffered another breakdown, which required several months of holiday for him to feel relief. On my return from America, we resumed our work together. But it was only after a couple of months that he felt able to express his real, negative, feelings about my absence.

The therapeutic crisis

In 2000 I was appointed to a university, and I subsequently left the company where I worked with my patient. By that time the career of my patient was failing disastrously due to his breakdowns, and his marriage was beginning to fall apart. At this time he often suggested that he would commit suicide, and that he was self-harming. He was complaining that his company held him in low estimation, and that his wife refused him sexual relations. He could not find any meaning in his life and felt that no one needed him. It was clearly a serious crisis for him and a crucial point in our work together. In order to help prevent him from self-harming, I thought that it was absolutely necessary for him to express his emotion outwardly, to me in our sessions. He seemed to be able to express some emotion regarding our impending final separation and the end of our sessions, and he struggled for a month to find a way to release his feelings.

Eventually, when we had only three sessions remaining, coming into the room, he said: 'I have something that I must absolutely tell you today . . . I will miss you a lot. You know, I am damaged by change very much and I had never imagined you would leave. I have clung to the idea that no one needs me, and I am always biting my nails.' 'Do you do anything else?' I asked. He replied, 'I hit myself.' 'How do you hit yourself? Terribly?' I asked. He then suddenly and violently hit himself in the face many times. I was too shocked at his sudden acting out to say anything. After a while, getting so sad, I asked him, 'Have you ever cried?' 'Never', he replied. I felt I completely understood his deep despair and absolute loneliness. I also realized that there was nothing that I could do for him. I subsequently stopped trying to do anything and, instead, found myself withdrawing, feeling a need to escape from the situation. I ceased to respond to him consciously, and I concentrated on the search within myself, to connect with my own feelings.

I closed my eyes and meditated with Hokkai-join, the hand sign of the dharma-dhatu mediation (Mitsumori and Okada 1995), which is used for Zen meditation as a method to improve concentration. Keeping silent, I simply waited for something (such as an idea or an image) to come to mind. I had never meditated in this way in front of my patients, and I did not know the full, experiential meaning of Hokkai-join. I do not know why I did such an unusual deed but it seemed natural or instinctual at the time. Soon, a fantastic vision emerged in my mind: a real, dark space, the universe, in which many galaxies with cool brilliance are slowly moving. Intuitively, I realized that the image represented the universe and the *Mahavairocana-tatha-gata* himself, who is the Absolute being reigning over the whole universe. I also impressively felt his vast and boundless mercy, which contained me and forgave me as a powerless therapist. The image released me from my rigid persona or role as 'therapist', and from my presumption that I alone, as therapist, could heal my client. The image enabled me to realize that there is a greater reality beyond our own wills, and that an Absolute Being governs us. Subsequently, my suffering patient was accepted, contained, relieved and led by the great mercy of the image that I experienced for both of us. I was sure he must find his way by himself though I did not know how, but I was confident that he and I would be guided by the transcendent aspect of the universe.

My heart swelled with conviction and hope, as the image brought me feelings of exultation and tears of joy. Opening my eyes, I found my patient gazing at me. I had never before observed such a serious look in his eyes. I did not tell him of my experience, of the image I saw, because it seemed to me that verbal communication was no longer needed. We spent about 20 minutes together in silence and we finished the session in peace.

After this episode, his rage, distorted aggression and self-destructive behavior disappeared. In our last session together, he calmly expressed his thankfulness to his wife for her devoted support, his happiness working at the company, and his appreciation to me for our long work together. After my departure, he decided to see a new female therapist, who had plenty of experience, and I assume he was able to get along well her, for, to my knowledge, he did not have another breakdown.

The therapist's response in crisis

Mario Jacoby gave a significant contribution to the theory of transference and countertransference in his book, The *Analytic Encounter Transference and Human Relationship* (1984). He discussed narcissism and transference, using the concept of 'mirror transference' in Heinz Kohut. Jacoby writes:

> Such a basic sense of isolation is often at the bottom of the suffering symptomatic of the extreme narcissistic personality disorder. Nobody is 'there' to give mirroring and empathic resonance. This may actually be true in reality, but usually it has to do with inner psychic difficulty: nobody can be trusted to come near enough to perform these vitally needed functions.
>
> (Jacoby 1984: 44)

In my case, it is obvious that the fundamental problem of my patient is a basic sense of isolation. While he always kept me at arm's length with his extreme aggression, he eagerly needed to be intimate with someone. Therefore, it is no wonder that when he experienced separation from the symbol of the mother, such as his mother country, Japan, or from me when I left him for 6 months, he experienced a breakdown. Good or bad, as long as I was playing the role of 'mother', the patient was apparently keeping his life, which supported him and enabled him to keep coming to our sessions for 8 years. When the patient and the therapist, who are involved in such an intense and unconscious transferential relationship, face separation, a serious crisis occurs for both. My patient's aggression had reached its peak, and it might have crushed both himself and me, as his therapist.

Jung said little about what the therapist should do in such moments, but his following description is suggestive: 'A genuine participation, going right beyond professional routine, is absolutely imperative, unless of course the doctor prefers to jeopardize the whole proceeding by evading his own problems, which are becoming more and more insistent' (1946b: 400). These words of Jung suggest to me that, at crucial points in therapy, it is important for the therapist to give up his or her persona, and to observe carefully and honestly what is happening within his or her psyche. I found myself being overwhelmed by powerlessness as a therapist, as well as feeling grief and rage due to feelings abandoned by the patient's decision of working with another therapist (even though this separation was due to my decision to leave him). In other words, my own narcissism, isolation, and aggression came under question, and not the patient's.

It is natural for people to assimilate new unconscious aspects when they encounter a serious crisis and their ego-central functions do not work. This is because, as Jung said: 'the unconscious yields an endless and self-replenishing abundance of living creatures, and wealth beyond our fathoming' (1946b: 366). Jung continued to say that the only way to get to these unconscious aspects is to try to attain a conscious attitude that allows the unconscious to cooperate instead of being driven into opposition (ibid.). Here is a reason why, at a crucial point in my therapeutic sessions with my patient, I ceased to consciously respond to him, and closed my eyes and withdrew instead. Of course, I had never done such a thing in front of my patient in sessions before, and my deed was unusual. I neither intended to do something, nor anticipated what would, or indeed did, happen next. But my belief which I had consolidated through my study of Jungian theory and experience of my training, enabled me to be spontaneous without any hesitation and fear, even when my patient had been violent moments before. It seemed to me the best thing I could do and it led us to a new stage of transformation.

The meaning of *Mahavairocana-tatha-gata*

Jung said:

> The doctor must go to the limits of his subjective possibilities, otherwise the patient will be unable to follow suit . . . It reveals a unity which nevertheless is – or was – a diversity. No longer the earlier ego with its make-believes and artificial contrivance, but another, 'objective' ego, which for this reason is better called the 'self' . . . These first indications of a future synthesis of personality . . . where they take the form of the mandala symbols.
>
> (1946b: 400)

In this case, it is extraordinarily important that the therapist touch the image of *Mahavairocana-tatha-gata* through dialogue with the unconscious. But what is this crucial image? *Mahavairocana-tatha-gata* (*Mahavairocana* means Great Sun) and is the main deity for esoteric Buddhism. Esoteric Buddhism appeared in India during the seventh and eighth centuries and was much influenced by Hinduism. *Mahavairocana-tatha-gata* is influenced by the Hindu concept of an original universal creator and it is seen as the symbolic all-embracing being of the *mandala* and of the universe itself. The Sun does not shine in shadow or at night. However, the radiance of *Mahavairocana-tatha-gata* is unlimited by time and space because it personifies the Dharma Body, the entire universe, and it is thought to unite the wisdoms and qualities represented separately in the many deities of esoteric Buddhism. Therefore, *Mahavairocana-tatha-gata* is always placed at the center of the *mandala*. Also the image of *Mahavairocana-tatha-gata* has the vast and boundless mercy of permits existence of even the evil, which lets one acknowledge one's dark aspects (Yamasaki 1988).

Radmila Moacanin, in *Jung's Psychology and Tibetan Buddhism Western and Eastern Paths to the Heart* (1986) examined 'visualization', a meditation method of esoteric Buddhism, which is also used in Japanese esoteric Buddhism, Shingon sect. Moacanin writes:

> Meditators are given deity, chosen according to their specific needs and spiritual capacities . . . Indeed they do not only contemplate the deity, they identify themselves as the deity. For a moment they have been transfigured into the divinity: the archetypal essence of it has been transferred into them. During that time of identification with the deity they generate the so-called 'divine pride', pride that one is Buddha. The core of visualization consists in this union with the deity. It is a dynamic process in which the meditator's ego, their ordinary consciousness, is abandoned and substituted with the higher consciousness of the deity. One could say, to use Jung's language, that the individual's ego has been sacrificed for the Self.
>
> (1986: 50–1)

Moacanin later refers to the Mahavairocana Buddha as an example of 'visualization' (ibid.: 52). I have never practiced the method of visualization. Furthermore, the image that I had differs from the one that is anticipated by rigid practice of Shingon school.[1] However, people encounter such images in their inner psyche when they have intense and emotional experiences such as grief, despair, rage, and exultation. They can encounter various images or symbols of the self, depending on their familial, national, ethnic backgrounds, and such images can be fruitful resources to create a new self. If I were a devoted faithful of the True Pure Land Sect – my familial religion – I may have had an image of Amitabha-Buddha, who is the main deity of the sect. Instead, my encounters of Buddhism through Jungian psychology encouraged the image of *Mahavairocana-tatha-gata* as the most accessible symbol of the Self. The crisis might have been a good opportunity to open the door to spirituality as a Buddhist, which I unconsciously inherited from my ancestors, and have absorbed through my daily life as Japanese. According to Jung:

> This inner unity, or experience of unity, is expressed most forcibly by the mystics in the idea of *the unio mystica*, and above all in the philosophy and religion of India, in Chinese Taoism, and the Zen Buddhism of Japan. From the point of view of psychology, the names or images we give to the Self are quite irrelevant, and so is the question of whether or not the Self is 'real'. Its psychological reality is enough for all practical purposes.
>
> (1946b: 532)

There is no doubt that the image of *Mahavairocana-tatha-gata* emerging from the therapist is a symbol of the Self, which carries the strong impression and intense sense of unification of the universe, the sacred or the transcendent.

These unifying images, which can be experienced by the therapist, are extraordinarily significant to the transferential relationship in the therapeutic setting. The image of the *Mahavairocana-tatha-gata*, for instance, healed me as a therapist, relieving me of my suffering and from my feelings of powerlessness, isolation, and aggression, and bringing me hope, self-confidence and trust in relation to my patient. It seems to me that when I, the therapist recovered my self-confidence and trust in the patient, the patient likewise recovered these things in himself, even though the image of *Mahavairocana-tatha-gata* was not communicated between us verbally.

Jungian psychotherapy progresses by interaction between a therapist and a patient, in conscious and unconscious relationship. According to Jung, 'the transference phenomenon is without doubt one of the most important syndromes in the process of individuation; its wealth of meanings goes far beyond mere personal likes and dislikes' (1946b: 539). I experienced the mysterious dynamics of transference and countertransference with my patient. Moreover, the image of the Self, which was communicated nonverbally between us, enabled the transformation of both of us, together and separately, restoring our relationship and our respective sense of autonomy and self-confidence.

Note

1 Mediators are encouraged by teachers to have a different image of the personification of the universe: an 8-year-old child in medieval costume of the king of India (Moacanin 1986: 52).

References

Jacoby, M. (1984) *The Analytic Encounter: Transference and Human Relationship*, Toronto: Inner City Books.

Jung, C.G. (1946a) 'Foreword, to "The Psychology of Transference"', *CW* 16, 1954.

—— (1946b) 'The Psychology of Transference', *CW* 16, 1964: 353–539.

Mitsumori, M. and Okada, K. (1995) *Butuzou Chokoku no Kansho Kisochisiki* [*Understanding Buddhist Sculptures for Beginners*], Tokyo: Shibundo.

Moacanin, R. (1986) *Jung's Psychology and Tibetan Buddhism Western and Eastern Paths to the Heart*, London: Wisdom Publications.

Papadopoulos, R. (1998) 'Jungian Perspective in New Contexts', in A. Casement (ed.) *Post-Jungians Today Key Papers in Contemporary Analytical Psychology*, London and New York: Routledge.

Takasaki, J. (1988) *Higashi Asia Bukkyo Shiso-shi* [*A History of Buddhist Thoughts in Eastern Asia*] in M. Nagao, T. Idutu, K. Fukunaga, S. Ueyama, M. Hattori, Y. Kajiyama and J. Takasaki (eds) *Higashi Asia no Bukkyo Iwanami Kouza Toyo Shiso*, vol. 12 [*Buddhism in Eastern Asia Iwanami Lecture Series for Eastern Thoughts*, vol. 12] Tokyo: Iwanami Shoten.

Yamasaki, T. (1988) *Shingon Japanese Esoteric Buddhism*, Boston, MA and London: Shambhala.

Part 4

Psychic revisions: towards a new mythology

Chapter 12

Envisaging animus: an angry face in the consulting room

Phil Goss

Animus: inhibition or inspiration?

A woman reports a frightening dream of a giant man, who is rampaging across the countryside, as thousands of terrified people flee in their cars, on horse-drawn carts and on foot. The woman comments that the image reminds her of Goya's painting (c. 1809–12), *The Colossus*. A man dreams of a group of working men who are tough, no-nonsense, and unwilling to countenance weakness or vacillation in others. These men congregate in their overalls and stare at the dreamer, who feels uncomfortable. Both of these are disguised examples (to which I will return), from my practice, of dream images of the masculine, which have an unsettling, threatening, quality. These negative forms of *animus* can show themselves in dreams, imagination and cultural forms of expression. It presents in both women and men, although often with differing emphases.

In this chapter, I want to take Jung's concept of animus and play with its possible uses in our twenty-first-century discourses about the individuating self, experiences of otherness, and gender (where 'gender' refers to one's identity as masculine or feminine). Jung meant by animus the image of man and the masculine principle found in the woman's psyche (Jung 1959). While aware that its presence can be deconstructed, for the purposes of this chapter I am treating it as a present image and entity in all psyches, as suggested by the way such powerful imagery – as in the material just examined – crops up in individual imagination and dreams, as well as in artistic expression (such as the Goya example cited earlier).

The task of envisaging animus is not helped by the context in which it was born, as the less attractive of the anima–animus dyad, the ugly twin brother to the alluring soul-quality of anima. Its shadow quality arises from the personal shadow of analytical psychology's founder, as well as from the collective shadow of Western patriarchy, which tends to leave it lurking somewhere in the background of our musings about the place of the gendered *other*. Jung thought nothing, within the norms of nineteenth century Swiss society, of following Freud's lead in assuming that women lacked something important men had and envied them for it (Freud 1905), although for Jung this was not the penis, but instead full consciousness. Man supposedly had to do woman's thinking for her. This awkward cultural throwback tarnishes what is otherwise an original and valuable concept, one which could, for example, offer a pointer to a more satisfactory developmental process in Jung's model. Here, animus could offer an equivalence to Freud's phallic stage and Lacan's symbolic order (Lemaire 1994), as a development on from a state of anima possession at birth (Casement, personal communication, 24 May 2006). I ask readers to bear in mind the provocative edge to animus and to be responsible for their own conscious responses to what I might suggest (and to what they may have read or heard previously) as I take responsibility for what I write too. Being conscious of when we each might be thinking, feeling or speaking from our own animus is key to making it possible to productively experiment with 'catching animus'.

This edge I allude to makes it important that our 'envisaging of animus' is not just meant with the aim of visualizing the different forms it can take in our imaginations, in the consulting room and in art forms across cultures. It is also important to 'envisage' in the sense of 'face up to', and confront what animus, particularly *negative animus*, may represent. This is where my emphasis will lie – in the shadow side of animus, rather than the light, strength and attractive authority of *logos*, spiritual meaning and intellectuality with which *positive animus* was portrayed by Jung. I am doing this because most writing on animus conveys a sense that it is hard to get to the *positive* version of animus as the negative connotations associated with it get in the way. This can be offputting, but it also suggests the negative animus is trying to tell us something.

This discussion pays heed to the well-developed post-Jungian discussion on gender and otherness, and the recognition that 'gender is where Jung is at his least post-modern' (Rowland 2002: 158). A postmodern take on animus, anima and syzergy, as Hauke (2000) argues, demands the kinds of grand, essentialist, narratives about gender difference and status – through which Jung construed his ideas – are recognized as outdated, unhelpful and, at times, sexist. However, the historical efforts to define the 'essence' of the feminine and the masculine haven't simply disappeared. Instead, one could say they have been driven underneath the more open and pluralistic thinking, which hallmarks current approaches. It is important, therefore, for us to locate consideration of animus within the falling away of patriarchal thinking (which raised up the masculine as the source of wisdom and logic) as well as the rise of feminist thinking.

My own take on gender nods towards a postmodern perspective as well as Samuel's caution against emphasizing *opposites*. Instead, so-called feminine and masculine attributes and behaviours are part of the repertoire of how we all 'are' (Samuels 1985: 217). One example he uses illustrates this approach:

'Active and passive define a spectrum of psychological possibilities around *activity* and *passivity* – nothing more.' So, attributing such qualities as either masculine or feminine has doubtful currency and echoes the perception, post-Jung, that features of anima and animus, as representing archetypal aspects of the psyche, can be found in both women and men.

Samuels also writes about the value of recognizing difference and articulating for example 'Not what being a woman is but what being a woman is *like*' (Samuels 1989: 297) – a useful shift towards experientially describing, rather than trying to academically define, gender differences. This area of 'what it is like' being a man or a woman is the one I have an interest in exploring, in clinical and wider contexts, as well as the possibility that these differences in 'what it is like' being either a man or woman in turn lend differences in how animus influences us.

My own academic and clinical 'work in progress' involves pursuing the idea that although attributes, behaviours and perceptions free-float and are shared between men and women, there are nevertheless some key differences in how women and men generally experience life, and in how they embody and present these shared elements. This intuition, as suggested, may have implications for the place and meaning of animus, as might the central tension inherent (and which I experience) in trying to open up discussion about it.

This tension involves, on the one hand, an intuition that animus, taken in its basic meaning ascribed by Jung, has a fertile (but challenging) resonance for both genders. This includes its erotic connotations of man-within-woman and the way it implies a profound influence on 'boy-within-woman' (i.e. mother–son) relationships. On the other hand, animus discussion gets inhibited by anxiety about Jung's outdated perception of what the consciousness of women is 'capable of' or what Hill has termed a 'distortion of patrivalent culture' (1992: 177), and as Woodman observes (1990: 132), uncovering the masculine in women is challenging when it has been, 'so bludgeoned by patriarchy that we can only imagine what creative masculinity is'. This makes it awkward to explore gender without the fear of falling into generalizations, which are contentious and unhelpful. In other words, we can be gripped by the fear that discussion about animus will end up governed and spoiled by the very tendency Jung rather clumsily ascribed to it – that is, to overturn balanced ego consciousness with irrational judgement and highly charged assumptions.

Jung famously, or rather infamously, framed this scenario in terms of what he felt was a woman's tendency to speak from her opinions, shakily constructed but rigidly and emotively adhered to. Because this kind of assignation of 'inferior' ways of operating to women compared to men seems so awkward, embarrassing and unacceptable to us, it renders full discussion of animus likewise awkward. As a man, I notice in myself this discomfort, as if my writing about animus is going to lead me into making generalizations about women and men that will appear stereotyped or even misogynist. There is a voice within which whispers this may be too risky a topic for a male analyst to explore. Nevertheless, this in turn flags up the possibility I have hinted at earlier: that animus has some important things to say and that it has been pretty skilled at hiding them from us through the clever ruse of holding up the prospect of possessing us and the way we talk about it if we dare to try.

Quick to judge, slow to understand: Jung's model of animus

The examples of Jung's attitude towards how animus speaks and regards the world are many and well known, such as when he described a woman's world as one that, 'outside her husband, terminates in a sort of cosmic mist' (1953: 338). Here, Jung only noticed one side of the imperative a woman may have to focus her energies on mothering and family and has not seen the powerful expressions of intellectual, creative and vocational drives that demand to be met beyond the 'cosmic mist'. In making this gross presumption Jung provided his own vivid example of animus possession.

For Jung, however, animus presents as the man-within who offers meaning and fact from 'out-there' through a filter of something childlike. Emma Jung stayed loyal to this idea of her husband's, writing that women who are animus possessed convey, 'instead of the thirst for knowledge, curiosity; instead of judgement, prejudice; instead of thinking, imagination or dreaming; instead of will, wishing' (Jung 2004: 16). However shocked our immediate responses are to this characterization of animus possession, it does expose the residue of the question begged by it, i.e. is there any value left in Jung's implication that the negative masculine hovers in women – in a form that closes down the possibility of incisive thinking and fruitful relations – in the same way that he asserts the negative form of anima swamps a man with sentiment and enfeebled relations with others? One way of seeing value somewhere in this is through the notion, discussed earlier, that animus possession can be constellated in both genders, whenever rash and irrational ideas and reactions take hold. This chapter refers to animus as 'it' rather than 'he' to reflect this. It has primitive qualities that leave people possessed by it, unconscious of the impact this may have on themselves or others.

My idea is that alongside this there may be ways in which animus presents differently in women and men. If there is any credibility (in a post-essentialist way) in this perspective, these differences could function via a conjunction of generalized ways of 'being' a man or woman, which have been imbibed from collective, archetypal, tendencies, on the one hand, and the filters of social influence and individualised narratives of postmodern living, on the other.

The difficulty in re-evaluating animus is that it was intertwined with Jung's personal shadow and cultural biases right from the start. In its negative form this loads animus as an archetypal masculine presence that is hard to approach, even to look at – like a man nobody wants to work or socialize with. Thus, the caricature of animus that Jung's formulation at times invites, can feed unhelpful caricatures of men and what have come to be perceived as spiritually bankrupt masculine values.

A recent example of this appears in an article on current understanding on differences between men and women from biological and neurological perspectives. This article was peppered with jokes, which all ridiculed men in terms of their supposed immaturity, domestic laziness and fixation on sex, as compared to women (for example, the question was asked, 'Why is psychoanalysis quicker for men than women?', and the answer given was, 'Because when it's time to recall childhood, he's already there' (Midgley 2006: 1)). This conveys an eerie animus quality, as if it were an unconscious compensation for the kinds of blanket generalizations about women associated with outdated patriarchal thinking as exemplified by Jung's ideas on animus.

This distaste towards animus is important, however. It raises the question of what versions of the masculine we might automatically dismiss as dogmatic, abusive, myopic or lazy. More importantly perhaps, it lends the temptation to dismiss animus as unworthy and irrelevant to the point where it no longer exists in our thinking about gender and relationship. I believe this is reflected in the general steering clear of animus in current thinking about gender, as well as the anticipated anxiety that arises when we imagine the difficulties we may get into when discussing it. The carefully calibrated neutrality on anima–animus that is currently de rigeur is perhaps another example of animus coaxing us into not getting too close.

So, how do we find a place for animus – if we think it deserves a place at all? My route into scrutinizing this question is, as I have suggested, via a consideration of the negative animus. I want to highlight three key features of it, encapsulated in the terms of animosity, lazy judgement and skewed meaning. These terms stand as counterpoint, though not necessarily in direct opposition, to these elements of positive animus: spiritual meaning, intellectual rigour and openness to competing truths.

Negative animus in the consulting room

Negative animus presents in the consulting room in ways that reflect the psychological realities it represents, as well as its power to reach into and across relationships. Three disguised examples from clinical experience (for which permission from patients has been granted) will be discussed. I will then draw on a particular story to convey where negative animus can be opened up and used to enrich relationships. My approach here is *experiential* and an attempt to be *playful* with animus, probably the last thing it – or the culture built up around it – wants us to be!

The first image is from a woman who dreamt a suave intruder with a gun breaks into her house – a man who she says 'knew what he was looking for' (with all the aggressive and erotic connotations this might carry). Meanwhile, her partner ignores what is happening and keeps working at his desk. She feels angry with this, but just sits and looks on as the intruder takes some items and leaves through the window. In her rage, she throws a book at her partner.

This, in turn, enrages the figure at the desk who shouts: 'I wanted him to take it! It belongs to him!' Here, animus takes both an active and a passive form and seems, among other things, to be suggesting this woman is in some area(s) of her life making assumptions which are not merited or are too hastily or lazily arrived at, something which was felt to be around in the transference too – not least in my noticing my countertransference responses to this woman as a little overpresumptive on my part at times. This level of animus possession in our work was made conscious through her growing awareness of polarized projections she began to own about men being either aggressive and cheating, or cowardly and self-absorbed.

The second example is one given in the introduction of a man who dreamt of a group of working men who didn't suffer fools or weakness and who congregated in their overalls and stared at the dreamer. This image hints at a kind of animus super-ego – not tolerating anything less than a fully fledged 'hard-day's-physical-graft' feel. The collective quality of this male image hints at Jung's original assertion that animus often presents in dream images that portray more than one figure, like 'an assembly of fathers' (1953: 332). He believed women supposedly needed to compensate for the singular, 'close-to-home' nature of their preoccupations. However, we know gender cannot be glibly ascribed as determining such attitudes.

If we open up this 'collective' image as a cross-gendered intolerant negative animus one, it suggests the need to move into investigating what is out there, in the collective, rather than in the familiarity of personal routine, with the challenge to be tough and get down to work on it. Here, the image pointed towards embracing adventure and culture, via the collective masculine.

The final vignette involves an older woman patient, who brought images of an inadequate father into the work, from dreams as well as from lived experience of a real father who had not focused his paternal energies on his family, but had got caught up in publicity and social outreach work for a political organization instead. This woman often revealed and expressed a deep-seated rage towards this version of the masculine, as that which had ignored, misunderstood and therefore betrayed her. As McNeely (1991: 90–1) argues, 'we don't have to attribute rage to the animus . . . (and) . . . women are capable of rage entirely on their own . . . a "just anger", not a narcissistic exhibition of strength'. However, in this case there was the presence of an animus expression of almost uncontainable judgement and disgust towards the father figure and the masculine generally. Inevitably, in our work I was often on the receiving end of this, as I became the father for this patient and caught her animus projections about the enfeebled and distracted father figure. Dream images that cropped up more than once were of an 'angry Jesus' and an 'angry giant' (as described in the opening lines of this chapter).

This seemed to capture well the feeling of animosity and distance, between her and her father and how that had got internalized in her lack of meaningful relations to men (and to life as a whole) – not to mention what may have been happening in the transference–countertransference. For this woman, there was no possibility as things stood, of a full relationship to life, and to the masculine in particular, because of its glaring role in apparently having undermined her psychological relationship to it. Negative animus had placed a barrier between her and the possibility of meaning in her life, particularly in the form of fulfilling relationships. The only possibility in the long term was to begin to notice the projection of this onto me and allow the active, aggressive and erotic animus components to become slowly available to her once more.

Summary of clinical observations

These three examples are suggestive of the negative power of animus – in the way it might close down thinking, split or undermine individual qualities through projection, make judgements and block the path to spiritual and/or psychological enrichment. It is worth noting the way that animus projections for the two women patients take the form of male figures, who are either weak, angry, untrustworthy, dangerous and/or distant. For the man, animus points the finger more directly at the dreamer. Although in no way claiming any confidence in this as a kind of gendered pattern, it does reflect the way, in my clinical experience, that animus dream material, projections and thoughts may tend to show themselves in *different ways of experiencing* between men and women. For men, negative animus may point out, in an often accusatory way, what the man is overlooking in himself and needs to act on. In women, it may portray the current polarization of the masculine in her psyche (for example, as alternating between dangerous and weak aspects), which gets projected onto men in reality if this is not made conscious. These projections may also reflect at a collective level a reaction to the legacy of centuries of patriarchal power, as constellated in the psyches of individual women.

These speculations obviously require further substantiation. One in particular – which is perhaps what Jung was so awkwardly trying to get at – is the idea that a man sometimes needs a woman to point out where his blindspots are and vice versa. However, because of the insidious influence of negative animus, the raising of consciousness that would ordinarily allow, becomes rigidified into dogmatic generalizations about men by women, and about women by men.

The theme I am promoting in this chapter is that animus constellates in women *and* men, but in differing ways. In its negative form, animus is often attacking and aggressive (or passively aggressive). I tentatively suggest that for women this can be more about projection onto male figures (internal and external), while for men it is more overtly an attack back on self – although this can take the form of aggressive thoughts or attacks outside themselves as a way of displacing the discomforting energy aroused. Either way, this theme sheds further light on why the notion of animus, in its negative form, is so hard to deal with – at first sight it just seems to want to sow blame, distrust and destructiveness. The quality of this apparently destructive energy feeding negative animus is clearly more *Thanatos* than *Eros*. Because Jung was seemingly unable to write about it without generating reactions and anxieties along these lines, this impression has become rigidified. However, a more positive form of animus can emerge from making these patterns conscious and this may be part of the reason for it being so problematic – it is for us to notice, confront and integrate, in similar fashion to (or maybe even part of) the task of integrating the *shadow*. This implies there is a value in immersing oneself in the negative animus and playing with its possibilities, including what it may reveal about possible differences in how life might be experienced by women and men.

Across Devil's Bridge: the gift of negative animus

When I was looking for a way of trying to conclude this chapter by encapsulating the way that negative animus can offer something ultimately healthy, I struggled to find a mythical template that might help, until I realized I had one under my nose. I live in the small market town of Kirby Lonsdale in the north of England. The town is built on the banks of the River Lune, which flows from the Cumbrian mountains down to Lancaster before emptying into the Irish Sea. There is a medieval bridge here, known as 'Devil's Bridge'; it is 700 years old but in a remarkably good state as well as a tourist draw.

It is the myth surrounding the construction of the bridge – or at least the most famous version, probably originating in the nineteenth century – which has currency for the negative animus theme. In this story (Armistead 1891: 156–9), a woman who lived in the town, and next to the river, wanted to cross it to recover her cow and pony who had gone through the water during the night and got stranded on the other side. While she lamented her misfortune, the Devil appeared and said he would build a bridge over the river if she gave him the first thing that crossed. He assumed it would be her, so he could claim her soul.

Next morning, when she arrived with her little lapdog (named *Cue*) she found that the bridge had been built in the night, and the Devil now tempted her to cross it to recover her animals. She, however, had the sense to throw a bun in front of her and let Cue run after it. She reminded the Devil of his bargain – so the dog was now his. The Devil disappeared in a rage and the woman crossed safely and returned with her horse and pony.

If we take the devil in his masculine, negative animus form rather than focusing on any predominantly *trickster* or *shadow* aspects (although they will be here too), then this woman's animus becomes posed as the possible bridge back 'home' (to the self?, or maybe just to a more grounded and balanced psyche) – but also as the barrier which could well block her safe return.

She had to make a sacrifice; the devil demanded the dog, or rather, animus demanded she sacrifice something instinctual in her in order to get past the negative, rigidified aspects of herself. She trusted in this process even though it involved risking the loss of something precious and the animus let her past. This is a particularly pertinent aspect of the story, as animus seems so often, through its resort to dogmatic (*senex*-like?), thinking, to represent something we have to face up to in ourselves – and sacrifice – before it will ease its grip on us.

The negative animus – as represented here by the powerful, manipulative Devil – is, however, open to negotiation. The story suggests that we sometimes need to go against our instincts when finding ourselves possessed by animus and confronted by an Other who may have activated this, particularly the gendered Other. In this case, a woman forces the Prince of Darkness to allow her across the bridge by taking her 'cue' from an instinct, which is ready to be sacrificed and hasn't been trapped across the river, away from her conscious control.

In the same way, we can too easily allow ourselves to be pulled across the bridge into a territory of lazy assumption, blame and closed thinking. Like the old lady we can only rescue our instincts and get home by sacrificing something – and maybe the aspect as represented by the dog is fundamentally our reliance on familiar, gendered roles and assumptions. That is where animus rears its head, in our close relationships it catches us and demands we play out binary rituals and routines of blame and projection.

This assertion could hold for gay as well as straight relationships, if we concur with the suggestion made above that animus (and anima) constellates in both genders. The challenges presented by negative animus – to notice and address rigidity of thinking about, and projections onto, the 'otherness' present in a partner – will remain for a same-sex relationship. However, the implications highlighted from my discussion of possible differences of presentation of animus in men and women requires further scrutiny for man–man and woman–woman relationships than this chapter can offer.

We have to sacrifice the power, the pleasure even, of our animus projections and cross the river, and go to where the gendered Other is, in order to use the presence of negative animus fruitfully. Otherwise, we fall into the dangers of gender 'certainty . . . (where) . . . the other gender is inferiorized' (Samuels 1989: 75). This applies I think, too, in our collective debates and arguments about gender. By keeping discussion of what its influence might really be taboo, animus retains the power to feed collective assumptions about the gendered Other – lazy assumptions made about men by women, and about women by men. These wider binary assumptions – and the negative power of animus – are sustained in part by our avoidance of it, as well as the possibility that animus may present differently in men and women. This avoidance snarls up the quality of discussion and closes down areas, which might not feel safe to explore. As a consequence, negative animus becomes a malevolent force that creates conflict and pain in relationships, and in collective projections between women and men – and it is this aspect of animus, I propose, which wants to stop us from examining, and therefore disarming, it.

To summarize, I make two propositions about animus: first, that it may present differently in men as compared to in women, and second, it thrives on being avoided and feared. Taking this into account, a new formulation for animus is needed and in this chapter, I have made an initial proposal that a cross-gendered version of animus operates in all of us, albeit with differing functions in women and men. In its negative form, its purpose seems to be to challenge us to overcome the tendency of being driven into a more primitive state of dogmatic and presumptive unconsciousness within our relationships with significant others (and, therefore, with ourselves). If such a new formulation cannot be found via fully 'envisaging animus' it will retain its powerful negative influence on gender relations, individual pathology and Jung's legacy.

References

Armistead, W. (1891) 'Tales and Legends of the English Lakes', in J. Westwood and J. Simpson *The Lore of the Land*, London: Penguin Books, 2005, pp. 761–79.

Freud, S. (1905) *Three Essays on the Theory of Sexuality*, A. Richards, The Penguin Freud Library, Volume 7, London: Penguin Books, 1991.

Hauke, C. (2000) *Jung and the Postmodern; The Interpretation of Realities*, London and New York: Routledge.

Hill, C. (1992) *Masculine and Feminine: The Natural Flow of Opposites in the Psyche*, Boston, MA: Shambhala.

Jung, C.G. (1959) 'The Syzygy: Anima and Animus', *CW* 9ii, 1959/1968: 20–42.

—— (1953) 'Anima and Animus', *CW* 7, 1953/1966: 296–340.
Jung, E. (2004) *Animus & Anima: Two Essays*, Dallas, TX: Spring.
Lemaire, A. (1994) *Jacques Lacan*, London and New York: Routledge.
McNeely, A. (1991) *Animus Aeternus*, Toronto: Inner City Books.
Midgley, C. (2006) *Lobal Warfare*, London, *The Times*, 9 August.
Rowland, S. (2002) *Jung: A Feminist Revision*, Cambridge: Polity.
Samuels, A. (1985) *Jung and the Post-Jungians*, London and New York: Routledge.
—— (1989) *The Plural Psyche*, London and New York: Routledge.
Woodman, M. (1990) *The Ravaged Bridegroom*, Toronto: Inner City Books.

Chapter 13

Plato's Echo: a feminist refiguring of the anima

Frances Gray

C.G. Jung represents the feminine in at least two related ways: as anima feminine and as maternal feminine. In this chapter, I argue that Jung's conception of the anima is closely related to Plato's conception of the irrational – or soul disorder – as feminine. I maintain that Plato's idea of mimesis or imitation is important in Jung's construction of the psyche. Just as Plato argues in *The Republic* that it is morally undesirable to mirror properties of women through imitation, so in Jung's work, it is undesirable for the moral imagination to be inspired by the anima feminine. The anima feminine has a functional role to play, however, as a source of moral caution, very like the irrational or womanly in *The Republic*: look at women and you will see what you should not be like. Luce Irigaray defies Plato's recommendation to avoid miming the irrational and her writing expresses this defiance. According to Irigaray, mimicry has been historically assigned to the feminine in the male symbolic. By strategically using *mimesis* – especially '*mimesis* as production which would lie more in the realm of music' (1985b: 131)[1] – women may be able to develop their own symbolic. In that symbolic 'the possibility of a woman's writing may come about' based on the use of productive mimesis. She argues that 'one must assume the feminine role deliberately. Which means already to convert a form of subordination into an affirmation, and thus to begin to thwart it' (ibid.: 76). For Irigaray, women are 'the mute outside that sustains all systematicity [and is the] still silent ground that nourishes all foundations [so they do not] have to conform to the codes theory has set up for itself' (1985a: 365). I claim that in Irigaray's defiance we find the seeds for a potential revolution of the individuation process for women, which takes a very different turn from that conceived and valorized by Jung. Thus, at the end of the chapter I respond to Jung's idea that it is sometimes appropriate for a devoted and self-sacrificing, unconscious woman to attack her insignificant husband.

Both Plato and Jung continue to exercise authority and to inspire admiration or contempt, as they are read and reread for their arguably valuable insights into human being and human relationship. Plato's philosophy underpins much of Western moral, political and theological thought,[2] and

Jung's thinking has emerged in our everyday ways of interpreting the world. But their respective views, and later interpretations of these views, diverge and clash. Among them we find feminist readings that contribute to the richness of this contested terrain.

Whether Plato and Jung are feminist or anti-feminist are debates that cannot be settled; instead they generate new questions and open up new territory.[3] Plato is not consistently pro-women or anti-women. He argues that cowardly soldiers are womanly, which suggests that there are some properties of women he thinks undesirable (Spelman 1988: 33). Yet he also thinks women can be superior to men (Plato 455d). The fact that Plato allows women to be guardians in his republic was in his time regarded as outrageous.[4] Even though Plato was once thought of as a champion of women because of this apparent concession to women, his pro-women stance has been problematized. Furthermore, even if he were pro-women (as he seems to be in Book V of *The Republic*) it does not follow from that that he was a feminist. Jung's apparent championing of the feminine through his development of the concept of the anima has its appeal and its detractors. Jung's ideas about the anima as a feminine principle follow, very closely, Plato's evaluation of the Athenian women, which we find in *The Republic*. In this chapter, I attempt to open up new territory by reading Jung as if he is a successor to Plato's anti-woman (and, possibly his anti-feminist and anti-feminine) stance. Furthermore, I argue that Plato's apparent pro-feminist stance – that some women can have the rights that some men can have in the republic, and thus by virtue of the kinds of souls they have, can be guardians – comes at a cost. That cost is abandonment of the feminine in favour of a narrow, privileged and privileging notion of the masculine. Lastly, I propose that Luce Irigaray's ironic appropriation of the Platonic feminine – a feminine found also in Jung's work – gestures towards a different kind of individuation for women from that envisaged by Jung.

Plato and mimesis as imitation

In *The Republic* Plato raises the question of the *moral* worthiness of imitation (mimesis). If practiced from a young age, imitation leaves an impression on 'character and nature, on body and voice and mind' (Plato 395d). We should not, Plato continues, allow future guardians:

> Who are men and men who must grow up good, to imitate a woman, whether she be young or old, either railing at her husband, or striving or vaunting herself against the gods, thinking she is happy, or overcome by misfortune, or grief, or tears; much less shall we allow them to imitate one who is ill or in love or in labour.

Guardians should also not imitate male or female slaves, mad men, bad men and women, and cowards, but they 'must know' of them (Plato 396a).

This 'must' is to be read as a moral imperative: it is morally desirable to be acquainted with different modes of being, but what *should* be imitated is limited to that which brings about order, harmony and knowledge of the good. Morality, which has to do with one's habits, turns on the notion of the habitual doing of that which brings about and maintains order. For Plato, morality imposes order, and order is necessary for society to flourish. Order is a key ideal in society even to this day. If we extrapolate Plato's directive beyond the guardian class, we find a principled approach for the living of any human life: seek out and imitate only what is good; do not imitate what is bad and seek to avoid it for fear of moral peril.

Plato argues that there are three forms of poetry and storytelling: simple narration, simple narration that includes imitation, and straightforward imitation. He argues that the speech of guardians should demonstrate a preference for simple narration including imitation, since a guardian should not be ashamed of imitating the actions and person of a good man (Plato 396d). Imitation of the actions and person of a good man would be consistent with the one task for which a guardian is suited; that is, to know the good and to practice that which promotes the good and thus the flourishing of the republic. The poet who can be admitted to the city or the republic, he concludes, should be austere and not twofold or manifold in his talents, because he will act as a model for educating the guardians. The poetry of the austere poet/storyteller will 'be to our profit' and the poet 'will imitate for us the diction of the good man and in saying what he has to say will conform to those canons which we laid down originally when we were undertaking the task of educating the soldiers' (Plato 398b). Poets are morally worthy, in other words where they exemplify the speech and actions of a good man; and this is the one thing they should be good at.[5]

Yet Plato also argues that mimesis is foundational in the making of our character. Mimesis grounds the moral imagination, and our perception and understanding of our world. Mimesis as imitation exposes us to various moral properties and characteristics, and as a form of representation it expresses the moral imagination. If we allow ourselves or another to imitate goodness or badness, then such exposure will affect our characters. So, mimesis distances us from truth because it is an imitation of it, yet mimesis is also instrumental in the development of the moral imagination which facilitates the apprehension of goodness and badness. We are influenced by the stories of poets and storytellers, either consciously or unconsciously.[6] As Charles Griswold puts it, Plato:

> Is asserting, though without filling out the psychological mechanisms in the detail for which one would wish, that from childhood up, mimesis shapes our images and our fantasies, our unconscious or semiconscious pictures and feelings, and thereby shapes our characters,

> especially that part of our nature prone to what he thinks of as irrational or non-rational.
>
> (Griswold 2005)

Mimesis can be intentional or unintentional. The pervasive influence mimesis has in our lives comes about through our being in the world: we learn by imitating and this is usually unconscious, so unintentional. Contrariwise, mimesis can also be intentional, as it is in the case of the poets. Mimesis, on this account, brings us closer to, and distances us from, truth. Mimesis acts as a mirror to the world, imitating and representing the objects of that world and its moral properties. It brings the world to us through words, images and associations; and takes us to the world through its constructive representation of ourselves in that world. Mimesis is instrumental in our epistemic access to, and moral relationships with, our worlds. Mimesis as imitation and as representation *is* morally worthy, with the caution that we can be deluded by imitation where effects are detrimental to our moral characters through exposure of the wrong kind.

Plato's directive that we should know what is bad and mad without imitating them, is instructive here in terms of gender conceptions. His examples of the mad and the bad allude to women and to what we might think of as anima–feminine properties. The properties of women that Plato requires men – especially those who are guardian of the republic – to avoid are those feminine properties that characterize Jung's negative conception of the anima.

Plato's view is that women are bad because they have disordered souls. In Plato's tripartite soul, reason brings us closest to truth: passion assists reason in its apprehension of truth, and desire is the errant factor of the soul which leads us astray. Thus desire is the element in us that is removed from insight. Desire is the least worthy aspect of the soul, obfuscating and leading us astray. To be ruled by desire is to be womanly and unreliable. Indeed, Plato holds in contempt those governed by desire. The exception is women who have manly souls ordered by reason.[7] These women can become guardians; furthermore, these women are superior to some men, for not all men have souls ruled by reason, and so not all men are potential guardians. In view of the fact that most women, according to Plato, are ruled by desire rather than reason, and are thus irrational, most women are bound to the bad, and are unworthy of imitation. Woman, the bad and the irrational form a triumgynate, the imitation of which leads to moral unworthiness, moral failure and immoral character.

Jung and mimesis as imitation

Jung's discussion of identification as imitation echoes Plato's analysis of imitation as a mode of mimesis. Identification is itself a mode of mimesis by virtue of its being unconscious imitation. Hence we can construe mimesis as an integral constructive mechanism of the Jungian psyche. Jung distinguishes conscious and unconscious imitation. He calls unconscious imitation 'identification' and cites the example of a son's adopting 'all of the father's ways of behaving, as though the son were the same as the father and not a separate individuality' (Jung 1921: 738). Jung holds that identification of aspects of oneself with that of another is beneficial until such time as one comes across something that requires that one give it up and perhaps become identified with a different object, or abandon identification completely. In this sense, a confrontation arises between the psychic identification with the other and the possibility of something else: the new object of identification or abandonment of identification. According to Jung, in this confrontation we see identification show its 'morbid character by becoming just as great a hindrance as it was an unconscious help before. It now has a dissociative effect, splitting the individual into two mutually estranged personalities' (Jung, 1921: 738).

Jung argues that conscious 'imitation is an indispensable aid in developing the youthful personality. It is beneficial so long as it does not serve as a mere convenience and hinder the development of ways and means suited to the individual' (Jung 1921: 738). Like Plato, Jung seems to have in mind the idea that intentional imitation is a springboard for the emulation of goodness. Jung's qualifying 'so long as . . .' brings our attention to the potential for becoming lost in the object of admiration, of slipping into unconscious imitation or identification. As individuals, we need to be aware that our way of being in the world is uniquely our own, and that to imitate another to the extent that one no longer is oneself, is to betray our obligation to our own subjectivity.

Becoming psychologically lost or slipping into unconscious identification reveals the psyche's projective directedness where subject and object are fused: I am no longer myself because I blur the boundaries between myself and the love object (or object of hate). In this light, imitation is the consort of projection, and together they initiate imaginative modes of engagement with the world. Through these imaginative modes and their instantiations, their relative dominance and recession over time, and the development of individual identity, mimesis and projection, reveal the dialectic between subject and the world. Projection and mimesis are means by which psyche and the world enact their mutual engagement, consciously and unconsciously in their intentionality or *directedness towards an object*. I make the world mine and I do that through mimesis. Imitation, in other words, is a fundamental disposition of the psyche. I learn how to be human because of mimesis, because I am disposed towards imitating as a way of learning and being. And I also learn about and encounter the moral domain.

As we saw, Plato argues that one should intentionally imitate *good* moral character, and that the danger of poetry lies in the possibility of assimilating the morally unworthy, and also in the deceptive assumption that poetry expresses truth. The moral dimensions of mimesis are intertwined with its constitutive existential function. Character is *moral* character: one's identity is always a *moral* identity. So that mimesis is not merely productive of a subject or a self. Insofar as one's character is one's identity, one is a *morally* situated and a *morally* permeated subject or self. On this view, the characterization of the Platonic soul as ordered or disordered is not simply an existential diagnosis, but also a *moral* diagnosis. And the same holds for Jung's analysis of the psyche.

Jung's elucidation of conscious imitation and unconscious identification suggests that each has a moral dimension presupposed by the disquietude evident in the struggle for individuation. The moral dimensions of mimesis traverse both conscious and unconscious. The crisis into which an individual is thrown centres on her identity: how she has previously understood herself and what kind of understanding she will now have of herself given this new dimension and the crisis in which she is embroiled.[8] Existential discombobulation poses questions about who one is but not only that, it raises questions about who one *ought* to be. This 'ought' is a moral ought conceived in terms of responsibility to oneself and to one's community. The notion of responsibility arises out of the relational aspect of mimesis. While I imitate you, I deny your integrity and individuality as I appropriate moments of your being which are not mine to appropriate. While I imitate you, I deny my own integrity, my own moments and places in the world by abrogating the responsibility I have to my own being qua my own identity. In other words, mimesis grounds the psyche as a moral domain from which arises notions of identity and of personal and community responsibility. This occurs at the level of identification and conscious imitation, and also at the level of moral caution.

The notion of appropriation is important here. In a sense we are all expected to imitate the values and practices of our communities. We are 'thrown' (in an Heideggerian sense) into collectives, which appropriate us at birth as potential community members. Through collective membership we develop as cultural identities – as women and men through the valorization and condemnation of modes of behaviour and attitudes. Plato's directive that men should not imitate women can be seen as a demand for the normalization of manly behaviour and disposition, and the pathologizing of womanly behaviour and disposition. His directive, in other words, is about appropriating bodies and behaviour for a masculine ideal that valorizes manliness and the masculine, and deprecates womanliness and the irrational feminine. Jung's interpretation of these gender concepts is not unlike Plato's.

We saw that in *The Republic*, Plato's characterization of the soul assumes a preference for one kind of soul over another, based on a gendered attribution of 'womanly' and 'manly' properties. Jung's elucidation of anima and animus follows Plato and ensures the overvaluation of the masculine or manly and the undervaluation of the anima feminine or womanly. It is not simply that the psyches of men are masculine psyches and those of women are feminine. Anima and animus are an acknowledgement of the internally gendered nature of the psyche. An examination of the properties of each and what each *does* in men and women, clearly demonstrates that a system of gender privileging similar to Plato's is operating in Jung's psychic architectonic. For example, Jung's discussion of the anima and animus as inferior functions sees them as contaminants of the larger personality (Jung 1953: 296ff). But, when we look closely, we see that contamination works *against* women and the anima feminine, and always *for* men and the masculine.

In a man, the anima is redeemed by the complementary role it plays in individuation – the moodiness of the anima abets the turn inwards. The feminine as anima is a kind of psychological catalyst for a necessary change in a man. Yet the obviously unflattering portrayal of the anima as a feminine principle reveals Jung's ambivalence about the anima feminine.[9] The notion of the anima feminine as a catalyst is supported by Jung's claim that the animus or male principle within a woman is corrupted and reduced to a petty utterer of dubious opinions (Jung 1953: 331). Indeed, we might think of both anima and animus as vehicles for a deeply misogynistic undercurrent in Jung's work.

The contaminating influence of anima and animus reflects the Platonic conception of the masculine and feminine, as well as the situation in the social world where men and women are disproportionately valued. The anima feminine is almost always malfigured with respect to the masculine; and it is undervalued even when its constitutive role in psychological development is acknowledged. One might wonder on this basis about the gendered nature of individuation. The notion of wholeness implicit in individuation is more closely aligned with Plato's conception of the ordered soul, and therefore with a masculine ideal of reason, than it is with a conception of balance between positive masculine and anima feminine characteristics. The notion 'positive feminine characteristics' becomes oxymoronic because the feminine and irrationality, or soul disorder, are synonymous. Jung's descriptions of individuation – as 'a process of differentiation having for its goal the development of the individual personality', and as a 'natural necessity inasmuch as its prevention by a levelling down to collective standards is injurious to the vital activity of the individual' (Jung 1921: 757–8) – affirms the moral, as well as the existential imperative, to become uniquely oneself. The experience of individuating means the experience of emerging from the collective by conscious endeavour, even though this might be initiated at an unconscious level. The individuated person is not only a person who knows what the mad and the bad are, but is also someone who does not imitate the mad and the bad. In other words, the mediating activity of the transcendent function – so central to the formation of the emerging self – directs the psyche towards a rational order in much the same way as reason mediates the dialectic between passion and desire in the Platonic soul. To be individuated is to abandon the anima feminine. In the case of a woman, it is to cede her disorder to the demand for rationality as order. It is to accept the moral demand that is imposed by non-imitation of the bad and mad, conceived in terms of order, where passion and desire are secondary to the rational. It is indeed to become more masculine or more manly.

Irigaray, individuation, and mimesis

Jung, when commenting on the 'nothing—but daughter', the 'woman who is so identified with her mother that her own instincts are paralysed through projection', remarks that:

> [T]hese women remind me – if I may be forgiven the impolite comparison – of hefty great bitches who turn tail before the smallest cur simply because he is a terrible male and it never occurs to them to bite him.
>
> (Jung 1938/1954: 182)[10]

This unsubtle characterization of the woman trapped by the mother archetype, of which she is not yet conscious, brings together excessive identification or unconscious imitation and the irrationality of the disordered soul. Such a woman cannot progress on the path of individuation unless she is able to confront her mother complex and resolve it in some appropriate manner. But what is appropriate is circumscribed by order, by the conscious weighing of psychological options made available through imaginative encounter with the unconscious and through dream analysis. Suppose, however, that the woman *does* bite the terrible male and that her modus operandi is *inappropriate*: instead of being lured by order, the woman embraces the anima feminine, the irrational which is not to be imitated. What would be the consequences of this? Luce Irigaray's wager is that women will, by ironic appropriation of the biting feminine, find a new feminine not constructed within the masculine symbolic. This new feminine can be thought of as a *feminine* feminine as distinct from the *masculine* feminine that biting feminine women are to deliberately imitate. Let us see how she works this out.

Using mimesis as a politico-ethical tool, Luce Irigaray defies Plato's directive to mime only that which is edifying. In the context of her assertion that 'any theory of the "subject" has been appropriated by the "masculine"' (1985a: 133), Irigaray corrupts standard academic methodology by deliberately adopting the Platonic feminine and its voice of disorder, of irrationality. This imaginative ploy sets in motion the possibility of gendered individuation, not through sameness of procedure but through acknowledgement and valorization of sexual difference. The unkempt feminine of the anima feminine becomes Irigaray's means for producing a potentially new feminine, characterized neither as anima nor as maternal. In Irigaray's work, we can identify a moral imperative to individuate over and against the dominating masculine.[11] How does she do this?

Irigaray redeploys the moral imagination in terms that do not conjoin and then valorize the good-as-rational-order. We saw in Plato's account of the soul and then in Jung's account of anima, that a key element of the good is its identification with the rational as an ordering of the psyche. One becomes good by imitating the good, and by making available only good models for mimesis. Where such models are not directly available, counter-examples are seen as morally cautionary and to be avoided. On this account, women are not good because they have, on the whole, womanly or feminine souls – the mark of which is disorder. Luce Irigaray maintains that this theory of subjectivity constitutes the feminine and women's identities through their being assigned the moral turpitude of the masculine and of men: Luce Irigaray regards the mad and the bad as important aspects assigned to women by the male symbolic. In other words, the feminine is a projection, but such a deeply entrenched projection that it is regarded as natural. We might think of the feminine in this context as a *masculine* feminine. The terms of Luce Irigaray's account are Lacanian: she claims that the symbolic and the imaginary are masculine. Thus masculine assumptions and power relations permeate representation. Luce Irigaray's intuition is that a *feminine* feminine can be retrieved by reappropriation of what is assigned to women (1985a: passim). She seems to be invoking a feminine that is present before little girls are initiated into the masculine symbolic (1985a: 13–129).

Hence Irigaray imagines a *feminine* feminine subject issuing from *masculine* feminine disorder. The former, is however, still embryonic and potential. Since writing is germane to theories of the subject, she deliberately subverts the discursive canons of philosophy and psychoanalysis by miming the *masculine* feminine – the irrational disorder by which women are represented (1985a: 72). This radical proposal entails a rethinking of the moral dimensions of the imagination and individuation. It boldly opens the moral imagination onto new oceans of possibility, and it has the potential to re-imagine the *masculine* feminine as more than an opposite derivative of the masculine psyche – as a *feminine* feminine with value in itself. Furthermore, the proposal implies a radical rethinking of the collective unconscious and its masculine gendered nature. As Lacan has pointed out, the symbolic and the unconscious are the same (2002: 469). He is speaking of the *collective unconscious*. The *feminine* feminine which will emerge is a *feminine* feminine symbolic, hence a *feminine* feminine unconscious. But mostly, with the making of a *feminine* feminine and resistance of women to the masculine symbolic, the masculine unconscious will force a refiguring of the masculine, which is not dependent on the notion of disorder or the anima feminine, or on the maternal feminine, all of which might be thought of as falling under the category of the *masculine* feminine.

Luce Irigaray's work opens up new ways of thinking about the feminine, mimesis, morality, and the relationship between men and women. In arguing that women are assigned a place in the symbolic, over which women have no control due to the insidious nature of that symbolic and its initiatory practices (Irigaray 1985a: passim), Irigaray is attempting to reconceive women within an existential–moral framework. The upshot of her work, which is highly controversial,[12] is that when we read her alongside Plato and Jung, we can see that her work intersects with major concerns and questions of these two thinkers: the nature of justice and goodness, the idea of identity as expressed in the soul and the psyche, and the meaning of individuation. And the task before us is to see through mimesis and take her argument to the making of new women and new men who embody their own forms of feminine and masculine being; and to imagine the possibilities for a new relationship between them.

Notes

1 Here Irigaray refers to Plato's two senses of mimesis: the productive to which I have just referred, and mimesis 'already caught up in a process of imitation, specularization, adequation, and production. It is the second form that is privileged throughout the history of philosophy'. Irigaray uses both forms of mimesis, but in her later writings, promotes the first. See also, Naomi Schor (1994) for a good discussion of this distinction. I thank Morny Joy for pointing this out.

2 Alfred North Whitehead famously remarked that:

> So far as concerns philosophy only a selected group can be explicitly mentioned. There is no point in endeavouring to force the interpretations of divergent philosophers into a vague agreement. What is important is that the scheme of interpretation here adopted can claim for each of its main positions the express authority of one, or the other, of some supreme master of thought – Plato, Aristotle, Descartes, Locke, Hume, Kant. But ultimately nothing rests on authority; the final court of appeal is intrinsic reasonableness. The safest general characterization of the European philosophical tradition is that it consists of a series of footnotes to Plato. I do not mean the systematic scheme of thought which scholars have doubtfully extracted from his writings. I allude to the wealth of general ideas scattered through them'
>
> (1979: 39).

In my view, it is not only the philosophical tradition that is in debt to Plato, but European/Western thinking in general.

3 See the edited collection by Nancy Tuana, *Feminist Interpretations of Plato*

(1994), which is an extended discussion of Plato's philosophy and political theory. On Jung, see Naomi R. Goldenberg (1976) 'A Feminist Critique of Jung'; Susan Rowland (2002) *Jung: A Feminist Revision.*

4 See Gregory Vlastos (1994).

5 The problem with poets however, Plato later argues, is that as imitators, they do not represent reality: the imitative man, of whom poets exemplify, have 'no knowledge of any value on the subject of his imitation; (and) that imitation is a form of amusement and not a serious occupation' (Plato 602b). Poets are three times removed from the truth as all imitation 'produces work that is quite removed from the truth, and also associates with that element in us which is removed from insight, and is its companion and is friend to no healthy or true purpose' (ibid.: 603b).

6 One of the effects of poetry is that it represents to us aspects of ourselves, of which we might be ashamed. In so doing, poetry forms our imagination by allowing us to think and feel in ways we would not readily admit to. This is one reason we need to be wary of poets. They enact mimesis in their work and while acknowledging their influence, we cannot be certain of the precise nature of that influence, of whether it is good or bad.

7 Elizabeth Spelman uses the terms 'manly soul' and 'womanly soul'. She argues that masculine nature and rational embodiment are closely linked. A manly soul is characterized by the dominance of reason and a womanly soul by the dominance of desire. A manly soul is ordered and a womanly soul is disordered. 'Rational' and 'order' are paired descriptors and 'disorder' and 'irrational' are paired descriptors, in both cases, paired by sameness rather than difference. According to Plato male soldiers who are cowards have womanly or irrational souls. Badness (and madness) are bad and mad because the soul is disordered. See *Inessential Woman*, Spelman, 1988.

8 We might think of the activation of the anima archetype in this way when the persona archetype fails as an existential option. A man unconsciously imitates what he takes to be an acceptable self in the world, projecting a version of himself in which he has great investment. The struggle that ensues once the anima is activated enacts a psychological crisis that can be settled only with the withdrawal of the relevant projection and the instigation of a new phase of psychic life.

9 '[S]he intensifies, exaggerates, falsifies and mythologizes all emotional relations with his work and with other people of both sexes. The resultant fantasies and entanglements are all her doing. When the anima is strongly constellated, she softens the man's character and makes him touchy, irritable, moody, jealous, vain and unadjusted' (Jung 1936/1954: 144).

10 It is significant that this comment occurs in 'Psychological Aspects of the Mother Archetype', Part 4, 'Positive Aspects of the Mother-Complex' (Jung 1938/1954).

11 I argue for this view of individuation in my forthcoming book, *Jung, Irigaray, Individuation.*

12 See, for example, Deutscher 2002; Grosz, 1989; Moi, 1985; Rowland, 2002; Schüssler-Fiorenza, 1992; Whitford, 1991; among others.

References

Deutscher, P. (2002) *A Politics of Impossible Difference: The Later Works of Luce Irigaray*, Ithaca, NY and London: Cornell University Press.

Goldenberg, N.R. (1976) 'A Feminist Critique of Jung', *Signs*, 2, 2, 443–9.

Gray, F. (2007) *Jung, Irigaray, Individuation*, London: Routledge.

Griswold, C. (2005) 'Plato on Rhetoric and Poetry', *The Stanford Encyclopedia of Philosophy (Summer 2005 Edition)*, E.N. Zalta (ed.), Online. Available at http://www.plato.stanford.edu/archives/sum2005/entries/plato-rhetoric/. Accessed 18 June 2006.

Grosz, E. (1989) *Sexual Subversions: Three French Feminists*, St Leonards: Allen & Unwin.

Irigaray, L. (1985a) 'Any Theory of the "Subject" Has Always Been Appropriated by the "Masculine"' in *Speculum of the Other Woman*, trans. G.C. Gill, Ithaca, NY and New York: Cornell University Press.

—— (1985b) *This Sex Which is not One*, trans. C. Porter and C. Burke, New York: Cornell University Press.

Jung, C.G. (1921) 'Definitions', *CW* 6, 1971: 672–844.

—— (1953) 'Anima and Animus', *CW* 7, 1953/1966: 296–340.

—— (1936/1954) 'Concerning the Archetypes, with Special Reference to the Anima Concept', *CW* 9i, 1959/1968: 111–47.

—— (1938/1954) 'Psychological Aspects of the Mother Type', *CW* 9i, 1959/1968: 148–98.

Lacan, J. (2002) *Ecrits*, trans. B. Fink, H. Fink and R. Grigg, New York and London: W.W. Norton.

Moi, T. (1985) *Sexual Textual Politics*, London and New York: Routledge.

Plato (1992) *The Republic*, trans. A.D. Lindsay, London: Everyman.

Rowland, S. (2002) *Jung: A Feminist Revision*, Cambridge: Polity.

Schor, N. (1994) 'This Essentialism Which Is Not One', in C. Burke, N. Schor and M. Whitford (eds) *Engaging With Irigaray*, New York: Colombia University Press, pp. 57–78.

Schüssler-Fiorenza, E. (1992) *But She Said*, Boston, MA: Beacon Press.

Spelman, E. (1988) *Inessential Woman: Problems of Exclusion in Feminist Thought*, Boston, MA: Beacon Press.

Tuana, N. (ed.) (1994) *Feminist Interpretations of Plato*, University Park, PA: Pennsylvania State University Press.

Vlastos, G. (1994) 'Was Plato a Feminist?' in N. Tuana (ed.) *Feminist Interpretations of Plato*, University Park, PA: Pennsylvania State University Press.

Whitehead, A.N. (1979) *Process and Reality*, New York: The Free Press.

Whitford, M. (1991) *Luce Irigaray: Philosophy in the Feminine*, London and New York: Routledge.

Chapter 14

Re-imagining the child: challenging social constructionist views of childhood

Shiho Main

Introduction

The aim of this chapter is to explore some of the issues related to adults' images of children from a Jungian perspective, in comparison with one of the current popular views on images: the social constructionist perspective. As one context in which images of children could be examined, I shall look at international legislation concerning children's rights, namely, the United Nations Convention on the Rights of the Child.[1]

The central question with which I shall engage is whether all child images are socially constructed, and if not, how can one challenge the predominant social frameworks for understanding childhood issues. I shall consider (1) the diversity of child images; (2) the social constructionist perspective on child images; (3) a Jungian perspective on child images; (4) a comparison between the aforementioned two perspectives on child images (using as an example debates around current international legislation about children's rights); and finally (5) an evaluation of the Jungian perspective on issues regarding child images. I shall suggest some ways in which a Jungian perspective might advance debates about images of children and childhood to which the social constructionist perspective has been making the most significant recent contribution.

Diversity of child images

There is increasing interest in issues related to childhood and need for various kinds of work concerned with children. Discourses about children's welfare and rights have been turned into not only charities but also international legislation.[2] Today's debates continue in the areas of development, education, health, poverty, delinquency, child protection, and child and youth culture, to name a few.

It is surprising how much we learn about adults once we start looking at issues about childhood. However hard adults try, children's minds are not directly accessible by adults. Instead, adults make inferences about children's minds, and present different theories and opinions about children, which often lead to heated debates. Researches on children – ranging from psychological to sociological, philosophical, historical, anthropological, ethnographical, sociolegal, and so on – are ultimately adults' enquiries and explanations of childhood (even when their methods employ an insider viewpoint). Socially constructed images and public discourses of childhood could be seen as adults' expectations and assumptions about childhood. Similarly, legislation about children is based on adults' knowledge and images of children and leads to adults' intervention in childhood. Thus, what prevents adults from accessing children's minds remains: it is adults' own minds that get in the way when speaking about children.

It has also been debated whether we need to include more of children's own voices, experiences, and views of childhood. Although this is another vital issue, it is a separate to the current one, and in this chapter I shall focus on adults' images of children. Nevertheless, the latter is not unrelated to the former, since adults' images of children is the very factor that often cannot be prevented from interfering in listening to children's voices and in understanding children's views.

The social constructionist perspective on child images

The social constructionist perspective, with its preference for cultural relativism, has greatly contributed to increasing awareness of diversities of child images in different places and at different times, and to making us cautious of taking whatever is talked about childhood at face value or as universal, predetermined, fixed facts (see James and Prout 1990; James et al. 1998; Jenks 1982, 1996; Montgomery 2003; Stainton-Rogers 2003; Stainton-Rogers and Stainton-Rogers 1989, 1992).

For instance, James and colleagues write that 'childhood does not exist in a finite and identifiable form' (1998: 27). They hold that 'knowledge of the child and its lifeworld depends on the social, political, historical and moral context' (ibid.). Suspending 'assumptions about the existence and causal powers of a social structure that makes things, like childhood, as they are', they emphasize 'the issue of plurality and [that], far from this model recommending a unitary form, it foregrounds diverse constructions' (ibid.).

For the social constructionist perspective meaning is constructed, and it is the process of subjective meaning making that brings about the rich diversity of child images. To some extent, the social constructionist perspective touches on the unconscious in the process of social construction. It attempts to probe beneath what is taken for granted and to bring what is found there to conscious recognition.

According to this perspective, all our images of children and childhood are to be seen as social constructions. This could be understood to mean that the origins of child images could be traced to particular values embedded in specific cultural contexts in particular times and places. The debate has moved on from Ariès' original claim that the idea of childhood did not exist in medieval society (1962: 463),[3] to many modern discourses about childhood (for instance, children as innocent, sinful, a blank slate, autonomous, rights holders).[4] Nevertheless, from the social constructionist point of view, all these images are products of particular societies and human meaning making. A question arises as to whether, from this viewpoint, this means that society and culture are the only source of, and a limit for, our imagination.

In short, from the social constructionist perspective:

- Images are social constructions.
- Meanings of images are taken-for-granted (unconscious) but there are conscious values underpinning them.
- Images are diverse depending on time, place, and culture.

A Jungian perspective on child images

The diversity of child images can also be observed in analytical psychology, particularly as manifestations of the child archetype. From a Jungian perspective, some images, including some child images, come from beyond the social realm. The collective unconscious is thought to be the realm of the psyche from which such images emerge. The archetype of the child in the collective unconscious manifests itself in the form of archetypal images. The archetype itself is unknown, universal and timeless, while the archetypal images are diverse. Such archetypal images are symbols (Jung 1940: 273, n.21; 1961: 481). Likewise, the collective unconscious is to be distinguished from the personal unconscious, the latter of which could produce images that are primarily based on personal, social or cultural experiences and contexts (Jung 1916).

From a Jungian perspective:

- Some images come from beyond the social realm.
- The collective unconscious plays a significant role in certain images.
- Diverse archetypal images are the expressions of the universal archetype.

The child archetype

In order to understand Jungian perspectives on child images, it is necessary to look more closely at the child archetype. The archetype of the child is one of the archetypes in the collective unconscious. The concept of the archetypes within Jungian psychology is not straightforward (see, for example, Hogenson 2004; Knox 2003). However, in order to pursue the dialogue with social constructionism with regard to child images, we will focus on the following aspects of the archetypes. As an archetype, 'the child' exhibits duality and integrates opposites – such as beginning and end; the pre-conscious and the post-conscious essence of humans; futurity and past; male and female; unity and plurality (Jung 1940: 271–300) – and many other paired elements. Similarly, like any other archetype, 'the child' could also be the source of unconscious projections (which need to be recognized in order to integrate them). 'The child' is not real but a motif, and manifests itself as symbolic images of the child, whose characteristics are archaic, autonomous, spontaneous, and numinous, while 'the child' itself is unknown.

Jung also writes that 'the child is a symbol of the self' (1946: 378, 531; 1952: 522).[5] The concept of the self as an archetype, too, cannot be introduced without complexities (see, for example, Colman 2006). Nevertheless, here we will continue the discussion with a current understanding that the child is in relation to, or intertwined with, a whole package of many other archetypes (such as senex, parental imagos, Great Mother, hero, God, hermaphrodite, and so on) in the collective unconscious; and that the self, which can be symbolized by the child, organizes all archetypes in the collective unconscious (see Main forthcoming). As symbolizing the archetype of the self, 'the child' could represent wholeness, the whole personality, and the totality of the psyche, which is worked towards through the individuation process.

In these ways, 'the child' could be seen as both the origin of symbolic images and the goal of individuation. Whether it is seen as being an archetype or as representing the self, or as the origin or the goal, 'the child' is not determined by age. The child archetype is, in Jung's view, an objective fact and beyond subjective experience or social and cultural conditions or contexts (Jung 1957: 562). This perspective presupposes an objective world in which all human beings and individual psyches participate. Therefore, the meaning is objective rather than constructed.

Comparison between the social constructionist and Jungian perspectives on child images

Having looked at the social constructionist and Jungian perspectives on child images, their differences can be summarized in terms of (a) sources of our images; (b) meanings; (c) diversity; (d) the significance of the unconscious; and (e) the relevance of age.

Sources of our images

The social constructionists observe all images as human constructions in specific cultural contexts (based on particular values). However, Jung views some images as symbolic, as manifestations of the archetypes, and hence beyond the social (and socially derived values).

Meanings

For social constructionists, it is human subjectivity that constructs meaning. However, for Jung, there is objective meaning, which can never be fully recognized but the human psyche needs to work towards recognizing. Both disagree with the meanings presented by the old paradigm of scientific approaches, which aim to establish objective, value-free facts, by questioning whether the methods and results of such scientific approaches truly reflect reality.[6] Nevertheless, while the social constructionists do not believe in objective meaning as such, and argue instead that subjective meaning making operates within all scientific approaches, the Jungian perspective does believe in objective meaning, but argues that objective meaning cannot be accessed adequately by mainstream scientific approaches on their own. For such approaches are, in Jung's view, one sided: they represent an extension of directed thinking (also called adapted thinking, logical thinking, reality thinking, or *thinking in words*) as opposed to archaic thinking (also called dream thinking, fantasy thinking, subjective thinking, non-directed thinking) (Jung 1911–12/1952: 4–46).

Diversity

For social constructionists, universality – being understood as something clear-cut, predetermined, and definite – does not exist. The social constructionists celebrate the idea of diversity as a way of getting away from universality, as observed earlier in their emphasis on diverse constructions of childhood over universal facts about it. Therefore, in their view, diversity and universality are only contrasted: the former as relative and the latter as absolute and clear-cut. However, for Jung, as represented in his theory of archetypes, universality, although multifaceted and inexplicable, is always there in the objective world, independent of any social or cultural factors. Diversity is the expression of universality. Therefore, in his view, diversity and universality are connected and are both multifaceted.

The significance of the unconscious

The social constructionist perspective touches on the unconscious influence of social contexts on individual's views. It could point to particular social conditions, cultural practices, and aspects of human subjectivity as the origins of child images, but it does not suggest a goal. However, from the Jungian view this applies only to the personal unconscious. It suggests that the child archetype in the collective unconscious is the origin or source of various child images and, at the same time, the goal to be achieved in the form of the self.

The relevance of age

The social constructionist perspective sees age as one of the strong factors that contribute to forming various child images. For age often provokes what adults consider to be appropriate or inappropriate for children: for instance, their appearance, moral understanding, and involvement in labour or sexual activity. However, from a Jungian point of view, since 'the child' could appear as an 'eternal child' (Jung 1934: 286; 1952: 755), age is irrelevant and not a determinant of what the child is. Even though youth is undoubtedly one of the commonest factors in manifestations of the child archetype, Jung does not define the child archetype in terms of age or appearance of age. Unlike the child images seen from the social constructionist perspective, the child archetype does not reflect adults' expectations about what is appropriate or inappropriate for 'the child'; rather, its autonomous and spontaneous characteristics often defeat any presumptions or expectations.

Some shared aspects

Not only these differences but also some similarities could be noted. Both the social constructionist and Jungian perspectives seem to suffer from the criticism that their foci on child images neglect actual, embodied children. James and colleagues, for instance, point out that social constructionists are in danger of replacing one reductionism with another – the child not as the product of nature and nurture interaction but as the effect of discourse (1998: 146–7). Likewise, Samuels distinguishes the symbolic child, which Jung is primarily concerned with, from a literal child (1989: 15–47). More importantly, the two perspectives seem similar in terms of their non-judgemental attitude when observing various child images, though taking very different approaches: the social constructionist perspective recognizes and accepts various social, cultural, and personal values as underpinning each image, while the Jungian perspective makes such values irrelevant or meaningless to the deeper layer of the psyche, and transforms subjective meaning into objective meaning. How adults' images of children, and their imaginations about the psyche of children, could be linked with actual children and their actual experiences of their world is an issue to be discussed elsewhere.

Example: 1989 UN Convention on the Rights of the Child

We shall now examine the social constructionist and Jungian perspectives in the light of a concrete example of some recent debates about childhood – some controversies surrounding the United Nations Convention on the Rights of the Child (CRC).[7] To introduce it briefly, the convention ensures rights for all children under 18 wherever they live in the world. It is made up of 54 articles, and Van Bueren characterizes its core elements as '4Ps': provision, prevention, protection, and participation (1995: 1–31). It has been ratified since 1989 by 191 countries (all countries in the world except the USA and Somalia). There are many contentious issues surrounding the convention, but in this chapter we shall address the following three: the balance between universality and diversity; the tension between protection and participation rights; and the concept of children as individual rights holders.

Universality and diversity

To reach international (universal) agreement on a definition of what children are and how they should be treated is extremely difficult (see Burr and Montgomery 2003: 139; Davin 1999: 33; King 1985: 53; Veerman 1992: 397–8). Such concepts as 'rights', as well as 'children', 'society', 'psychological needs', and 'justice' are thought to be relative, and their interpretation to depend 'on the particular ideological position held by its interpreters' (King 1985: 53). Also, there are difficulties in deciding which to prioritize: local cultural practices or the setting of universal standards (Burr and Montgomery 2003: 139).

The social constructionists observe that such concepts depend on time, place, cultures, and specific contexts. From this point of view, universal images of children do not exist. They argue that various social discourses coexist in different places and times or even within the same culture. This perspective could be employed in two ways. Seen cautiously, universal agreement would be an idealized, unrealistic goal and cultural diversity would be a challenge for achieving such a goal. Seen optimistically, universal agreement would be a potential goal and cultural diversity would be a key to a solution. Either way, the universality of child images is regarded as something trouble free and straightforward, and diversity is preferred as a rich containment of many complex images.

However, for Jung, universality is primary, and diversity is a secondary product of the former, when the archetype of the child is seen as universal and archetypal images of the child as diverse. Also, diversity could be primary and universality could be secondary, when the focus is on a particular aspect of the child archetype, which Jung equates with a symbol of the self. From the Jungian viewpoint, universality is not just an idealized or potential goal; it is the basis (as an unknown and yet objective fact, which is already and always there, without being dependent on individual experiences or personal choice). For Jung, diversity is not a problem or a source of conflict, but is the natural expression of archetypes. Paradoxically, diversity itself is a necessity for universality (for universal and timeless archetypes to manifest themselves and be recognized). As we have seen, age is irrelevant to the child archetype, which suggests that it has many different roles to play. Here, the universality of 'the child' is at the same time both the origin and the goal to be worked towards. Thus, the universality of 'the child' is seen as a containment of diversity, partly emerged and partly still emerging.

Protection and participation

It has been pointed out that there is a tension between children's protection and participation rights (Burr and Montgomery 2003: 144–51). Protection rights are based on the idea that children are vulnerable and innocent, whereas participation rights assume that children are competent and knowledgeable. Protection rights try to separate children from the adults' world, in order to protect children against exploitation and abuse, whereas participation rights encourage children to get actively involved in the world as much as adults do, emphasizing respect for children's choices and their autonomy.

The social constructionists allow that contradictory discourses could coexist (Montgomery 2003: 48). In this case, one of the historical views of an idealized child (a child as innocent and pure) and the newly emerged view of a child (a child as autonomous, individual, knowledgeable and competent) contradict each other. Therefore, the tension between the two rights simply gets down to the conflict between these particular opposing images of a child.

Jung also recognizes the coexistence of the opposites, but he would go further by seeing this as a healthy aspect of such international legislation. From this viewpoint, the contradiction is not problematic but helpful at the psychological level. This view encourages us to embrace the inevitable irrational aspects of law rather than be simply tolerant of them, thus reflecting the true nature of the human psyche. Therefore, the tension between the two rights reflects the inevitable contradiction of the opposites, which are different aspects of the same thing. From this perspective, for law not to be inclusive of the opposites would, in fact, be problematic.

Children as individual rights holders

It has also been argued that the concept of children as individual rights holders does not apply to all cultures and societies in the world (Burr and Montgomery 2003: 157–9; Veerman 1992: 397).

The social constructionists take the view that this is a concept specific to Western cultures where individuality is regarded as one of the important human qualities, and the concept is therefore a challenge to non-Western cultures in the rest of the world (Montgomery 2003: 68–72). Veerman observes that 'the child, conceptualized in the Western World, especially in a Western monopoly of pedagogies, does not apply to a "global village" of the whole world, which also includes children living in the so-called "Third World"' (1992: 397). Moreover, attempts to globalize an idealized notion of childhood based on Western culture are thought to create and reinforce further negative images of children in the South (Burman 1994: 32; Holland 1992).

However, from a Jungian viewpoint, to present this concept as specific to the West and a challenge to non-Western cultures (or to the South) would, in fact, be problematic. For such a view would not demand psychological engagement on the personal and individual level, as it mainly focuses on a political division on a global level (albeit in our mind) created by the politicization of certain child images. Alternatively, a Jungian perspective would encourage engaging more deeply with such newly emerging images of children as autonomous rights holders; it would encourage, not least in contexts where discourses about rights are not prominent, encountering such images of children as something that already exists in the unconscious. Such engagement could, from a Jungian viewpoint, lead to one's psychological development by means of an integration of something unconscious into consciousness, and achieving a better balance between consciousness and the unconscious. This process at the individual level could eventually bring about a change in collective views of children's issues including rights.

It needs to be noted that Jung's idea of the universal, timeless child is different from that of an idealized child produced by any particular society (criticized as the global child based on Western values). In Jung's idea, the child is nothing like the representation of an ideal. Rather, a Jungian perspective encourages us to re-imagine what is often not associated with a child in any culture.

Conclusion

In this chapter, I have made comparisons between the social constructionist and Jungian perspectives on child images in terms of the sources of images, their understanding of meaning, diversity, the unconscious, and age. I have examined their approaches with reference to some issues related to the CRC. I have suggested some of the ways in which a Jungian perspective – in particular the concept of the child archetype – could challenge or add to the social constructionist view in current debates about child images.

When a Jungian perspective is introduced into an interdisciplinary field, explaining particular concepts and theories such as archetypes and individuation often poses a problem. The field of childhood studies, in which children's rights issues have been widely debated, is no exception. Some of the difficulties would be not to oversimplify the debate, and to strike a balance between clarifying a Jungian perspective for comprehension outside its own discipline and conveying many disputes within that discipline. As we have seen earlier, one of the criticisms of Jung is that, as in social constructionism, actual embodied children are neglected in favour of child images.

However, there are some potential contributions that a Jungian perspective could offer to understanding images of children. The Jungian perspective:

- suggests the view of self-oriented diversity rather than ego-oriented diversity
- presents a view of multifaceted universality rather than of clear-cut, definable, predetermined universality
- demands deeper psychological engagement with certain child images at the individual and possibly collective levels rather than politicizing them.

Thus, a Jungian view suggests an alternative way of conceptualizing the diversity of child images. Whereas the social constructionist view of diversity could be seen as ego oriented (mainly concerned with the conscious and partly with the personal unconscious), a Jungian view of diversity could be seen as self-oriented (involved in the conscious and the collective as well as the personal unconscious). In other words, the social constructionist view of diversity only reflects the process of human meaning making – forming a collection of specific images without any universal ground – while the Jungian view of diversity reflects the process of the whole psyche involved in the objective world – forming a collection of specific images as emerged out of a universal ground. A Jungian perspective on diversity does not dismiss universality but holds a strong relationship with universality. Diverse child images are not fragmented; they are universal in terms of their roots, processes of manifestation, and various psychological functions. Therefore, instead of limiting the sources of our diverse child images to the social realm, a Jungian perspective suggests a wider and profounder ground for our imagination, in which consciousness is closely connected with the collective unconscious.

Similarly, a Jungian perspective could suggest an alternative way of conceptualizing the universality of child images. Whereas the social constructionist view of universality assumes clear-cut, definable, absolute truth (as the opposite of diversity), a Jungian view of universality suggests a multifaceted, objective world (parts of which could be mirrored in diverse forms in our psyche). Therefore, the alternative way of conceptualizing the diversity and universality of child images suggested by a Jungian perspective could help us to realize a closer and more engaging relationship between the two, rather than seeing them as remote from each other, or even at the two ends of a spectrum.

Furthermore, a Jungian perspective could bring about change to the potential of our imagination (rather than merely looking back at the products of our imagination). The social constructionists seem to remain at the level of simply suggesting that one's images could be so deeply embedded in culture that it is difficult to realize how they have been influenced. Even though this perspective is employed for accepting different child images from one's own, it still seems to be the case that one is simply acknowledging images other than one's own, rather than integrating them into oneself. However, a Jungian perspective creates expectations of encountering and engaging the opposite (the 'shadow') of one's own point of view (such as the interpretations or implementations of law, images of children, attitudes towards children, the roles of adults, etc.) rather than dismissing or denying or trying to conquer this opposite by strongly sustaining one's own view. Above all, before rushing to any conclusion concerning current issues about children and childhood, a Jungian perspective could be employed as a powerful and effective method to encounter one's own child images and face one's inner world on the more objective level.

Having suggested these potential theoretical contributions from a Jungian perspective to some current debates about child images, there would still remain difficulties in utilizing them in practice. Nevertheless, even though a Jungian perspective cannot finally solve global and local disagreements on issues about children, it at least provides us with an opportunity to re-imagine reality and set our imagination free beyond the limits of social constructionism.

Notes

1 For further discussion of Fordham's idea of children as individuals in relation to the children's rights movement, see Main forthcoming.

2 For the history of the children's rights movement, see, for example, Fottrel 1999; Freeman and Veerman 1992; King 1985; Montgomery 2003; Van Bueren 1995; Veerman 1992.

3 Cunningham points out the problem in the translation of the French *sentiment*, used by Ariès, as the English 'idea', which fails to convey the meaning of the original word, i.e., 'the sense of a feeling about childhood as well as a concept of it' (1995: 30). He argues that, by using this particular word, Ariès attempted to make a clear 'distinction between a "*sentiment*" about childhood and the way adults treated children' (ibid.).

4 For further details of histories of children and childhood, see Cunningham 1995; Clarke 2004; deMause 1974; Lowe 2004; Pollock 1983; Shahar 1990.

5 Jung equates the child archetype with the self as well as the circle (1946: 378; 1952: 738), quaternity (1946: 378), God image (1940: 268), etc.

6 For Jung's disagreement with the old paradigm, see Main forthcoming.

7 For further details, see Burr and Montgomery 2003; Fottrell 1999; Freeman and Veerman 1992; General Assembly of the United Nations 1989; Veerman 1992.

References

Ariès, P. (1962) *Centuries of Childhood: A Social History of Family Life*, trans. R. Baldick, New York: Vintage Books; London: Jonathan Cape.

Burman, E. (1994) 'Poor Children: Charity Appeals and Ideologies of Childhood', *Changes*, 12, 1, 29–36.

Burr, R. and Montgomery, H. (2003) 'Children and Rights', in M. Woodhead and H. Montgomery (eds) *Understanding Childhood: An Interdisciplinary Approach*, Milton Keynes: Open University; Chichester: Wiley.

Clark, J. (2004) 'Histories of Childhood', in D. Wyse (ed.) *Childhood Studies: An Introduction*, Oxford: Blackwell.

Colman, W. (2006) 'The Self', in R. Papadopoulous (ed.) *The Handbook of Jungian Psychology: Theory, Practice, and Applications*, London and New York: Routledge.

Cunningham, H. (1995) *Children and Childhood in Western Society since 1500*, London and New York: Longman.

Davin, A. (1999) 'What is a Child?', in A. Fletcher and S. Hussey (eds) *Childhood in Question: Children, Parents and the State*, Manchester and New York: Manchester University Press.

deMause, L. (ed.) (1974) *The History of Childhood*, New York: Psychohistory Press.

Fottrel, D. (1999) 'Children's Rights', in A. Hegarty and S. Leonard (eds) *Human Rights – An Agenda for the 21st Century*, London: Cavendish.

Freeman, M. and Veerman, P. (eds) (1992), *The Ideologies of Children's Rights*, International Studies in Human Rights, vol. 23, Dordrecht, Boston, MA, and London: Martinus Nijhoff.

General Assembly of the United Nations (1989) *The Convention on the Rights of the Child*, adopted by the General Assembly of the United Nations on 20 November 1989. Online. Available at http://www.unicef.org/crc. Accessed May 2007.

Hogenson, G.B. (2004) 'Archetypes: Emergence and the Psyche's Deep Structure', in J. Cambray and L. Carter (eds) *Analytical Psychology: Contemporary Perspectives in Jungian Analysis*, Hove and New York: Brunner-Routledge.

Holland, P. (1992) 'Crybabies and Damaged Children', in P. Holland, *What Is a Child? Popular Images of Childhood*, London: Virago.

James, A., Jenks, C. and Prout, A. (1998) *Theorising Childhood*, Cambridge: Polity; Oxford, Blackwell.

James, A. and Prout, A. (1990) *Constructing and Re-constructing Childhood: Contemporary Issues in the Sociological Study of Childhood*, Brighton: Falmer.

Jenks, C. (ed.) (1982) *The Sociology of Childhood – Essential Readings*, London: Batsford.

Jenks, C. (1996) *Childhood*, London: Routledge.

Jung, C.G. (1911–12/1952) *Symbols of Transformation, CW* 5, 1956.

—— (1916) 'The Structure of the Unconscious', *CW* 7, 1953/1966: 442–521.

—— (1934) 'The Development of Personality', *CW* 17, 1954/1970: 284-323.

—— (1940) 'The Psychology of the Child Archetype', *CW* 9(i), 1959/1968: 259–305.

—— (1946) 'Psychology of the Transference', *CW* 16, 1954: 353–539.

—— (1952) 'Answer to Job', *CW* 11, 1958/1969: 553–758.

—— (1957) 'The Undiscovered Self (Present and Future)', *CW* 10, 1964/1970: 488–588.

—— (1961) 'Symbols and the Interpretation of Dreams', *CW* 18, 1977: 416–607.

King, M. (1985) 'Are Rights Relevant?', *Educational and Child Psychology*, 2 2, 49–57.

Knox, J. (2003) *Archetype, Attachment, Analysis: Jungian Psychology and the Emergent Mind*, Hove and New York: Brunner-Routledge.

Lowe, R. (2004) 'Childhood through the Ages', in T. Maynard and N. Thomas (eds) *An Introduction to Early Childhood Studies*, London: Sage.

Main, S. (forthcoming) *Childhood Re-imagined: Images and Narratives of Development in Analytical Psychology*, London: Routledge.

Montgomery, H. (2003) 'Childhood in Time and Place', in M. Woodhead and H. Montgomery (eds) *Understanding Childhood: An Interdisciplinary Approach*, Milton Keynes: Open University; Chichester: Wiley.

Pollock, L.A. (1983) *Forgotten Children: Parent-Child Relations from 1500 to 1900*, Cambridge: Cambridge University Press.

Samuels, A. (1989) *The Plural Psyche: Personality, Morality and the Father*, London: Routledge.

Shahar, S. (1990) *Childhood in the Middle Ages*, London and New York: Routledge.

Stainton-Rogers, W. (2003) 'What is a Child?', in M. Woodhead and H. Montgomery (eds) *Understanding Childhood: An Interdisciplinary Approach*, Milton Keynes: Open University; Chichester: Wiley.

Stainton-Rogers, R. and Stainton-Rogers, W. (1989) 'The Social Construction of Childhood', in W. Stainton-Rogers, D. Harvey and E. Ash (eds) *Child Abuse and Neglect*, London: Open University Press.

—— (1992) *Stories of Childhood: Shifting Agendas of Child Concern*, London: Harvester Wheatsheaf.

Van Bueren, G. (1995) *The International Law on the Rights of the Child*, International Studies in Human Rights, vol. 35, Dordrecht, Boston, MA, and London: Martinus Nijhoff.

Veerman, P.E. (1992) *The Rights of Children and Changing Images of Childhood*, International Studies in Human Rights, vol. 18, Dordrecht, Boston, MA, and London: Martinus Nijhoff.

Chapter 15

Discourse of illness or discourse of health: towards a paradigm shift in post-Jungian clinical theory

Birgit Heuer

Introduction

This chapter explores the dynamics of psychotherapeutic healing in a contextual field that links quantum field research with mystical experience and clinical theory. The intention is to rethink the way in which clinical theory conceptualizes and contextualizes the therapeutic process. It has been argued, that clinical theory and practice always relate to an underlying clinical paradigm (Grünbaum 1984; Heuer 1998; Papadopoulos 2006). Here 'clinical paradigm' will be approached as a set of basic assumptions – about the nature of reality, causality, illness and health and their interrelation – that make up the analyst's felt experience of clinical reality. Such underlying assumptions tend to colour and shape clinical discourse in clinical practice teaching, supervision and clinical writing. The main question posed in this chapter is whether the current post-Jungian clinical paradigm is preoccupied with notions of illness rather than notions of health. In other words, is there the assumption underlying clinical practice that a preoccupation with illness or pathology will somehow bring about positive change or health? How are health and healing assumed to come about clinically? Does healing have to be predicated on suffering? And finally, is it possible to imagine a clinical paradigm preoccupied with notions of health and healing, rather than suffering – a 'sanatology' rather than a pathology? Such shifts would need to be anchored in shifting views of the nature of reality, as evidenced in quantum field research and theory, and which now emerge in many sciences (including biology, biochemistry, mathematics, medicine, philosophy, physics). Very broadly speaking, research findings suggest an emergent worldview that resonates strongly with the mystical universe, which informs much of Jung's clinical psychology. In this chapter, I shall argue that, in our field, the implications of quantum field research lead to a 'sanatology' – a clinical theory of health and healing, which complements the ever growing complexity of clinical knowledge in the area of pathology. Finally, I shall outline the epistemological shifts based on quantum field theory, which might contribute to a clinical discourse of health and healing where the dynamics of pathology might be a somewhat lesser and receding preoccupation.

The healing agents in analysis: what is it that heals?

I would like to begin this part with a general observation from my own clinical practice. When I started practising as a psychotherapist 26 years ago, it seems to me that the underlying questions that motivated patients were: 'Why do I experience as I do?' 'What are the reasons for my suffering?' and, ultimately, 'What is my story?' In the last couple of years these questions seem to be changing focus from 'why' to 'how'. The underlying question motivating patients now seems to be: 'How can I heal myself?' One might see these observations as indicators of a change in zeitgeist, but also as an invitation to reflect on clinical paradigm. Do we have a clinical paradigm that is equal to this new question? How do we conceptualize clinically a healing process? What are our ideas on psychic health and the factors that promote it? It is interesting to delve into clinical accounts with these questions in mind. In the absence of statistical research data, I have to generalize and describe trends. It is still possible to observe that the focus of conception seems to be the clinical evaluation of the patient's pathology unfolding in relation to the analyst, or, depending on orientation, the patient's inner or outer lives. It is noticeable that this approach is, generally speaking, through an underlying focus on the negative and that analysis tends to conceptualize its subject negatively through the lens of pathology.

In the historiography of psychoanalysis, Freud's clinical pessimism is well known, whereas Jung held a more ambiguous position. He was perhaps at his most optimistic when, in a somewhat heated talk with Professor Hisamatsu from Kyoto University, he was asked whether his method aimed at healing the patient completely and, after some deliberation, he finally answered in the affirmative (Meckel and Moore 1992: 111). The classical clinical tool is interpretation, which is implicitly held to be a healing *agens*. This is most clearly thought out in Stracey's idea of the mutative interpretation. Here the therapeutic factor is implied to be the patient's capacity for insight and their understanding of the dynamics of their pathology. More recent approaches are concerned with the analyst and the analytic attitude as facilitating environment. With Jung, transpersonal, archetypal healing factors come into play, such as analysis as an alchemical opus, the Self as central organizing principle, and the ego–Self axis. Here the healing *agens* is implied to be a transpersonal factor and the healing process is anchored transpersonally. Thus the three clinical factors thought to be therapeutic seem to be first, interpretation insight; second, curative experience; and, third, a transpersonal *agens*, while, at the same time, the patient tends to be constructed through the lens of pathology.

Another curative concept held by current clinical discourse is the idea that the patient's capacity to tolerate his or her reality is an indicator of growing psychic health. Here it is assumed that a capacity for engaging with pain is therapeutic and that change is contingent on suffering. This view of reality is informed by the lens of pathology and a belief in the necessity and validity of psychic pain. It seems that clinical discourse tends to conflate negativity and reality or conceptualize reality in terms of negativity. Such a bias towards negativity leaves a conceptual gap, as it does not tell us how to positively imagine the dynamics of the therapeutic process. In practice, however, analysis – generalizing broadly – does heal. Could it be that the current clinical paradigm has, in some way, not yet caught up with the deeper curative processes of clinical practice? Might this be because the complexities of healing are difficult to put into words in a pre-quantum paradigm?

Quantum reality

It is helpful, at this point, to sketch the contrasting world view that emerges from quantum field research, where the implications invite a much more positive picture. One characteristic of this emerging worldview is its closeness conceptually to the mystical world. As the findings of quantum field research are being assimilated by the scientific community, and in turn by the rest of the world, it is as if the nature of reality itself – of what is felt to be real – might change. What are these findings and, more importantly, the implications to be drawn from them?

It is extremely challenging to say anything meaningful about quantum theory in such a short chapter, as it is a complex subject that has been around for roughly the same time as analysis. Its latest developments are to be found in string theory, which I will not discuss here, and in zero-point field theory, which I will focus on. I will engage with the empirical research in a manner that lies somewhere between the literal and the symbolic. For this purpose, mystical language suggests itself, as its implicit ratio – logically paradoxical yet vibrating with meaning – resonates with quantum rationality.

Zero-point field theory represents a further development of traditional quantum mechanics, which held that quantum principles only operate in an inanimate subatomic world. The chief properties discovered in traditional quantum physics were non-locality and non-causality. The quantum physicist Amit Goswami explains:

> A quantum object (for example an electron) can be at more than one place at the same time (the wave property).
> A quantum object cannot be said to manifest in ordinary spacetime reality until we observe it as a particle (collapse of the wave).

> A quantum object ceases to exist here and simultaneously appears in existence over there, we cannot say it went through the intervening space (the quantum jump).
> A manifestation of one quantum object, caused by our observation, simultaneously influences its correlated twin object . . . (quantum action-at-a-distance).
>
> (Goswami 1995: 9)

If quantum particles, once connected, continue to influence each other instantaneously wherever they are, then the idea of time and space recedes, and if quantum events do not relate to causes, then the idea of cause and effect recedes also. The ideas that replace time and space are 'attunement', 'resonance' and 'coherence'. Causality turns into probability and also into non-local, discontinuous quantum collapse, or quantum leaps. The physicist Jude Currivan writes:

> Until observed the quantum building blocks of the entire universe exist only as probabilities. But experiments show that when we observe a quantum entity – or, significantly have the intention to do so – it becomes coherent and is realised or, as quantum physicists say, 'actualised'. Such evidence reveals that we can no longer consider an observer and what is observed as separate . . . This recognition is profoundly associated with one of the most intriguing aspects of quantum behaviour. Termed non-locality, it is the experimentally proven fact that quanta can be instantaneously connected and are effectively a single entity – even if separated by the entire universe.
>
> (Currivan 2007: 11)

Zero-point field theory represents research findings that strongly suggest that quantum laws cannot be neatly consigned to an inanimate world of small particles, but that they extend and underpin the living world and human consciousness also. The zero-point field is a world of subatomic particles or waves of potentiality that are in constant motion through exchange of energy, 'an ocean of microscopic energy in the space between things' (McTaggart 2001: xxi). It is thought to hold an extraordinary amount of information stored in wave interference patterns, i.e. all memory of all time, because it is thought that all physical events are interlinked with quantum events. It is also thought to hold an unimaginable amount of energy, with the energy in one cubic metre of space being enough to boil all the oceans in the world. Zero-point field energy is thought to be responsible for the stability of matter, so that all atomic structures would collapse without it. The German physicist Fritz Albert Popp was the first to discover quantum data in living cells in the 1970s. Out of his, and other similar findings, grew the idea that all processes of life might be linked into the zero-point field and could be conceptualized as quantum processes. If this is the case, then not only our assumptions about the nature of reality, but also our felt experience of it, might change radically. It would then seem that we are all connected, and in subtle ways constantly influence each other. All kinds of intuitive and psychic phenomena could be explained and might be thought of as quite natural. This includes the subtle clinical phenomena of the transference and countertranference, which are a vital yet unexplained part of clinical discourse.

A multitude of experiments (McTaggart 2001) suggests that consciousness itself might be quantum in nature, able to function both as wave and particle, and that it might be consciousness that creates material reality out of probability (Goswami 1995). The PEAR Lab (Princeton Engineering Anomalies Laboratory) studies and the work of the mind–machine consortium (Jahn 2001) examined the effect of the conscious and unconscious mind on random events-generating computers and came up with striking results. They theorized that quantum consciousness is linked to a process called superradiance – 'a rippling cascade of subatomic coherence' (McTaggart 2001: 160) – a very high degree of order by which consciousness spreads out into the environment and creates material events. This creative consciousness was found to be at its most active when linked to archetypal or religious imagery, which suggests that we create out of our unconscious; and that, at this level, it might indeed be a case of 'mind over matter' via a quantum link between the unconscious mind and the unconscious of matter; and furthermore, that an inherent capacity for order – in the sense of healthier and more helpful preconfigurations – is potentially stronger than the forces of entropy. Entropy, or the second law of thermodynamics, holds that material reality, with the passage of time, always tends towards disorder and disintegration. This law applies only if the world is conceived of as a closed system. In contrast, the suggestion of an enormously high degree of order, capable of outweighing the forces of entropy and the implication of an inherent tendency towards holistic and holographic order, rather than disorder, challenges our current view of the nature of reality. The physicist Jude Currivan writes:

> One of the most significant aspects of the holographic principle is that the entirety of the whole object is re-created in every part of its three-dimensional image. So, if a holographic projection is subdivided into millions of pieces, every single piece will incorporate a tiny and complete representation of the whole. The mathematics that describes the hologram enables any physical pattern to be transformed into waveforms and converted back to its original shape . . . Their harmonic nature is seen both in their self-similarity, where each part is similar to the whole, and in their scale-invariance, whereby their inherent patterns remain unchanged whether scaled up or down in size.
>
> (Currivan 2007: 6)

She continues, weaving together quantum theory and mystical concepts:

> Scientifically, the description of the Cosmos in holographic terms is relatively new, yet the idea is millennia old. The teaching ascribed to the archetypal wisdom bringer known as Toth to the ancient Egyptians, 'As above so below', describes the One as manifest in the diversity of the many and the microcosm as embodying the totality of the macrocosm. This perfectly reflects the reality of the hologram.
>
> (ibid.)

Elisabeth Targ (1997), and others (Greyson 1996; Harris 1999; Miller 1982; Stanford 1969), have researched intensively into the effect of positive intention, spiritual healing and prayer on physical and emotional well-being and have found statistically significant links. It seems that the ability of humans to influence each other positively could be ultimately unlimited. All forms of positive concentration – from gentle wishing through prayer to distant healing – seem to have a faster than light positive effect that increases in relation to faith. The new paradigm of reality that emerges here is about the human ability to influence and create vis-à-vis a responsive universe. We might be the creators of our experience in a far more literal way then has ever been thought scientifically, but also the responsive universe might be of an inherently harmonically ordered and benevolent nature. This kind of order operates essentially outside of time, space and causality and is therefore best conceived as a symbolic or mystical type of order. It then seems possible to say that we create, partially unconsciously, in relation to a quantum universe, whose inherent tendency it is to respond with a higher degree of holographic order, which, in mystical language, could be read as agape, love and grace. Of course, this research is too new and the implications perhaps too radical to have informed a generally held scientific paradigm or a generally held experience of the nature of reality. In my view, paradigmata, be they scientific or generally held, become reality through a process of collective 'making real' in the Winnicottian sense. From this perspective, a new paradigm might be as much collectively 'imagined' as it is scientifically 'found', so that a combination of such imagining and finding creates a new reality and we might, in time, collectively grow into quantum reality.

Quantum reality is greatly important for clinical theory because it enables us to conceptualize and explain positively how and why we heal. This might, in turn, facilitate some fundamental changes in clinical theory and practice. Generally speaking, quantum reality suggests a clinical paradigm that would be guided by an underlying fundamentally positive outlook, similar to views suggested by faith, and particularly by mystical experience or gnosticism. If human beings are linked into the zero-point field on all levels – physical, emotional and mental – so that all human processes are rooted in quantum processes, then there might be no limit to creativity and the capacity to heal.

The underlying principle seems to be: 'I create therefore I am'. If the zero-point field contains all knowledge of all time, stored in wave interference patterns, then everything that is needed to heal is already there in potentiality (Jones 2002). And if were are in constant, albeit mostly unconscious, interchange with the field, then there might be access to unlimited healing potential. This implies an innate ability to heal and to be healed – far greater than hitherto imagined – which in turn gives rise to therapeutic optimism. This therapeutic optimism could extend into how we conceptualize the patient clinically. How would it be if we conceptualized the patient positively, in relation to their innate goodness and their potentially unlimited creative capacity? We would then be concerned with the specific shape, form and dynamics of the patient's goodness, their creativity and their potential and this would be a primary clinical concern. Clinical accounts would look at the patient through a positive lens, intent on catching any minute detail that reflects positively on the patient. A belief in innate goodness is related to the question of entropy. The second law of thermodynamics entails a belief in the predominant power of an innate destructiveness. Zero-point field research, with its suggestion that the creative force is potentially the stronger one – both externally and internally – presents a view hitherto only accessible by faith. We might, however, only be in the process of making real a quantum universe, which would mean that the forces of negentropy (i.e. creativity and goodness) might become stronger and more accessible as we become more knowledgeable about them. Analysis – and particularly Jungian analysis – could make a contribution here by moving beyond the implicit conflation of negativity and reality. However, it needs to be conceded that, at this point, the relationship between zero-point field research and clinical theory is one of utilizing its findings in an interpretative and amplificatory manner.

Conceptualizing a positive, creative, and potentially healed patient has another advantage according to zero-point field theory. As we constantly create physical reality from the field via unconscious/conscious imagination, the way our clinical paradigm imagines the patient might actually contribute to either facilitating or impeding a healing environment. The current clinical paradigm, with its bias towards pathology, links positive change to the capacity to tolerate inner and outer reality, and links this in turn to the capacity to tolerate psychic pain – to suffer consciously rather than unconsciously. This is called into question if human learning and change becomes a quantum process, as clinical change then might also relate to a capacity to unlearn suffering and to tolerate and learn reality in the form of innate, but individually specific, goodness.

Research also indicates specific patterns – albeit non-linear and acausal ones – in which materiality is created from the zero-point field and its intrinsic holographic and holistic properties. From the point of view of materiality, this is experienced in the form of quantum leaps, which means that something miraculously occurs out of nothing, without a logical cause and unrelated to time and space. I suggest that this forms the pattern of the healing process when clinical change is conceptualized in a quantum theoretical way.

Clinical change then, is essentially neither linear/causal nor spiral/cyclical (although from a materialistic point of view it might be experienced as such) but is seemingly acausal and miraculous. In mystical language, clinical change or healing is patterned by grace. It flows from the space between things and between thoughts. It is always available and carries with it intricate holographic pre-patterns or, in mystical language, the invisible and indivisible face of the divine. Clinically speaking, change as a quantum process, enables us to expect our patients to literally 'come on in leaps and bounds'. In his very last paper, the late Donald Meltzer expressed a growing awareness of such processes thus: 'I am (becoming) miracle-perceptive' (Meltzer 2005: 132).

Zero-point field research has also explored the role of the so-called creative observer, i.e. the circumstances and attitudes which contribute to creating quantum reality (Jahn and Dunne 1997; McTaggart 2001). Thus, it seems that the quantum flow of grace cannot be coerced, but is intensified by gentle, as well as intense, wishing or desiring, when this is, at the same time, given up to the unconscious. This brings to mind the Jungian concept of an ego–Self axis (Edinger 1973), meaning that the creative observer is most effective when his or her gentle wishing is aligned between ego and Self. I would like to suggest that in a quantum clinical paradigm, the therapist's role is much like that of the creative observer in a quantum field experiment, i.e the observer's or therapist's attitudes, feelings, actions and state of being can all have a positive effect. Thus it has been shown, that the more coherent state of mind – that is, the more meditative, alpha brain-wave state of mind – induces coherence in other minds. Prayerlike or prayerful states of mind in the therapist are thus considered most helpful and Bion's clinical dictum – that the analyst be without memory or desire – is validated.

Having interpreted the effects of quantum research for clinical discourse, it is now possible to sketch some aspects of a clinical theory of healing, a 'sanatology'. A 'sanatology' is anchored in a quantum view of the world. It suggests that we heal in quantum leaps, that healing is a creative process that emerges from the space between things and thoughts. Its dynamics are essentially non-linear, acausal and not bound by time, seemingly coming out of nowhere and therefore miraculous. In mystical language we heal by grace, which is ever present and ever flowing but does not coerce. Grace is the stronger force, capable of outweighing the effects of entropy, while its way is always to soften and to flow. Healing in clinical terms is co-created by the therapist, whose role is multifaceted. One facet is the therapist's capacity to function like the creative observer in zero-point field experiments. This includes the knowledge that the patient's healed states already exist in potentiality, a therapeutic form of faith (Jones 2002). The therapist as creative observer is able to constellate a healing environment via his or her gentle wishes for the patient to heal, the ability to conceptualize the patient positively and a predominance of meditative states of mind. In other words the therapist helps to wish and dream the patient into health, which might be his or her quantum birthright.

Conclusion

In this chapter I have explored the implications of quantum field research for clinical discourse. Quantum reality facilitates a shift in the intrinsic outlook of the current analytical clinical paradigm, enabling the paradigmatic lens of pathology to recede and be complemented by a 'sanatology', a clinical theory of health and healing. I have described the various opportunities for therapeutic optimism that such paradigmatic change allows. I have used the mystical term 'grace' to evoke the chief aspects of a quantum clinical paradigm, which seems fitting in the light of Jung's own clinical orientation and interest in quantum theory. And finally, I hope that all my colleagues who are currently seeking to integrate their spirituality with their clinical work will feel encouraged and empowered.

References

Currivan, J. (2007) *The 8th Chakra*, London: Hay House.

Edinger, E.F. (1973) *Ego and Archetype*, Harmondsworth: Penguin Books.

Goswami, A. (1995) *The Self-Aware Universe: How Consciousness Creates the Material World*, New York: Tarcher/Putnam.

Greyson, B. (1996) 'Distance Healing of Patients with Major Depression', *Journal of Scientific Exploration*, 10, 4, 447–65.

Grünbaum, A. (1984) *The Foundations of Psychoanalysis*, Berkeley, CA: University of California Press.

Harris, W.S. (1999) 'A Randomised, Controlled Trial of the Effects of Remote, Intercessory Prayer on Outcomes in Patients Admitted to the Coronary Care Unit', *Archives of Internal Medicine*, 159, 19, 2273–8.

Heuer, B. (1998) 'Sein oder Nichtsein. Überlegungen zur Körperlichkeit und Seinserfahrung in der Analyse', *Analytische Psychologie*, 29, 830-98.

Jahn, R. (2001) 'A Modular Model of Mind/Matter Manifestations', PEAR Technical Note 2001.01, May 2001 (abstract).

Jahn, R. and Dunne, B. (1997) 'Science of the Subjective', *Journal of Scientific Exploration*, 11, 2, 201–24.

Jones, A.M. (2002) 'Teleology and the Hermeneutics of Hope: Jungian Interpretation in the Light of the Work of Paul Ricoeur', *Journal of Jungian Theory and Practice*, 4, 2, 45–55.

McTaggart, L. (2001) *The Field. The Quest For The Secret Force Of The Universe*, London: HarperCollins.

Meckel, D.J. and Moore, R.L. (eds) (1992) *Self And Liberation. The Jung/Buddhism Dialogue*, Mahwah, NJ: Paulist Press.

Meltzer, D. (2005) 'The Role of Projective Identification in the Formation of Weltanschauung', in N. Field with T. Harvey and B. Sharp (eds) *Ten Lectures on Psychotherapy and Spirituality*, London: Karnac.

Miller, R.N. (1982) 'Study on the Effectiveness of Remote Mental Healing', *Medical Hypotheses*, 8, 481–90.

Papadopoulos, R.K. (2006) 'Jung's Epistemology and Methodology', in R.K. Papadopoulos (ed.) *The Handbook of Jungian Psychology: Theory, Practice and Applications*, London and New York: Routledge.

Stanford, R. (1969) '"Associative Activation of the Unconscious" and "Visualisation" as Methods for Influencing the PK Target', *Journal of the American Society for Psychical Research*, 63, 338–51.

Targ, E. (1997) 'Evaluating Distant Healing: A Research Review', *Alternative Therapies*, 3, 6, 74–8.

Chapter 16

Evoking the embodied image: Jung in the age of the brain

Honor Griffith

Over the past 20 years exciting new explorations have been taking place in the fields of neurobiology, attachment theory, and trauma research. Out of the convergence of studies in these formerly disparate domains, a new paradigm for understanding and treating psychopathology is emerging. As Jungians, our challenge is not only to rethink our theories and practices in the light of these latest scientific discoveries, but also to join the discussion that is taking place in the larger psychological community; a discussion in which researchers such as Jean Knox (2003), and Margaret Wilkinson (2006a, 2006b) already have begun to participate.

My own interest in this new territory has been stimulated not only by the remarkable results brought about by incorporating the eye movement desensitization and reprocessing protocol (EMDR) into my psychotherapy practice, but also by the significant correlations that I have found between Jungian theories and developments in these new fields. Combining techniques such as the bilateral stimulation used in EMDR with a growing understanding of brain functioning in the areas of memory, early attachment, identity formation, and trauma have given me more effective theories and tools with which to help my patients resolve a negative complex, integrate shadow material, activate the ego–Self axis and facilitate the individuation process.

In this chapter I examine Jung's theory of the complex – both its formation and its healing – in the context of attachment theory, brain research and the effects of trauma. I illustrate some of my insights with the case history of a client with whom I used the bilateral stimulation method of EMDR.

When an adult comes to therapy part of the work is to help the patient analyze negative aspects of his or her complex, thus enabling the energy formerly held in the unconscious to become available for the individual's transformation and growth. My thesis is that the healing of painful symptoms and dysfunctional behavioural patterns comes about when the client is able to integrate, on a deeply experiential level, the images, thoughts, affects, feelings and sensations that constitute aspects of the complex. I describe this process as *evoking the embodied image*. Incorporating the EMDR protocol into a Jungian-based practice may greatly enhance this work.

But what is the eye movement desensitization and reprocessing protocol?

Developed by Francine Shapiro in the 1980s, EMDR has become the most extensively researched treatment for patients suffering from posttraumatic stress disorder (PTSD) (Maxfield and Hyer 2002; Van Etten and Taylor 1998). When an individual experiences a traumatic event, stress-induced hormones are released resulting in brain disorganization and the consequent shutting down of neuronal pathways of the corpus collosum and anterior commissure. These are the parts of the brain normally used to integrate information between left and right hemispheres (Krebs 1998; Siegel 1999, 2002). Hence, the logical and language functions of the neocortex are not available to 'store' the event – along with its emotions, physical sensations, and visual images – as would normally take place when events are processed into long-term memory. Instead, the traumatic memories perseverate along narrow associative pathways 'trapped' in an 'unmetabolized' form in the nervous system. The individual has no language for, or coherent autobiographical story about, what took place. Also, in cases of severe trauma, activity in the right amygdala is increased, but, because reactions here are recorded in implicit, not explicit memory, one has no conscious recall of the events. Yet the person becomes highly sensitized to those triggers in the external world which are reminiscent of an aspect of the original trauma (Mollon 2005; Siegel 1999, 2002).

Processing the traumatic event with the protocol of EMDR seems to allow for normal 'digestion' of the experience (Mollon 2005; Shapiro 2001). The client is asked simultaneously to bring up an image that represents the trauma, associated emotions and sensations, as well as an internalized negative cognition about the self in regards to the event. Meanwhile, the therapist induces a bilateral stimulation of the brain either through alternating tapping on the client's knees or hands – with or without an electronic tapping device – through alternating audio input provided by earphones or through oscillating eye movements produced by asking the client to follow the side-to-side motion of the therapist's hand. The modality used is determined by the patient's preference. The client then simply notices any images, feelings, thoughts, and body sensations that occur, and, from time to time, reports on what is happening.

The bilateral stimulation, which is evoked by any one of the chosen modalities, seems to bring 'online' a far wider network of neuronal pathways, including verbal and cognitive functions along with affective and sensorimotor systems, than were available at the time of the trauma (Siegel 2002; van der Kolk 2002). Hence, a much larger repertoire of information is available from which to sort, organize, eliminate, and integrate representations of the original event. When the activation of images, emotions, and physical sensations is combined with the individual's verbal report of them, a connection between the emotion-processing right brain and the linguistic left brain is facilitated (Bohart and Greenberg 2002), 'resulting in a story that can be told, rather than an experience to be endlessly relived like a waking dream' (Mollon 2005: 8). Changes subsequently take place at the neurobiological level, allowing new synaptic pathways to form in place of the perseverative patterns of traumatic arousal. Because healing is embodied, rooted in physiology, paying attention to the sensations associated with the image is a critical component of the protocol.

EMDR, attachment and affective neuroscience

I have found that incorporating the EMDR protocol into a traditional depth psychology approach has proven immensely successful in the treatment of many of the problems that my clients bring to psychotherapy that are not caused by apparent trauma. These problems usually stem from dysfunctional internalized representations of the self, which have been formed in the relationships with early caregivers. Understanding attachment trauma as well as the psychobiology of affective development can shed light on why the EMDR protocol is sometimes so effective in healing early wounds.

Overwhelming evidence from research in attachment theory (Bowlby 1988) and neurobiology (Schore 1994, 2003a, 2003b; Siegel 1999, 2002) is proving how critical a role the primary caregiver plays in the child's physiological and psychological development. They further reveal how these early relationships lead to an internal working model of self and other, which forms the basis of an individual's adult behaviour and identity. When the caregiver is not capable of adequately meeting the baby's needs, the child's neurobiological system responds as if it were experiencing trauma.

According to Fordham (1976), the very early stage of life is wholly archetypal, that is, dominated by affects, sensations and emerging images, which arise out of the biological needs of the infant. It is the task of the mother to attune empathically to her child's experiences – of both terrifying fragmentation and blissful oneness – so that she might contain them for her infant and give them symbolic representation through words and non-verbal ways that express attunement. In this way, the child begins to make meaning of, 'name', and give symbolic form to, the archetypal, raw, primitive affect that partly constitutes the experience of infancy. Gradually, through the personal digestion of the archetypal contents mediated by the mother, these raw affects become humanized in the growing child.

When the mother is incapable of emotionally responding to her infant – for either physical or psychological reasons – the absence of the mother leaves the infant bereft of the containment that is essential to assuage its excessive anxiety, terror, frustration, and anger. Without such holding, the overwhelming affects are simply too much to bear. The infant resorts to defending itself against them by splitting them off from the developing consciousness of the ego (Kalsched 1996; Sidoli 1989, 2000). As a result, the affects, rather than becoming humanized, remain in their raw, undigested state far from consciousness. As the child develops, the ego becomes more and more proficient at erecting defences, which block awareness of the terror and pain that still lurk in the depths of the psyche. Much of the work of analysis, of course, is about identifying these defences and healing the wounds they conceal.

What psychoanalysis has known intuitively for many decades, research in affective neuroscience has unequivocally confirmed: that the attachment bond between mother and infant is the foundation not only for the physical but also for the psychic growth of the child. From a neurobiological perspective, the reciprocal process between baby and mother is designed to create a stable, properly balanced pair of organisms. The interpersonal relationship that is established through attachment is essential so that the infant's immature brain can actually 'use the mature functions of the parent's brain to organize its own processes' (Siegel 1999: 67).

Because five-sixths of the growth spurt of the human brain takes place after birth, the nature of that growth is greatly influenced by the mother (Schore 1994, 2003a, 2003b). Although the infant is genetically programmed to evolve brain structures in the direction of a predetermined hierarchy of greater and greater complexity, the mother's caregiving is an essential component in the release of these inherent structures, particularly the limbic and cortical areas of the right hemisphere where affect and emotion are registered (Schore 1994). The attachment style that develops between mother and infant determines the actual neuronal structures of the limbic system.

In the first 2 years of life – before the 'cognitive' left hemisphere is fully 'online' – pathways for self-regulation form through interactions with the mother. She is the one who initially quells the over active amygdala with her soothing responses, enabling her infant gradually to learn to do so for itself. The mother who is capable of responding to the reciprocal love evoked in the mother/infant dyad produces an abundance of serotonin, which in turn, regulates the infant's psychobiological state by soothing and reducing pain. Through internalizing these experiences, the baby establishes its own increasing capacity for self-regulation, hence laying the neuronal foundations for an affectively healthy adult life.

In extreme cases, if the mother is in a dysregulated state, such as that of terror or rage, the infant will register that state in the stress-sensitive corticolimbic regions of the brain, at a time of critical growth, when left hemisphere functioning is usually not yet established (Siegel 1999, 2002).

Representations of these traumatic experiences are held unconsciously in procedural memory ready, at any time, to be triggered by environmental cues or affect states linked to these memories. These early experiences then become structurally encoded as unconscious behaviour patterns.

The complex

These structurally encoded unconscious behaviour patterns are very similar to what Jung (1948) refers to as a complex: a split-off psychic fragment, something like an autonomous sub-personality, which has a life of its own and over which we have little control. At the centre of the complex is an image with a very strong feeling tone attached to it. Complexes comprise a loose cluster of feelings, images, behaviours, associations, experiences and beliefs, which are incompatible with our conscious personality. Many complexes begin to take shape around our very earliest experiences with our caregivers, often forming at the pre-verbal stage, and are gradually built up, in a piecemeal way, through what we experience in the repetitions of our interactions with our environment.

Jung emphasizes the fact that intensity of affect is central to the formation of the complex. Jung attributes the most common cause of a complex to trauma or emotional shock, or to a moral conflict in which it appears impossible to affirm the whole of one's nature. In such circumstances, a fragment of experience – replete with its representations – splits off from consciousness, setting up its own sub-personality, and subsequently creating a field that attracts to it similar experiences with the same affect. When we are in the grip of a complex, we are not able to respond spontaneously and freely to a given situation. Neither can we trust our emotions to give us the true picture of what is going on.

EMDR and the complex

It is my experience that the EMDR protocol can help to 'metabolize' the negative complexes that have kept clients stuck in painful patterns of thinking and behaving created in childhood. As with any form of therapy, it is essential that a strong therapeutic bond exists between therapist and client before the EMDR protocol is introduced into the analytic process. However, as soon as it is introduced it can feel as if therapy is being conducted at warp speed. The sheer number of memories that emerge, the enormous abreactions that can take place with a client not previously in touch with his or her emotions, and the shift in the client's feelings about the self – all within one session – often leave both patient and therapist awe struck. It would seem that the bilateral stimulation – along with the focus on visual, emotional, cognitive, and sensate experience – activates affective corticolimbic structures in the right hemisphere along with cognitive, verbal structures in the left, making available a vast network of associations which the brain/mind can then bring to bear on the current problem. The imagination is then 'freed up' to play a central role in integrating the undigested material by drawing on whatever bits and pieces of experience – both conscious and unconscious – that are evoked during the process. What also stands out is the inexorable tendency of psyche to move in the direction of healing and growth, as Jung claimed.

One of the most intriguing consequences that I have found using the EMDR protocol is that, in the very process of unravelling aspects of a complex, we are able to glimpse how it was constructed in the first place. I will now illustrate the workings of using the EMDR protocol, focusing on this particularly interesting aspect, with a case history.

Case history

Jennifer is a highly intelligent, well-educated, professional woman who returned to therapy because she had anxiety and depression. Recently engaged, and participating in a long-distance relationship with her fiancé, Peter, she found that their telephone conversations had activated feelings of intense jealousy and mistrust. She recognizes this behaviour as a pattern that was experienced in her previous two marriages, and for which she has had many years of therapy.

Jennifer is exhibiting classic symptoms of being caught in a complex. She has very little control over her excessive jealousy and intense anger that manifest when she thinks she is not being listened to or when her partner socializes with female colleagues, and also of her general irritability when she and Peter are talking on the phone. Rather than responding spontaneously and freely, she finds herself trying to control Peter's behaviour. In saner moments she knows that she is overreacting and that her feelings are not giving her a true picture of the relationship.

I worked through several threads of Jennifer's complex with her over eight sessions. In our first session, I asked Jennifer to re-invoke the overwhelming feelings of anxiety and hopelessness that had been triggered by a recent telephone conversation with her fiancé and to notice where in her body those feelings resided. I then asked her to notice any memories or images that might surface. Immediately, she recalled the incident, at about the age of 10, of an attempted molestation by a doctor, which her own resistance and her mother's appearance in the room had aborted. Although troubled by the doctor's behaviour, Jennifer's most distressing memory was of her desperate need to tell her mother what had taken place. The image that attached itself to this disturbing affect was that of lying on the couch, wishing that her mother would stop her obsessive busyness and come to her and ask her the 'right' questions.

I instructed Jennifer to focus on this image, and simultaneously, to pay attention to her feelings and body sensations, as I began rhythmically tapping on her knees. (Jennifer's preference was for the tapping modality as it enabled her to close her eyes and visualize better.) As was typical throughout every one of our sessions, a massive amount of material was evoked: ideas, images, and memories spanning her entire life, as well as enormous affect and abreaction, including feelings of nausea, confusion, fear, and anger. The material that spontaneously emerged, however, always pertained to aspects of the particular complex which had been constellated with Peter.

As Jennifer focused on the image, her frustration of not having been able to speak about the incident with her mother significantly increased, and she experienced an overwhelming feeling of not being safe. She recalled memories of other powerful, malevolent male figures in her young adulthood and experienced utter despair at not knowing how to protect herself from people like this in the world. In order to remain safe and to defend against these feelings, she became suspicious of people, withdrawing and actively looking for signs that proved to her that she could not trust people.

By the end of this first session, Jennifer had begun to make conscious aspects of this complex: she realized that her intense anxiety was related to feeling unsafe, and that her inability to trust was getting in the way of her relationship with Peter. She understood that she defended against her feelings by looking out for signs that affirmed her need to distrust, which was precisely what she was doing in her relationship with Peter and in all her intimate relationships.

Although Jennifer had ended the first session feeling much calmer, she returned after a week with her fiancé reporting that she felt hopeless, pathetic, stuck and immobilized – like a child. She was irritable after intimacy and she knew that she was putting up a wall between Peter and herself. The fact that she felt this way indicated that the enactment of the complex ran deeper than the incident with the doctor, and subsequent disturbing experiences with powerful figures in early adulthood. Instead, these incidents must be feeding into an already well-established complex. It was no surprise then that Jennifer brought to the next session two stories from her childhood of being hospitalized and kept apart from her mother: once for 2 weeks at the age of 18 months for a gastric condition, and again at the age of 3 for tonsillitis. Even though Jennifer had no memory of these incidents, she understood how terrifying it would be for a child to have been torn away from the safety of its mother and placed in the hands of strangers at a time of such vulnerability. Also, we talked about how at 18 months she would not yet have developed a cohesive enough ego to have any conscious memory of this event. Yet it would be encoded in her sensory emotional system of implicit memory, unconsciously influencing the way in which she related to others and to herself.

Because Jennifer had no conscious memories of these incidents, we focused again with the image of her lying on the couch. As soon as I began tapping, she immediately felt enormous anxiety and a desire, once again, for her mother to ask her about the incident with the doctor. She was overcome with the hopeless feeling that her mother was never there for her. Very quickly the image of being on the couch morphed into being in a crib, which was accompanied by a feeling of unending blackness and unbearable anxiety. Jennifer had accessed a state – until now well defended against – of unprocessed archetypal rage and aggression. She exclaimed, 'It feels like a storm inside me. I want to escape. I want to rip and kill someone. Stay away from me!' As the session progressed, the scene changed from that of her earlier hospitalization to that of her tonsillitis operation. She became enraged at her mother's betrayal, particularly because she had been promised she would never have to go to hospital again. She expressed primal hatred towards her mother, and despair which, in turn, reminded her of the anger she had felt on rare occasions with her first husband.

As I tapped and she continued to metabolize these feelings of rage and aggression, her emotions became less intense and her understanding grew. She re-experienced the strategies she has used to defend against these desperate feelings: staying in control by withdrawing; numbing herself to relieve the anxiety; being overly careful about what she might say; and the painful internalized belief that whatever she wanted made no difference to her life as no one would listen.

During this second session she had been able to associate the feelings she had on the phone with Peter to her feelings after the incident with the doctor, which, in turn, opened her to the memory of her mother's not being available for her. As she worked backwards in time, it became clear why her mother's inability to ask the right questions and Jennifer's perception of her mother's unavailability fed right back to that devastating experience of being abandoned, twice, in hospital. It also explained, in part, why she had such an excessive need to control all aspects of life in an intimate relationship.

Remaining sessions

As we worked together throughout the remaining sessions, Jennifer continued to experience sensations, intense affect, thoughts and images from across the lifespan – not only of painful memories but also of happy times with parents, siblings, friends, former husbands, and boyfriends. By the end of the third session she said that she felt safe for the first time in a long time. By the sixth session the jealousy had diminished to the point that when Peter mentioned having had dinner with a woman friend, she was not the least bit upset. She was amazed at how remarkably different her reaction was. She also brought up more family history and we were able to piece together other experiences that had gone into the making of this complex. Because of her father's profession, he was away from home for 4 months every summer. According to Jennifer's mother, during these absences Jennifer would lose developmental achievements. For example, when he left shortly before her first stay in hospital, she had stopped walking. So, from her perspective as a baby, both her mother and father had abandoned her. The superimposed images in one session of her being left by Peter and then of her father leaving her is testimony to the way in which the primal fear of abandonment had been constellated in her intimate relationships.[1]

Commentary

Jennifer's situation is a very good example of the way in which a complex erupts into the everyday life of a fairly well-functioning adult. The overwhelming anxiety triggered by her new relationship is really about what happened early in life. By following her current feelings, with the aid of the bilateral tapping and a safe therapeutic container, she is eventually led back to the 'storm inside' and the 'rip-and-kill' experiences, which reveal undigested aspects of archetypal affect that lie at the core of this complex. Alone in hospital and falling apart with no mother to help metabolize the suffering for her, Jennifer is left to guard against these unbearable affects as best she can by erecting defenses.

The fast-track work using the EMDR protocol provides a window through which to observe how the feeling-based ideas at the core of the complex were formed in the first place. The image of lying on the couch and the enormous frustration that her mother would not ask her the right questions was the aperture through which she tumbled, like Alice falling down the rabbit hole, into the world of that unbearable first abandonment in the hospital at 18 months, re-experienced at age 3, compounded by her father's absences during the summers and then later by the arrival of two siblings. Insights are very quickly gained into the many different aspects of this complex: the images, emotions, bodily sensations, ideas, or cognitions about the self and others, which have been woven together from infancy right through childhood and adult life. It becomes vividly apparent how this loose collection of associations cohere through a common affect creating a 'field' which pulls all similar feeling-toned experiences into its orbit.

Not only do these eight sessions provide a window through which to observe the forming of the complex, it also allows one to witness its unravelling. In 'Psychological Aspects of the Mother Archetype' Jung writes:

> A complex can be really overcome only if it is lived out to the full. In other words, if we are to develop further we have to draw to us and drink down to the very dregs what, because of our complexes, we have held at a distance.
>
> (1954/1959: 98–9)

The very intensity of the abreactions, the physical sensations that Jennifer experienced, and the multitude of images, memories and ideas that she processed, vividly illustrate what it means to drink those dregs.

With the activation of a wide network of neuronal circuits in both hemispheres of the brain and the concurrent digestion of the emerging material which such activation helped to facilitate, Jennifer has become much more conscious of the way in which the complex has 'had' her. By making aspects of the complex conscious, she now has more 'repertoire', as Jung would say. She has a larger story about herself and she is no longer stuck (perseverating) in the old story of inevitable abandonment in intimate relationships. That story, which formerly took up a large space in her psyche, has shrunk to relative insignificance. Most importantly, she has been able to disarm the defence system that was erected to save her from the unbearable primal terror and rage which she experienced at her original abandonments. Hence, incorporating bilateral stimulation into the sessions enabled her not only to fully embody the images, sensations, intense affect, and ideas that constituted aspects of the complex, but it also enabled her to metabolize early experiences in a way that allowed those traumatic events to become simply autobiographical history.

Conclusion

This case is only one illustration of the way in which emerging theory and practice may profoundly enhance our work as Jungian psychotherapists. In fact, I believe that to ignore research from fields such as neurobiology and to eschew protocols such as EMDR not only deprives us of tools that could greatly augment our work, but it marginalizes us even further from the mainstream scientific debate taking place in psychology today. To do so goes against the spirit of Jung, who himself stayed current with the latest scientific discoveries of his day.

Incorporating the EMDR protocol into our work would mean radically rethinking a number of assumptions underlying Jungian analysis: for example, the timeframe in which shifts in psyche can take place. Because the EMDR protocol dramatically speeds up the healing process, for many patients it would decrease the length and frequency of treatment. For example, Jennifer was able to de-activate the powerful negative charge at the core of a lifelong complex in eight sessions. In a traditional Jungian analysis it probably would have taken many months, perhaps even years, to reach a similar state.

Not only the speed, but the depth of transformation that can take place in an individual is something we do not expect without many years of intensive psychotherapy. In a traditional Jungian analysis, we typically work with dreams, fantasies, active imagination, and transference–countertransference material to slowly unpack the layers of the complex. Gradually, the patient integrates formerly split-off fragments into consciousness. Rather than reacting automatically when a situation engenders strong affect, the individual begins to recognize when a complex has been triggered and consciously to choose how to respond.

In contrast, the EMDR protocol, when it is successful, seems so completely to metabolize the affect at the core of the complex that the emotions no longer become triggered at all. For example, when Peter told Jennifer that he had dined with a woman colleague – someone she had recently been profoundly jealous of – she had no emotional reaction whatsoever. It was just an event. She did not go through a process – as we would expect her to – of becoming conscious of a twinge of jealousy triggered by Peter's tale, recognize that this was the reaction to an abandonment complex from early childhood, and then choose to respond to Peter without trying to 'control' him. She was not jealous, period! It was an automatic non-reaction. In fact, because the charge is no longer there, individuals often do not recognize that their behaviour has changed until later.

A third area of radical rethinking would be the role that the transference analysis should play in healing, especially in light of the fact that concentrating on the patient/analyst relationship has become the primary tool for many therapists in analytical psychology as well as psychoanalysis. However, not everyone agrees with this excessive focus on transference. Both Mollon (2005) and Samuels (2006) have suggested that it may actually get in the way of healing. At the other extreme, no analysis of the transference is made at all when using the EMDR protocol. The process is considered entirely intra-psychic. Van der Kolk (2002) even argues that, with severely traumatized patients, techniques that *avoid* relying on a trusting relationship may be necessary in order to help prevent the re-enactment of the original trauma.

Even though transference analysis as such is not part of the EMDR protocol, I believe, contrary to van der Kolk, that building a trusting relationship with a client is essential before introducing the EMDR protocol into the therapy. Also, I suspect that a strong ego–Self connection within the therapist unconsciously supports a similar connection within the client while the protocol is underway.

Although we do not analyze the transference during EMDR, I see similarities in the process to Jung's (1946) alchemical image of transference. For example, together, my client and I first build a sturdy vessel to contain the deep work of transformation, often by using the tools of a traditional Jungian analysis, including, when appropriate, transference analysis. (This may take anywhere from two or three sessions to many months.) When we feel ready to apply the EMDR protocol to an issue, we gather the raw images, ideas, emotions, and sensations that need to be transformed into the container we have created between us and apply the bilateral stimulation. The latter is comparable to turning up the heat, enabling the *prima materia* to cook. The therapist's role, as Jung says, is simply to help the client follow psyche as the intra-psychic processes of transmutation take place. Nature (psyche), which naturally tends towards healing, does the rest.

The question arises whether EMDR is more conducive to a shorter term counselling model than to the Jungian long-term work of analysis. Although suitable to both, I believe that the protocol lends itself particularly favourably to a depth approach. As Jungians, our goal in therapy is not only to help clients resolve issues at the level of the personal unconscious but also to help them access the archetypal energies of the self. As Stein describes it:

> At the heart of treatment lies the analysis (dismemberment) of the complexes and the synthesis of an ego attitude that can support what Jung called the transcendent function, the bridge between ego consciousness and the deeper layers of the unconscious.
>
> (1996: 88)

What frequently prevents us from accessing these deeper layers and the healing potential that naturally takes place when the transcendent function is activated are the dysfunctional childhood complexes. Again I quote Stein:

> In order for nature to do its healing, it is often the case that the pathways by which it can do this work are blocked and need to be opened and cleared of obstacles . . . Faulty and malignant conscious attitudes and developments, acquired usually through traumatic and hurtful experiences in early life, prevent nature's healing processes from having much effect.
>
> (1996: 80)

As we saw with Jennifer, the EMDR protocol was profoundly effective in helping her clear the blocked pathways acquired from early childhood trauma, access the healing energies of the self, and activate the transcendent function. With the deactivation of the powerful affect at the core of her complex, she has been able to follow the deeper demands of her soul and fully embrace an artistic side of her nature, which she had formerly stifled due to intense disapproval from both family and peers.

Another reason why EMDR specifically suits depth work is that the protocol helps to bring about what Jung considered essential to individuation: the integration of the biological/instinctual with the spiritual/archetypal sides of psychic life. 'The archetype as an image of instinct is a spiritual goal toward which the whole nature of man strives' (Jung, 1954/1960: 212). Active imagination is a method that Jung discovered to help facilitate that goal. He writes:

> By means of 'active imagination' we are put in a position of advantage, for we can then make the discovery of the archetype without sinking back into the instinctual sphere, which would only lead to blank

unconsciousness or, worse still, to some kind of intellectual substitute for instinct.

(1954/1960: 211)

The EMDR protocol engenders a spontaneous process which remarkably resembles active imagination. During the bilateral stimulation, the psyche activates movement back and forth between the instinctual level of early wounds, as we saw with Jennifer's archetypal rage and aggression, and the imagistic/ideational level which gives meaning to experience. So often, after the traumatic memories and associations have been processed, my clients encounter a profoundly numinous image, which they describe as enabling them to feel connected to a centre larger than their 'small' self. These images are no 'intellectual substitute for instinct'; they arise out of the patient's encounter with the somatic and affective layers of psyche and are deeply embodied.

I have argued that incorporating emerging new theory and practices from fields such as neurobiology would enhance our Jungian work. I have tried to demonstrate why the EMDR protocol specifically is such a good fit with the aims of Jungian analysis. I want to end by stressing the importance of depth psychology's active engagement with the ongoing dialogue that is taking pace in the larger field of psychology today. I believe, as Glen Slater (2006) so chillingly but perceptively argues in his paper on 'Cyborgian Drift', that as a species we are nearing a crossroads. On the one hand, the multidisciplinary scientific research which Schore's (1994, 2003a, 2003b) work exemplifies has shown the importance of loving, empathic relationship, embedded in a supportive community, as the criteria for creating healthy, embodied, soul-filled individuals. However, much of mainstream cognitive and behavioural psychology, which still exercise primary control over *our* field – the tending of psyche – along with the technological and pharmaceutical institutions, operate from a paradigm that reduces psychological life to brain function and brain function to machine/computer. In such a paradigm there is little patience for embodiment, let alone for the language of soul – myth, poetry, religion, the numinous.

Since Jung's day, technology has already changed how we experience ourselves as humans. The ever present intrusion from electronic gadgetry – from iPods, to cell phones, to computers, etc. – distances us from our bodies, feelings, and intuitions. Mood altering medications, standard 'remedies' for any form of dis-ease, as well as all pervasive street drugs, numb us from our pain and the underlying messages such pain might carry – disembodying us even further. Most disturbing is Slater's (2006) description of the current drift towards the human–machine hybrid, resulting in a condition which virtually detaches us from our instinctual and archetypal roots altogether.

At this point in history, it is essential that we Jungians, whose primary work is concerned with the disease caused by loss of soul, fully engage in the project of the brain, so that we might give back to the interdisciplinary world of psychology our deeply embodied experiences of tending soul. Were psychology to disassociate from soul, we, as a species, could end up losing the imaginative capacity with which to dream any myth onwards.

Note

1 However 'good enough' her mother was, the fact that a sister was born when Jennifer was just over 2, and a brother a year later, meant that her mother's attention had to be withdrawn to care for the other two siblings. In any family, there would be the horrible experience of being supplanted. However, in Jennifer's situation, her sister's arrival only 6 months after her first hospital experience of abandonment, her father's departure, and her brother's birth close to the time of her second hospitalization would be reinforcing a well-established negative complex.

References

Bohart, A.C. and Greenberg, L. (2002) 'EMDR and Experiential Psychotherapy', in F. Shapiro (ed.) *EMDR as an Integrative Psychotherapy Approach*, Washington: American Psychological Association.

Bowlby, J. (1988) *A Secure Base: Parent–Child Attachment and Healthy Human Development*, London: Routledge.

Fordham, M. (1976) *The Self and Autism*, L.A.P., vol. 3, London: Karnac.

Jung, C.G. (1946) 'Psychology of the Transference', *CW* 16, 1954: 353–539.

—— (1948) 'A Review of the Complex Theory', *CW* 8, 1960: 194–219.

—— (1954/1959) 'Psychological Aspects of the Mother Archetype', *CW* 9i, 1959/1968: 148–98.

—— (1954/1960) 'On the Nature of the Psyche', *CW* 8, 1960: 343–442.

Kalsched, D. (1996) *The Inner World of Trauma: Archetypal Defenses of the Personal Spirit*, Hove and New York: Brunner-Routledge.

Knox, J. (2003) *Archetype, Attachment, Analysis*, Hove and New York: Brunner-Routledge.

Krebs, C. (1998) *A Revolutionary Way of Thinking*, Melbourne: Hill of Content.

Maxfield, L. and Hyer, L.A (2002) 'The Relationship between Efficacy and Methodology in Studies Investigating EMDR Treatment of PTSD', *Journal of Clinical Psychology*, 58, 23–41.

Mollon, P. (2005) *EMDR and the Energy Therapies: Psychoanalytic Perspectives*, London and New York: Karnac.

Samuels, A. (2006) 'Transference/Countertransference', in R. Papadopoulos (ed.) *The Handbook of Jungian Psychology*, London and New York: Routledge.

Schore, A. (1994) *Affect Regulation and the Origin of the Self*, Hillsdale, NJ: Lawrence Erlbaum Associates.

—— (2003a) *Affect Dysregulation and Disorders of the Self*, New York and London: W.W. Norton.

—— (2003b) *Affect Regulation and the Repair of the Self*, New York and London: W.W. Norton.

Shapiro, F. (2001) *Eye Movement Desensitization and Reprocessing*, New York and London: Guilford Press.

Sidoli, M. (1989) *The Unfolding Self*, Boston, MA: Sigo Press.

—— (2000) *When the Body Speaks: The Archetypes in the Body*, London: Routledge.

Siegel, D.J. (1999) *The Developing Mind*, New York and London: Guilford Press.

—— (2002) 'The Developing Mind and the Resolution of Trauma: Some Ideas about Information Processing and an Interpersonal Neurobiology of Psychotherapy', in F. Shapiro (ed.) *EMDR as an Integrative Psychotherapy Approach*, Washington: American Psychological Association.

Slater, G. (2006) 'Cyborgian Drift: Resistance is Not Futile', *Spring: A Journal of Archetype and Culture*, 75, 1, 171–95.

Stein, M. (1996) *Practicing Wholeness*, New York: Continuum.

van der Kolk, B.A. (2002) 'Beyond the Talking Cure: Somatic Experience and Subcortical Imprints in the Treatment of Trauma', in F. Shapiro (ed.) *EMDR as an Integrative Psychotherapy Approach*, Washington: American Psychological Association.

Van Etten, M.L. and Taylor, S. (1998) 'Comparative Efficacy of Treatments for Posttraumatic Stress Disorder: A Meta-Analysis', *Clinical Psychology and Psychotherapy*, 5, 126–44.

Wilkinson, M. (2006a) 'The Dreaming Mind-Brain: A Jungian Perspective', *Journal of Analytical Psychology*, 51, 1, 43–59.

—— (2006b) *Coming into Mind*, London and New York: Routledge.

Index